The Cruel Sea Retold

By the same author

The Cruel Sea Retold

A New Look at Nicholas Monsarrat's Epic Story of a World War 2 Convoy

Bernard Edwards

NAVAL INSTITUTE PRESS
Annapolis, Maryland

First published in Great Britain in 2008 by
Pen & Sword Military
an imprint of
Pen & Sword Books Ltd
47 Church Street
Barnsley
South Yorkshire
S70 2AS

This edition published and distributed in the United States of America
and Canada by the Naval Institute Press, 291 Wood Road
Annapolis, Maryland 21402-5034
www.navalinstitute.org

Library of Congress Control Number 2008940169

ISBN 978 159114 145 7

Typeset in 11pt Palatino by Mac Style, Beverley, UK
Printed by the MPG Books Group
in the UK

Contents

This book is for Captain Philip Morgan Cheek, R.N.R., Master Mariner

Did it really happen or did it not
Or is it that I forgot?
Was there a dark ship swishing through the freezing night
With staring eyes to glimpse some tiny bobbing light
To guide us on and keep in line
And save us from a lurking mine?

Was there a heaving deck and needle spray
And thumping engine down below to keep us on our way
And spinning line and wheel which logged the miles each day?

Was there a shimmering sea with boiling sun alight
And darting flying fish that skimmed and glinted bright
And watch bells clanging in the night?

Yes, there was a crashing bow that cleaved the seas
Which always rose to proudly shake its head
And all those grinning mates who sailed and drank with me
Where do they lift their glasses now and which decks do they tread?

Lesley Owen, 'Old Shipmates'

Author's Note

This is the story of a gallant company of little ships, the short-sea Mediterranean traders, sloops and corvettes that rode shotgun on them in the early days of World War II.

The merchant ships were undermanned and overloaded, their escorts slow and lightly armed. Yet together they ran the gauntlet of the U-boats and Focke-Wulfs that terrorised the road to Gibraltar. Their losses were grievous, but their determination to fight their way through was never in question.

Convoy OG 71, in which Nicholas Monsarrat sailed as lieutenant in the corvette HMS *Campanula*, was immortalised in his best-selling novel 'The Cruel Sea'. His fictional character Lieutenant Commander George Eastwood Ericson, RNR was based on Lieutenant Commander Charles George Cuthbertson, RNR; Ericson's ship *Compass Rose* was Cuthbertson's corvette HMS *Zinnia*.

The Author regrets to record in this book yet more examples of the despicable treatment of some survivors from British merchant ships by those who ran things ashore. Although these men were still in shock after having their ships blown from under them, their only remaining possessions being the salt-stained clothes they stood up in, they were treated as if their unfortunate plight was of their own making.

Sadly, this same attitude prevails to this day. Those who survived the horrors of war at sea – 30,000 of their shipmates still lie in watery graves – asked for a medal to call their own. A grateful nation awarded them a tin badge, thereby equating their part in the war with that of the Women's Land Army and the Bevin Boys.

Bernard Edwards
Llanvaches, April 2008

PART ONE

OG 71 Liverpool–Gibraltar

CHAPTER ONE

Departure

Wednesday 13 August 1941: it was high summer in England, and dawn broke early over the River Mersey. Bombs had fallen on Liverpool again during the night, and the smoke was still rising from the shattered remains of several buildings near the docks when two grey-painted warships nosed their way up river and anchored off the Landing Stage. As they swung to the tide and brought up smartly to their anchors, the men-of-war revealed their rust-streaked sides and salt-caked funnels to the shore. These were tired ships, hard-pressed by the savage battle raging out on the Atlantic convoy routes, but business-like still.

The larger of the two warships flew the red and blue ensign of His Royal Norwegian Majesty's Navy in exile. She was the four-funneled destroyer *Bath*, ex-USS *Hopewell* and veteran of another war. Handed over to the Royal Navy, along with forty-nine of her sisters, under the Anglo-American Agreement of September 1940, she was part of a gesture by an American anxious to protect its shores without abandoning its neutrality. Built in 1918 at Newport News, the *Bath* was armed with four 4-inch and one 3-inch guns, and in her heyday had boasted a top speed of 35 knots. Now, twenty-two years later and thousands of miles of steaming on, she was no longer front-line, but under the command of Lieutenant-Commander Fredrik Melsom with a Norwegian crew of 127: she still had plenty of fight left in her.

Bath's companion, the Grimsby-class sloop HMS *Leith*, was younger by a decade and a half, well armed with two 4.7-inch guns and a 3-inch dual purpose, but at 16½ knots she was under a huge disadvantage when it came to chasing U-boats. She was a veteran of many Atlantic convoys, as were her commander, Lieutenant Commander E.C. Hutton and his crew – and this was a war in which experience counted for more than mere hitting power.

Shortly after 2 o'clock that afternoon, when the tide was right, the lock gates of Brunswick Dock swung open and the vanguard of Gibraltar-bound Convoy OG 71 made its entrance into the river. One by one, each with a tug pulling on the bow, five drab grey merchantmen eased clear of the dock wall and canted round to head downstream. The tugs were cast off, and with black smoke rolling back from their funnels as they picked up speed, the departing ships formed line astern in the wake of their naval escort, HMNorS *Bath* and HMS *Leith*, who were leading the way to the open sea.

At the head of the column of merchantmen was the Convoy Commodore's ship *Aguila,* a 3255-ton steamer owned by the Yeoward Line, from whose bomb-scarred offices in James Street the smoke of the outward bound vessels was just visible. Built in 1917 at the Caledon Shipyard in Dundee, the *Aguila* was a cargo/passenger ship for whom the road south was a well-trodden path. In times of peace, now a rapidly fading memory, the *Aguila,* and her sisters of the Yeoward Line, had run regular cruises from Liverpool to Lisbon, Madeira and the Canary Islands. At £21 for a round voyage of twenty-one days there was rarely a berth vacant, and the ships were filled with the sound of the laughter and passengers at play in the sunshine on well-scrubbed teak wood decks. Then the only threat was from choppy seas of the Portuguese Trades.

On this summer afternoon, two years into a bitter war, the *Aguila* was a changed ship. Her company colours were masked by dark Admiralty grey, paravane davits projected from each bow, a long-barreled 4-inch anti-submarine gun was mounted on her poop, and her bridge bristled with machine guns. Her cargo holds were still full of the usual general cargo, 1288 tons of machinery, spare parts, tinned food, textiles – the war had not changed that – but the *Aguila's* passengers were a very different breed from those she had carried on her popular peacetime cruises to the Canaries. Her comfortable, if somewhat outdated accommodation was occupied by eighty-four naval personnel, of which twenty-one were members of the Womens' Royal Naval Service and one was a nursing sister, Kate Gribble of the Queen Alexandra's Royal Naval Nursing Service. They were all volunteers, and under the command of Second Officer Christine Ogle, WRNS, were in transit to Gibraltar to man the Navy's wireless and cipher station on the Rock. Filled with enthusiasm, these young women were embarking on what promised to be the greatest adventure of their young lives. They had no inkling of the dark storm clouds gathering ahead.

Behind the *Aguila* came General Steam Navigation's *Stork*, loaded to the gunwales with cased petrol, her sister-ship *Lapwing*, Ellerman Wilson's *Spero*, and the ex-Danish, now British-flag, *Ebro*, all with general cargo and military stores for Gibraltar. They were small ships, burdened with far heavier loads than the Load Line Rules allowed. But then, this was war, and the rules were for bending.

On the bridge of the *Aguila*, her master, Captain Arthur Frith had some misgivings about the forthcoming voyage. At the convoy conference in India Buildings prior to sailing he had been informed of a change in the planned route for the convoy. The original and customary route for OG 71 was due west from the North Channel to longitude 16° W, then southwest to 22° W, passing 700 miles off the French Biscay coast, now home to Admiral Dönitz's U-boats. Only when abreast of Lisbon was it considered safe to edge in towards the Straits of Gibraltar. This route prolonged the passage by at least 500 miles and an extra three days steaming, but it considerably lessened the danger of enemy attack.

Examining the Admiralty's revised passage plan for OG 71, Captain Frith was not at all happy to see that it would mean passing 200 miles closer to the U-boat bases. He did, however, derive some comfort from the news that, for the first time, this Gibraltar-bound convoy would be under escort by the Royal Navy all the way, rather than until clear of the Western Approaches as before.

It was not that Arthur Frith was of a nervous disposition, as *Capitano di Covetta* Giulio Ghiglieri of the Italian submarine *Barbarigo* had discovered when he threatened the *Aguila* in August 1940. In a running gunfight, with the *Barbarigo* on the surface chasing the *Aguila*, Ghiglieri came very near to being blown out of the water by Frith's 4-inch, and was forced to retire from the conflict.

At Captain Frith's side on the *Aguila's* bridge was the Convoy Commodore Vice-Admiral Patrick Parker. They were contrasting pair, fifty-one-year-old Arthur Frith, short of stature, but a fastidious dresser, outgoing, radiating optimism and good humour; sixty-year-old Parker tall, slim, taciturn and dignified. The Admiral, like many of his contemporaries, had been called out of retirement for convoy duty, and given the almost impossible job of holding the notoriously independent merchantmen together. To assist in communicating his orders to the ships, Parker carried with him a staff of seven signalmen, led by Yeoman of Signals Fred Buckingham. Like Captain Frith, Admiral Parker was far from satisfied with the new route, but he kept his reservations to himself, indicating that perhaps he was aware of the reason for the change.

The rays of the hot summer sun struck silver from the muddy waters of the River Mersey as the long crocodile of ships, signal flags fluttering from every yard arm, moved downstream. The *Aguila's* Wrens lined the rail as she passed close inshore to the Rock Light, laughing and waving to the few idle watchers on New Brighton Pier. Except for the grim reminder of the naval uniforms, the Yeoward ship might well have been setting out on one of her peacetime cruises.

The departing ships reached the Bar light vessel shortly before sunset. Their quickest and easiest route to Gibraltar lay through the Irish Sea and the St.Georges Channel, a passage of some 1,200 miles. Unfortunately, that easy option was no longer open to them.

When, following the evacuation of the remains of her beaten army from the beaches of Dunkirk, Britain lay in imminent danger of invasion, and drastic measures were needed to defend her seaward approaches. The Irish were openly hostile, and refused to allow British naval ships and aircraft to use bases in the Republic. Consequently, the South-Western Approaches, easily accessible to the U-boats, were too dangerous for British ships to negotiate.

On 1 December, Winston Churchill wrote to the Chancellor of the Exchequer:

The straits to which we are being reduced by Irish action compel a reconsideration of the subsidies (to Ireland). It can hardly be argued that we can go on paying them till our last gasp. Surely we ought to use this money to build more ships or buy more from the United States in view of the heavy sinkings off the Bloody Foreland.

Pray let me know how these subsidies could be terminated, and what retaliatory measures could be taken in the financial sphere by the Irish, observing that we are not afraid of their cutting off our food, as it would save us the enormous mass of fertilisers and feeding stuffs we have to carry into Ireland through the de Valera-aided German blockade.

Churchill's threat to cut off the Irish subsidies was not carried out, but in order to cover Britain's south-western flank and protect the vital Bristol Channel ports, the Mersey and the Clyde, a huge minefield was laid stretching from The Lizard to Fastnet. From then on the only access to the west coast ports was through the North Channel.

By the time the vanguard of OG 71 came abreast of the Bar light vessel, the fickle English weather had done an about turn. Grey clouds were rolling in from the sea, and a strong northwester was blowing straight into Liverpool Bay, making it impossible for the merchant ships to disembark their pilots. Admiral Parker assured the Liverpool-based pilots that they would be landed in Belfast, and the convoy carried on.

While the ships of OG 71 prepared to do battle with the deteriorating Atlantic weather, some 300 miles to the south, U-201 was safe behind the breakwaters of the port of Brest, but making ready for sea. For the forty-four members of her crew the day had begun long before dawn when, bleary-eyed after an over-indulgent night ashore, they had manoeuvred their newly-painted boat alongside the ammunition pier on the west bank of the River Penfeld to begin taking on board the fourteen torpedoes that made up U-201's main armament. Manhandling the fourteen 1½-ton missiles into the bow, stern compartments and reserve lockers on deck took most of the daylight hours, reducing the men to a state of complete physical and mental exhaustion. And even when the torpedoes were at last safely stowed there was no rest. The 88mm shells for the deck gun, 220 in all, were next, to be followed by boxes of ammunition for the 20mm guns. The back-breaking work went on well into the night.

Next morning, U-201 returned alongside the depot ship, where she refilled her diesel tanks, at the same time taking on board provisions for the coming voyage. Only when the last loaf of bread and the last piece of salami had been passed below and stowed into every remaining nook and cranny of the cramped hull, was there time to rest – but only for an hour or two. The *Admiral* himself, Karl Dönitz, the *Befehlshaber-der-U-boote (BdU)*, had given orders for U-201 to return to sea without delay. She had a rendezvous to keep in the North Atlantic.

U-201 was a Type VII C U-boat, displacing 864 tons when submerged, 67 metres in length overall, having a top speed of 17.6 knots on the surface and 7.6 knots underwater, with a radius of action of 8,500 miles at 10 knots. She was one of the twenty-four front-line boats of Admiral Dönitz's elite First U-boat Flotilla, based in Brest, and led by *Korvettenkapitän* Hans Cohausz. Twenty-eight-year-old *Oberleutnant* Adalbert Schnee, who seven months earlier had brought U-201 out of the Germania Werft in Kiel, was in command. He was an experienced submariner, having learned his trade aboard U-23 with the legendary Otto Kretschmer before gaining his own command. Schnee was born in Berlin on 31 December 1913, on the eve of a year that saw Germany embarking on a terrible war that was to cost her 2 million dead and many years of economic and political chaos. Schnee grew up in a country turned sour by mass unemployment and rampant inflation, and when Adolf Hitler came to power offering new hope to Germany, young Adalbert joined the Navy, entering the submarine service in 1937.

Schnee's first war patrol in U-201 proved to be a disappointment. He sank only two British ships, totaling 14,000 tons gross, damaging one other. His second patrol was even worse, with not a single torpedo fired. U-201 returned to Brest on 19 July 1941 with no victory pennants flying, and after nearly a month in port, Schnee and his crew were anxious to return to sea and get to grips with the enemy.

As darkness fell on the evening of the 14 August, fog rolled up river from the Atlantic, and when, shortly after 2000, U-201 slipped her moorings, the visibility was down to 300 metres. This suited Adalbert Schnee well, providing a cloak to hide his command from the prying eyes of the French Resistance. Giving his orders in a voice only a little above a whisper, he turned the boat short round and headed down the Penfeld towards the open sea. Only the muffled beat of U-210's diesels betrayed her slow progress down river. Outside the breakwaters of Brest harbour, the shadowy shapes of two guard boats took station on the U-boat, and Schnee set course to the west.

Meanwhile, Convoy OG 71 was engaged in gathering in its full complement of ships and arranging its defensive screen for the coming voyage. At around the same time that U-201 was leaving her berth, a prearranged rendezvous was made to the north of Anglesey with the Milford Haven section of the convoy, eleven ships escorted by two armed trawlers. Among the newly joined merchantmen were two Limerick Steamship Company ships, the *Clonlara* and the *Lanahrone,* both 1200-tonners, unarmed and under the neutral flag of Eire. The *Clonlara* was commanded by Captain Joseph Reynolds, a veteran of the Spanish Civil War, and the *Lanahrone* by Captain William Tyrrell, who had served for many years in British ships. Both ships had loaded coal in South Wales for Lisbon.

Normally, the Irish ships would have been sailing alone, flying their neutral colours and with all lights blazing at night, but following a recent edict issued by Berlin declaring all neutral ships to be legitimate targets, they had sought the protection of British convoys. The *Clonlara* and *Lanahrone* were not, however, particularly welcome additions to OG 71, as they were sailing in their peacetime colours, which included distinctive red and white funnel markings, easily seen by enemy aircraft. Furthermore Irish ships were also unused to convoy routine, and notorious for showing lights at night while at sea.

After an exchange of signals, the sixteen merchantmen formed into two columns abreast, and altered onto a north-north-westerly course. Having rounded the southern end of the Isle of Man, the convoy then headed up for the North Channel. At this point, the Norwegian destroyer *Bath* was detached for Lough Foyle to top up her bunkers. Lieutenant-Commander Melsom had orders to rejoin the convoy at dusk.

When off Belfast, the Liverpool ships entered the lough to land their pilots, who then faced a ferry ride home. In compensation for their enforced detention on board ship, they would have the opportunity to shop in Belfast for few luxury items unobtainable on the mainland at this stage of the war.

With the Liverpool ships back with the convoy, the escorting trawlers from Milford Haven were detached, and OG 71 entered the North Channel. That night, as the rays of the setting sun turned the heather-clad slopes of the Mull of Kintyre a deep mauve, the ocean-going tug *Empire Oak* joined from Oban, and took her place in the ranks of slow-moving merchantmen.

At 0630 on the morning of the 15th, when within sight of the island of Inishtrahull, OG 71 began to assume its final shape with the arrival of six more ships from the Clyde, escorted by the Flower-class corvettes *Bluebell, Campanula* and *Hydrangea*. A little later, *Bath* rejoined, and with her came two more corvettes, *Campion* and *Wallflower*. Now the signal flags fluttered and lamps flashed as Admiral Parker, in the *Aguila*, chivied the twenty-two merchantmen into forming seven columns abreast. Lieutenant Commander Hutton's escort force then took station around them like sheepdogs around their flock, with *Bath* and *Leith* scouting ahead, *Bluebell, Campanula, Campion* and *Wallflower* guarding the flanks, and *Hydrangea* on the starboard quarter. At 1600, HMS *Zinnia*, another Flower-class corvette, arrived and took her station on the port quarter. The convoy was now complete and ready to challenge the Atlantic and its dangers, both natural and man-made.

By this time, U-201 was already twelve hours out of Brest. Motoring through the night at maximum speed on the surface, Oberleutnant Schnee had put 200 miles between himself and the coast of Occupied France, and felt that much safer for it. When it was fully light, he took U-201 down to periscope depth to avoid the attentions of RAF Coastal Command's long-range aircraft, which flew regular patrols over this area.

It was a fine summer's morning in the North Atlantic, and Adalbert Schnee, scanning a horizon sharp as a knife's edge, found time to reflect on the disappointment of his previous patrol, when he had spent five weeks at sea without the opportunity to fire a single torpedo. When he was on the point of returning to port empty-handed, when Lorient had given him a chance to redeem his fortunes. U-201 was ordered to join nine other boats of the flotilla in an attack on the forty-three ship convoy HX 133 which was passing south of Greenland, bound eastwards.

HX 133 was an 8½ knot convoy, escorted by the Canadian destroyer *Ottawa*, plus one British and three Canadian corvettes. With the exception of the British corvette, this was a relatively inexperienced escort force, the Canadian corvettes in particular being manned by raw recruits to the RCN. When the convoy was attacked, the Canadians put up a spirited defence, but the ten-strong U-boat pack simply outclassed them. In a running battle lasting three days six merchantmen totaling 38,269 tons gross were sent to the bottom along with their precious cargoes, while two others were damaged. U-201 joined in the attack with great enthusiasm, but by this time HX 133's escort had been reinforced by another five corvettes from Iceland. To his immense frustration, each time Schnee tried to break through the screen he was beaten back until, finally, running low on fuel, he was forced to retire from the fight and return to Biscay with all his torpedoes still on board. On this patrol he was determined to exact his revenge on the enemy, but first he had to find him.

In the early days of the war, radar was only a distant promise for Dönitz's U-boats, and the German submariner's horizon was limited to how far he could see from his conning tower – perhaps 5 miles in good weather. The Atlantic being a wide and largely empty ocean in which individual ships, and even whole convoys, might be lost to sight for days or weeks on end, finding a target was very much a matter of chance. When Lorient had news of a convoy putting to sea, the only tactic available to Dönitz was to station a line of U-boats across its track and hope that the enemy sailed into his net. This might work if the convoys stuck to predictable courses, which they very rarely did. Kept informed of the dangers ahead by the Admiralty, they took frequent evasive action, and all too often bypassed the U-boat line without being seen.

This all changed in January 1941, when Karl Dönitz persuaded Hitler to place twelve long-range *Focke-Wulf* 200 aircraft under his command to provide reconnaissance for the U-boats. The *Focke-Wulf 200*, or Condor as it was aptly named, was a formidable aircraft. Based on an airliner developed in 1938 for Lufthansa's transatlantic service, the four-engined Condor had a range of 2,210 miles and a cruising speed of 224 mph – the ideal aircraft for maritime reconnaissance. The military version was manned by a crew of seven, two pilots, two wireless operators, a flight mechanic, and a rear gunner. It carried four 500lb bombs, and was armed with one 20mm cannon, three 13mm and two 7.9mm machine-guns. By September 1940, the Condors had destroyed nearly 100,000 tons of Allied shipping, and had been dubbed by Winston Churchill 'the scourge of the Atlantic'.

Based at Mérignac near Bordeaux, and commanded by *Oberstleutnant* Martin Harlinghausen, the twelve Condors of KG 40 allocated to the U-boats began regular reconnaissance sorties. Two planes a day flew deep into the Atlantic searching the convoy routes, before turning north to land at an airfield in Southern Norway. After refueling and resting their crews, they retraced their steps back to Mérignac.

KG 40's first success came early in February 1941, but not in the role it had been assigned. Late on 8 February, Convoy HG 53, northbound from Gibraltar, was sighted 220 miles west-south-west of Cape St. Vincent by Nicolei Clausen in U-37. He sent a sighting report, in response to which five Condors took off from Mérignac to intercept. They found the convoy next day and attacked immediately, sinking six ships. Clausen, meanwhile, had sunk two more. Although in this case the sighting had been made by the U-boat rather than the aircraft, cooperation between the two services had resulted in half the ships in the convoy being sent to the bottom, and Admiral Dönitz was understandably very pleased.

It was not until fifteen days later that the *Focke-Wulfs* began to fulfill their intended role. On 23 February a Condor spotted the eastbound convoy OB 288 south of Iceland and called in the U-boats, who then wreaked havoc, sinking eight ships in the first five hours of the morning of the 24th.

From the time he was first appointed *Führer der U-boote* in September 1935, Dönitz had been training his crews in the *Rudeltaktik,* or group operation, which entailed U-boats hunting in packs rather than alone. It was not until early 1941 that the Admiral had sufficient boats operational to implement the 'wolf pack' system, and this he did with the help of the Condors of KG 40. Convoy OG 71 was to be the guinea pig.

Soon after 8 o'clock on the evening of 15 August, with the blue hills of Donegal fading into the coming night, OG 71 was 90 miles out into the Atlantic. The commodore ship, *Aguila,* was lead ship of column No.4, while the vice-commodore, MacAndrew Steamship Company's 1809-ton *Ciscar,* commanded by Captain Edward Hughes, led column No.2. Following their lead, the others steamed in orderly lines at a leisurely 7 knots. Moving at a speed equivalent to that of a horse-drawn wagon, the ships were pathetically vulnerable behind their thin screen of escorts. Many of the merchantmen were capable of at least 3 knots extra but their progress was dictated by the slower members of the convoy.

OG 71 was essentially a small-ship convoy, being composed largely of short-sea traders under 2000 tons gross. In pre-war days they had sailed regularly between British ports and the Mediterranean, taking coal and manufactured goods out, returning laden with ore cargoes topped off with fruit, wine and brandy. It was a trade that had existed since Roman times –and seemed to have changed little since. There was one ship sailing in OG 71 that, metaphorically, stood head and shoulders above the others. She was the 4274-ton *Grelhead* of the Cardigan Shipping Company, bound for Gibraltar in ballast, and consequently riding high out the water. She was conspicuous, but no more so than the two Irish ships, *Clonlara* and *Lanahrone*. Neither was over 1200 tons, but they were resplendent in their Limerick Steamship Company colours, complete with red and white painted funnels. They so contrasted with the sombre grey of the other ships that they stuck out like sore thumbs. It was hoped that they did not attract the attentions of the enemy.

The bridge of the *Aguila*, normally a quiet haven populated only by the officer of the watch, a helmsman and a lookout, was a bustle of activity. Vice-Admiral Parker and his staff of seven, were preparing for the coming night with a flurry of signals by flag and lamp to the other merchantmen. Yeoman of Signals Frank Buckingham and his 'bunting tossers' passed warnings about the need to keep station, to pay attention to blackouts, and the necessity of keeping radio silence, none of which were really needed by the British ships who had two years of convoy work behind them. It had never been easy for the merchantman, long accustomed to sailing the broad oceans alone and unhindered, to conform to convoy discipline. Shepherded into columns, with 1000 yards between each column and only 400 yards between ships in line astern, there was no room for error. On a dark, moonless night – and they were numerous – station keeping was a nightmare lived over and over again. Unable to show lights, and with no radar to guide them, those keeping watch on the bridge were like blind men tap, tapping their way along a crowded pavement. They were reduced to peering into the night looking for shadows, making minute adjustments of course, and reducing or increasing speed a few revolutions at a time. This, in turn, required the engineer on watch below to be at the controls at all times, and in a constant state of alert. Ships straggled and romped, and often the convoy was in a state of disarray when daylight came, but there were surprisingly few collisions, which says much for the quality of the men in the ships.

For OG 71's escorts, stationed on the periphery of the convoy and with plenty of room to manoeuvre, station keeping presented few problems. Some had radar, they had the advantage of a good turn of speed, and all carried large complements, and thus could afford numerous pairs of eyes watching the horizon at all times. Their only disadvantage lay in the fact that they were virtual strangers to each other, never having worked or exercised as a team before. The senior escort, HMS *Leith* had been involved in many hard-fought Atlantic convoys, and there was no lack of expertise in her; *Bath*, on the other hand, was new to the routine, having worked with Group 5 of the Liverpool Escort Force for just a few months. The corvettes had even less experience. As yet, Lieutenant Commander Hutton had no means of knowing what dangers the voyage ahead held. Of one thing he was certain – the U-boats would waiting for them.

The German occupation of France had completely changed the war for Admiral Dönitz's U-boat arm, putting at their disposal ports on the French Atlantic coast from Dunkirk to the Spanish border. The rocky Biscay coast offered excellent shelter, and bases were quickly set up at Brest, Lorient, St. Nazaire, La Pallice and Bordeaux. The long hazardous passage from Kiel, around the north coast of Scotland became a thing of the past and, effectively, as the distance to sail to the North Atlantic convoy routes was reduced by nearly 500 miles, the number of U-boats available for deep-sea operations was doubled. Dönitz moved his headquarters to Lorient, set up a powerful communications network, and the Battle of the Atlantic had begun in earnest.

CHAPTER TWO

Rudeltaktik

German U-boats communicated with each other and with their shore bases using the Enigma cypher machine, an ingenious coding device invented in 1919 for commercial use, and not taken up by the military until the 1930s. Resembling a portable typewriter, the Enigma machine used very complicated electrical circuits activated by a system of code wheels. It was capable of billions of permutations, and its message could be read only by a similar machine. Despite all the efforts of the brilliant code breakers at Bletchley Park, Enigma remained exactly what its name implied, and finding the U-boats was a game of hide and seek for the Royal Navy. Then, in 1941, came an unexpected breakthrough. It was discovered that German weather ships, two of which were stationed in the North Atlantic, used the same Enigma machine and codebooks as the U-boats.

On 7 May 1941, the weather ship *München* lay hove to off Iceland, rolling in the long Atlantic swell. The *München*, in earlier life a trawler owned by the *'Nordsee' Deutsche Hochseefischerei* of Wesermünde, now Weather Observing Ship No.6, was a long way from her usual fishing grounds in the North Sea. Her crew of seventeen, reduced to servicing the needs of the four meteorologists on board, found the days long and largely empty, with little to do but to lean on the rails with fishing lines over the side. They were thus occupied, on this cold Arctic morning, when the British destroyer *Somali* steamed over the horizon.

Somali opened fire with her 4.7-inch guns as soon as she was within range, lobbing shells all around the *München*, all deliberately aimed to miss. This was enough for the German trawlermen, who took to the boats in a panic. An armed party from *Somali* boarded the weather ship, and returned to the destroyer in triumph bearing the *München's* Enigma machine and a number of codebooks. Two days later, another extraordinary incident occurred which completed the picture for Bletchley Park.

On 9 May, U-110, commanded by *Kapitänleutnant* Fritz-Julius Lemp, who had earned notoriety by sinking the unarmed passenger liner *Athenia* within a few hours of the declaration of war in 1939, was involved in an attack on the westbound convoy OB 318 in mid-Atlantic. Operating on the surface at night, Lemp sank two British merchantmen, and was about to torpedo another when the corvette *Aubretia* appeared out of the darkness, heading straight for the U-boat at full speed. Lemp crash-dived to avoid being rammed, but *Aubretia's* depth charges followed him down, the blast so damaging the U-boat that she was unable to limp away. *Aubretia* was joined by the destroyers *Bulldog* and *Broadway*, and the combined depth charges of the three warships blew U-110 to the surface. Fritz-Julius Lemp was killed in the mêlée, and a boarding party from *Bulldog* captured U-110 before any move was made to scuttle her.

The rewards from the taking of U-110 were considerable, and included her Enigma machine and most of its associated code tables. As a result of this action, Bletchley Park was able to read the U-boats' Enigma messages within hours of them being transmitted. Unfortunately, halfway through June the Germans changed the Enigma settings, and the advantage was lost. Not to be deterred, on 25 June the Royal Navy set out to capture another weather ship. On the 28th, the destroyer HMS *Tartar* surprised the weather ship *Lauenburg*, hiding behind an iceberg to the north of Iceland. *Tartar* opened fire, and boarded when her crew abandoned ship in a hurry. The destroyer's boarding party came away with the Enigma machine settings for July, thus enabling Bletchley Park to carry on reading the German Navy's coded messages. The *Lauenburg* was sunk, and her crew taken prisoner.

As a direct result of these actions, the number of Allied ships sunk by U-boats in the North Atlantic fell dramatically from sixty-one in June 1941 to twenty-two in the July. Crucially, the capture of these Enigma machines and code tables remained a closely guarded secret until many years after the war. Although he suspected that all was not well, Admiral Dönitz was completely unaware that his wireless traffic was being read by the British.

At sunrise on Sunday 17 August, OG 71 was 90 miles due west of Bloody Foreland, on Ireland's west coast, and so far as was known, remained undetected by the enemy. Although the weather had held good, progress over the previous twenty-four hours had been painfully slow due to a number of the merchant ships experiencing engine problems. As the sun lifted above the horizon, the commodore ship *Aguila* rejoined, having fallen astern during the night with a jammed steering gear. No sooner had she resumed her place at the head of Column 4, than the *Grelhead* dropped back, her master reporting that his firemen were unable to maintain steam. However, the steamer rejoined the convoy within half an hour – her difficulties no doubt solved by the threat of fines and entries being made in the Official Log Book – and the convoy resumed its south-westerly course at 7 knots. This was a dangerously slow speed under the circumstances, but the best that could be done if this assembly of ageing cargo ships was to be held together.

Later in the morning, with breakfast over and the calm seas and a warm sun shining down out of a blue sky, an air of pleasant relaxation had once again settled over the convoy. Being Sunday, other than watchkeeping, there was little work being done in the ships. On the *Aguila*, the deck chairs had been taken out of their lockers, where they had lain unused for two years, and the Wren passengers were enjoying the sunshine. Their talk was all of Gibraltar, where it was certain that the sun shone all day, every day, and rationing was unknown. After the austerity of windswept Scarborough, where the Wrens had been based, this sounded like the Promised Land.

On the bridge of the *Aguila*, Captain Arthur Firth and Vice-Admiral Patrick Parker stood side by side, watching the horizon ahead, each wrapped in their own separate thoughts. They might have been an odd contrast in character and appearance, but both were old hands in this game of war. They were not fooled by the sunshine, the blue skies and the empty horizon. The hidden dangers that lay ahead constantly exercised their minds.

The first sign that storm clouds were gathering came all too soon. Shortly after 10 o'clock that morning, a patrolling British aircraft contacted HMS *Leith* by radio telephone warning that an enemy plane was approaching the convoy from an east-south-easterly direction. This was confirmed twenty minutes later by a W/T signal received from the Admiralty which read: 'Long range enemy aircraft are operating in your vicinity.' The *Focke-Wulfs* were airborne and searching for OG 71.

Leith immediately dropped back to cover the rear of the convoy, and at the same time the other escorts moved closer to the merchantmen, tightening the defensive screen around them. While the escorts were taking up position, a large unidentified aircraft was sighted astern of the convoy. The issued became confused when, at 1035, a Wellington bomber appeared on the port bow. The British plane was challenged by *Bath*, but gave the wrong reply, whereupon the Norwegian destroyer opened up with her AA guns. Meanwhile, the stranger loitering astern was identified as a *Focke-Wulf Condor*, and *Leith* also opened fire. For a time, it seemed that OG 71 was under attack both from ahead and astern, and there was a rush to man the guns in all ships. Both aircraft kept well out of range, and a great deal of ammunition was wasted. However, the fire had the desired effect. First the Wellington – no doubt unhappy at her unfriendly reception from so-called friendly ships – flew off to the north, while the *Focke-Wulf* continued to keep her distance. Signals picked up by the merchant ship *Spero*, D/F guard ship for OG 71, indicated the enemy aircraft was probably reporting the position of the convoy.

The *Spero's* wireless operator was not mistaken. The Condor was in fact one of KG 40's Air Reconnaissance section, then on the final leg of a long patrol from Mérignac, and running low on fuel. She reported the convoy to be 'to the west of Porcupine Bank, on a course of 230°'. The position given was vague, Porcupine Bank being one of the main fishing grounds worked by the deep-sea trawlers, lying 150 miles off the west coast of Ireland. Several U-boats picked up the *Focke-Wulf's* message and took D/F bearings of her transmissions. The resultant fix showed the convoy to be in approximately 53° 21'N 15° 35' W, which is some 180 miles off the coast of Ireland, due west of Slyne Head. The south-westerly course being steered indicated it was probably a Gibraltar-bound convoy. This information was passed to Admiral Dönitz at his chateau headquarters at Kerneval, near Lorient.

This was the opportunity Dönitz had been waiting for, a chance to put into practice his *Rudeltaktik* – an attack in force. Unfortunately, only a handful of U-boats were close enough to intercept the convoy, one of which was Adalbert Schnee's U-201. When the signal came in from Lorient, Schnee was in position 51° 50' N 15° 40' W, and steering a north-westerly course at 7¼ knots on the surface. He was, in fact, only 50 miles north-east of OG 71 and crossing astern of the convoy. On receipt of BdU's signal, Schnee altered course to intercept, and an hour later sighted traces of smoke on the horizon to the south-west. This he reported to BdU, who ordered him to close the convoy and shadow it closely. He was soon joined by Jürgen Oesten in U-106, one of the larger Type IX boats, which was homeward bound after attacking shipping in West African waters.

Schnee was first to make contact with OG 71, sighting the ships at 2130 on the 17th, reporting them to be in 52° 51' N 17° 05' W, and on a south-westerly course. At the time the wind was blowing WNW'ly force 5, and generating sufficient white horses to provide good cover for a U-boat trimmed well down. Schnee commenced shadowing at a discreet distance, and at 2345 reported that the convoy had altered onto a westerly course, and was making 8 knots.

With the orderly lines of slow-moving merchant ships clearly visible, at midnight Schnee decided to attack independently, but as he manoeuvred into position two escorts, probably a destroyer and a corvette, moved between him and the convoy. The escorts were sweeping the sea with their searchlights, indicating that they might have been alerted to the presence of U-boats in the area. Schnee sheered away, and attempted to pass astern of the convoy and attack from the other side, but the escorts seemed to be everywhere. Eventually, he was forced to drop back and continue shadowing at a distance. As the night wore on, heavy rain squalls set in, at times reducing the visibility to a mere 500 metres. At 0330 on the 18th, Schnee reported to Lorient that he had lost contact with the convoy. It seemed that OG 71 had vanished into the night like a fleet of ghost ships.

As Adalbert Schnee suspected, the convoy had been warned of the presence of the assembling wolf pack, which in addition to U-201 and U-106 now consisted of Walter Kell's U-204, Hans Heidtmann's U-559, and U-564, commanded by Reinhard Suhren. Unfortunately for them, the U-boats had still not learned to keep silent, and were making free of their radios to talk to one another. As always, British ears were listening. HMS *Leith* had earlier received an urgent signal from the Admiralty that read: 'More than one U-boat may be following the convoy'. Shortly before noon that day, this was followed by 'D/F bearings indicate three or four U-boats may be in your vicinity'. The Admiralty's assessment was correct, for U-559, U-564 and a newcomer on the scene, U-552, under the command of *Korvettenkapitän* Erich Topp, were homing in on U-201's signals. Meanwhile, some confusion reigned in the plotting room at Kerneval. At 1115 a patrolling *Focke-Wulf* had reported sighting the convoy in 50° 39' N 15° 35' W. However, cross bearings taken of signals from U-201, U106, U-204 and U-559, who all believed they were in the vicinity of OG 71, showed that the U-boats were in fact between 40 and 100 miles to the west of the convoy.

Following the appearance of the *Focke-Wulf* in the morning, there was a general acceptance throughout the ships of the convoy that an attack by U-boats would not be long delayed. But, for the moment unmolested, and sailing south in warm sunshine, a benign mood had descended on OG 71. The Commodore had warned all ships of the imminent danger from

U-boats, and as a result all guns were manned, and extra lookouts posted. Nevertheless, few really believed that the tranquillity of their voyage was about to be cruelly interrupted.

The first sign of impending trouble came not from beneath the waves, but from the sky, when, at 1730, the heavy drone of engines was heard, and two twin-engined aircraft appeared out of the clouds astern of the convoy. The planes began to circle out of range of the guns, but they were easily identifiable as Ju 88 low-level bombers. The mood in the ships suddenly changed to one of nervous alertness.

The Ju 88s kept their distance for half an hour, then they disappeared into the clouds. At first, it seemed that they must have flown away, but then they suddenly reappeared on the starboard side, and swooped on the *Grelhead,* the third ship in Column 6. Being by far the largest ship in the convoy she was an obvious target.

Momentarily, the Welsh tramp and the others around her were caught unawares, but their guns were still manned, and the diving Ju 88s were met by a fierce anti-aircraft barrage. The German planes flew straight through the curtain of fire, and each released a stick of four bombs aimed at the *Grelhead,* straddling her before she had time to take evading action. The ship disappeared behind a wall of spray thrown up by the eight bombs, but she had been built on the Tyne in an age when strength took precedence over convenience and she came sailing out the other side unharmed.

Soon after the enemy bombers had flown away, the Admiralty signalled *Leith:* 'D/F bearings between 1548Z and 1644Z indicate 4 or 5 U boats are in the vicinity of Convoy OG 71. It is probable OG 71 was reported by one of them'. This was passed to the Commodore's ship *Aguila* by lamp, and Admiral Parker hoisted the flag signal 'Submarines in the vicinity. No smoke or lights to be shown'. The C-in-C Western Approaches, meanwhile, signalled the destroyer HMS *Wanderer,* which was operating further to the west, instructing her: 'Proceed OG 71 and carry out sweep astern of convoy for two hours before returning. Convoy is being shadowed by U boats'.

Five hundred miles to the east, in Kerneval, Admiral Dönitz plotted to draw the net closer around OG 71. U-201 had now regained contact, and Schnee was following the ships at a safe distance, sending in regular reports of its progress. U-124 and U-126 were to the south and racing northwards to intercept, while U-204 and U-559 were approaching from the north. Dönitz planned to send in aircraft from KG 40 on the afternoon of the 19th, and in the confusion of the air attack, the U-boats, by then all in position, would move in with torpedoes.

The evening of the 18th was fine and the twilight long, with a southerly breeze creating enough of a sea to give the ships a gentle pitching motion. Despite the knowledge that the enemy was close at hand, the apparent tranquillity of this warm summer's evening again gave rise to a feeling in the ships that all was well. Aboard the Commodore's ship, *Aguila,* the passengers were holding an impromptu concert, and the sound of their voices raised in song carried across the water to the other ships. On her bridge, Admiral Parker and Captain Firth stood side by side conversing in subdued tones. Both men were aware that the danger was great, and increasing with every hour, but on a night such as this, even for them, reality was hard to accept.

On the bridge of the *Leith,* scouting ahead of the convoy, Lieutenant Commander Hutton shifted uneasily in his pilot chair. HMS *Wanderer* had not yet arrived, and with no ship covering the rear of the convoy Hutton felt very vulnerable. Reluctantly, he eventually decided to send *Bath* back, instructing Lieutenant-Commander Melsom to take station between 2 and 3 miles astern of the convoy, sweeping from quarter to quarter in the hope of flushing out any U-boat that might be shadowing. *Bath* was to return again as soon as darkness closed in. Unknown to Melsom, as he reversed course and steamed down the orderly lines of merchant ships. U-204, coming from the north, had overshot the convoy, and was now coming up astern of the rear ships.

When the long summer twilight finally came to an end at about 2300 and *Bath* had not returned to her station on the port bow of the convoy Lieutenant Commander Hutton assumed she had temporarily lost contact. As the Norwegian destroyer was equipped with radar, he was confident that she would have no difficulty in returning to the screen. Two hours later, however, when there was still no sign of *Bath,* Hutton became concerned for her safety.

Bath had, in fact, been on the point of returning when, at about 0110 on the 19th, her radar operator picked up a firm target close on the port bow. Although the echo was large, Melsom suspected it might be a U-boat, and altered to investigate, only to find that the contact was the 1584-ton steamer *Alva,* which was then straggling astern of the convoy. Five minutes later, *Bath's* radar showed another echo, small this time, and on the destroyer's starboard beam. Melsom, convinced that this was a submarine on the surface, immediately put the helm hard to starboard, and increased to full speed to ram.

Walter Kell was another man with a mission to fulfil. U-204 had sailed from Brest on 22 July, and after a month ceaselessly combing the waters of the Atlantic, she was yet to sink a single enemy ship. When Kell, aware that he was approaching the convoy, peered into the darkness and saw the unmistakeable silhouette of a four-funnelled ship ahead, he knew the moment he had waited so long for had at last arrived. He bent over his conning tower sight, and aiming carefully and deliberately, fired a fan of two torpedoes.

Bath was zig-zagging at 12 knots, but at 308 feet long on the waterline she was too easy a target to miss. One of her lookouts saw the torpedo tracks coming from starboard, racing towards the ship. Breathlessly, he reported to the bridge, where Lieutenant Commander Melsom made an attempt at evasive action. This was too late. Both Kell's torpedoes went home in *Bath's* engine-room on the starboard side, the thunderous double explosion blowing a huge whole in her thin hull plates. The sea poured into her engine spaces, and the stricken destroyer simply broke in two under the shock, both halves sliding below the waves in the space of two to three minutes. To put the seal on the disaster, as the stern section went down, two depth charges set at 100 feet, and not made safe, exploded, sending a lethal shock wave through the waters around the sinking ship, killing many of the men left struggling in the sea.

Captain Edward Hughes, commanding the vice-commodore ship *Ciscar*, sailing at the head of Column 2, recorded his impression of the attack:

Weather on the night of the 18th/19th August was fine, with a southerly wind force 4–5. We steamed at 7 knots and at about 0100 BST on the 19th we altered course to 190°. About this time, I am not sure whether it was just before or just after we had altered course, the 2nd Officer, who was on watch, called me to report that he had seen a bright flash and heard a loud explosion away towards the centre of the convoy, on our starboard quarter. I went onto the bridge, but could see nothing of what had happened, except that I noticed flares being sent up, presumably by the escort. There were no aircraft about at the time and these flares were definitely being fired from a gun, although several of my officers thought at first the convoy was being attacked from the air. I told them in my opinion it was a torpedo attack, and ordered everyone on deck, lifejackets to be worn, guns manned, and had the boats made ready with blankets etc...

The flash of the explosion that sank the Norwegian destroyer was also seen on board the corvette *Hydrangea*, stationed astern of the convoy. Lieutenant Woolfenden, sensing the urgency of the situation, immediately turned back and raced to the rescue. Twenty minutes later, *Hydrangea* reached the patch of floating debris and oil marking the sudden end of HMNorS *Bath*.

The night was extremely dark, and as the lifejackets carried by *Bath* were not equipped with red lights, it was necessary for the corvette to show lights to search for survivors. As at least one U-boat was known to be in the area, Woolfenden was aware that he was putting his ship at grave risk, but with the terrified cries of the drowning men ringing in his ears, he threw caution to the winds. The starboard skiff was lowered, and by the light of *Hydrangea's* searchlight and signal lamps, the rescue began. As luck would have it, *Wanderer* was then approaching the convoy from the west, and was guided in by *Hydrangea's* lights. The destroyer also lowered a boat, and between them the two escorts plucked forty-two survivors from the oil-covered water. Lieutenant-Commander Fredrik Melsom and eighty-three of his crew went down with HMNorS *Bath*. Two others died aboard the *Hydrangea* after rescue.

That so many men had been saved from the *Bath*, which went down in less than three minutes, was due in no small way to the prompt and determined rescue efforts of Lieutenant Woolfenden and the men of HMS *Hydrangea*. A report submitted by Woolfenden to the Vice Admiral Commanding North Atlantic illustrates the lengths he and his men went to:

I would like to draw your attention to the gallant but unavailing attempt to rescue a man from the water by ERA A.J. Tilling.

This rating went over the side into the water on a bowline at great personnel risk to endeavour to sling a line around him. The man was so covered in oil that all attempts were unsuccessful. The surface of the water was covered in oil fuel. Although a line was slung around the man, he being so exhausted that he was dead weight, each time an attempt was made to hoist him out of the water the bowline slipped from his body.

These attempts lasted for about a quarter of an hour, until the man slipped away and was lost in the darkness.

For OG 71 the sinking of the destroyer *Bath* was only the curtain raiser for a long night of horror to come. U-204 was not alone when she fired the opening shots. She had, by then, been joined by U-559, under the command of *Oberleutnant* Hans Heidtmann.

U-559, a Type VIIC built in the Blohm & Voss yard at Hamburg and commissioned at the end of February 1941, was on her first war patrol, having sailed from St. Nazaire on 26 July. She was yet to fire a shot in anger, as was her commander. Twenty-seven-year-old Hans Heidtmann was a career Navy man who had enlisted in 1934, and served on the light cruiser *Deutschland* before transferring to the U-boat Arm. He had then sailed in command of three U-boats on training patrols, but U-559 was his first operational command.

Homing in on U-201 signals, Heidtmann approached the convoy on the surface from the west. His first sighting of the enemy ships was shortly after midnight, when vague shadows on the horizon ahead hardened into a collection of high-sided merchantmen steaming south in orderly lines. On such a dark night manoeuvring into position was not difficult, and at 0112 Heidtmann fired a spread of four torpedoes at the leading ships.

A few minutes earlier, when the night sky astern of the convoy had been turned into day by the brilliant flash of Walter Kell's torpedoes striking *Bath*, all eyes in the other ships had been turned aft. This included Chief Officer C. Speller on watch on the bridge of the 1584-ton *Alva*. The *Alva*, owned by Glen & Company of London, and carrying a full cargo of coal from the Clyde to Lisbon, was the leading ship of Column 6. While Speller was still staring aft, struggling to come to terms with the awesome message of the flash, one of Heidtmann's torpedoes found its mark just forward of the *Alva's* bridge on her starboard side.

The explosion completely wrecked the starboard side of the *Alva's* bridge. Speller, who was keeping watch in the port wing, was showered by coal dust, but suffered no injuries. When his head cleared, he lunged for the engine-room telegraph and rang it to 'Stop'. Seconds later, he was joined on the bridge by Captain Cyril Palmer, who called for an assessment of the damage. The news was not good. Hans Heidtmann's torpedo had hit the *Alva* in her No.3 hold below the waterline, and she was taking on water at an alarming rate. With the starboard list increasing all the time, Palmer ordered all boats and rafts to be cleared away ready for launching, and the crew mustered on the boat deck. A few minutes later, with the ship settling by the head, he gave the order to abandon ship.

There was a considerable westerly swell running, but spurred on by the urgency of the situation Palmer and his men succeeded in launching both *Alva's* lifeboats and two rafts. All twenty-five crew, including five DEMS gunners, left the sinking ship without mishap or injury. Two minutes after they cleared the ship's side, they lay back on their oars and watched the

Alva take her last plunge. Fortunately, rescue was not long in coming, the deep-sea tug *Empire Oak* was on the scene within a few minutes: she picked up the men on the rafts and those in the *Alva's* starboard boat. The tug was followed ten minutes later by the Irish ship *Clonlara*, which dropped back to pick up those in the port boat, including Captain Palmer and Chief Officer Speller. While they were engaged in the rescue, the merchant ships were covered by the corvette *Zinnia*. Considering the blackness of the night and the troublesome swell running, the rescue operation was carried out remarkably swiftly. The *Empire Oak* and *Clonlara* were back on station with the convoy within the hour, when a roll call revealed that only the *Alva's* cook was missing.

The two naval ships, *Hydrangea* and *Wanderer*, continued to search the area for further survivors until daylight, by which time *Leith*, with the starboard quarter of the convoy unprotected, was calling for *Hydrangea* to resume her station. At 0715, satisfied that no more men were alive in the water, Lieutenant Woolfenden transferred most of his survivors to *Wanderer*, retaining nine seriously injured men on board, and at 0820 parted company with the destroyer. *Wanderer*, now running dangerously short of fuel, then set course for Lough Foyle. At 1150, in position 48° 34'N 17° 39' W, *Hydrangea* stopped to bury two of *Bath's* survivors who had died of their wounds after being rescued. They were named as Messboy Erling Gulbrandsen and T.G.M. Meller, a Royal Navy seaman serving in the Norwegian destroyer.

The enemy's ranks were also depleted by the departure for Biscay of U-204 and U-559, both being dangerously low on fuel. This left only Schnee's U-201 and Oesten's U-106 in contact with the convoy.

CHAPTER THREE

In the Darkest Hours

Leading the convoy, *Leith* was zig-zagging from bow to bow at high speed, sweeping with her Asdic and firing starshell to flush out any U-boats that might be ahead of the ships. With both the corvettes *Hydrangea* and *Zinnia* away picking up survivors from *Bath* and the *Alva*, Lieutenant Commander Hutton was becoming increasingly concerned that the rear of the convoy was now almost unprotected. And he had good reason to be concerned. Now that the U-boats had made contact, Adalbert Schnee had abandoned his role as OG 71's shadow, and was fast closing in on the convoy, intent on making good the deficiencies of U-201's previous patrol.

The impromptu concert aboard the *Aguila* had finished early on the previous night with a rendering by the WRNS contingent of a popular song of the day "The World is Waiting for the Sunrise". With the war so near – far closer than any of the young girls realised – this was a brave gesture and a fitting finale for an evening so full of hope. As the twilight closed in, passengers and crew drifted away to various parts of the ship, some to while away another hour or so yarning on the hatch-tops, some to take up a watch, and others to take advantage of an early night in their bunks

Captain Frith remained on the bridge, where he had been since early in the day, uneasy in the knowledge that the convoy was now inching its way across the mouth of the Bay of Biscay and within easy reach of German U-boat and bomber bases in Occupied France. The night promised to be a long one, but then, as master of a merchant ship, Arthur Frith was no stranger to long nights spent pacing the bridge.

Frith's reluctance to leave the *Aguila*'s bridge proved justified when, soon after one o'clock next morning, the night sky astern burst into flame as first the old four-stacker *Bath*, and then the *Alva* fell to the torpedoes of

Walter Kell's U-204 and Hans Heidtmann's U-559. Careful not to start a panic, Frith passed the word quietly for all passengers to be made aware of the danger and warned them to wear their lifejackets at all times. He also gave orders for the Wrens to assemble fully dressed in the ship's library, which was close to the boat deck. The happy and relaxed atmosphere of the previous evening suddenly evaporated, to be replaced by a nervous air of anticipation.

The night wore on, the frenzied activity astern subsided, and by 0300, with little more than an hour to go before daybeak, it seemed that the enemy must have withdrawn. Frith was not fully convinced that the danger had passed, but he did give permission for the passengers to return to their cabins, providing they did not undress and continued to wear lifejackets.

It was now very dark, the darkest hour before the dawn, and under cover of this darkness the convoy made a pre-arranged alteration of course thirty degrees to starboard. They hoped this would shake off any U-boats that might be shadowing. When the *Aguila* was settled on the new course, Captain Frith prepared to see out the rest of the night on the bridge. He would have done so, had Admiral Parker not hinted strongly that he should go below for a rest. It was only then that Frith who, sustained by endless mugs of coffee and cocoa, had not left the *Aguila's* bridge for more than forty-eight hours, realised how desperately tired he was. Reluctant though he was to take the Commodore's advice, he was forced to accept that in his present exhausted state his judgement might be lacking in an emergency. Finally, he agreed that, in view of the apparent lull in the attack, he could be spared for an hour or two. Instructing the officer of the watch to call him at the slightest sign of trouble, he retired to his accommodation immediately below the bridge. As he descended the ladder to the deck below, U-201, hidden in the darkness, was painstakingly manoeuvring into position to fire her torpedoes.

Yeoman of Signals Fred Buckingham, the senior hand of Admiral Parker's staff, was free to go off duty after the convoy was settled on its new course, but an uneasy feeling that all was not well kept him on the bridge. A few minutes after three o'clock, when he was obliged to slip below to answer a call of nature, his premonition was justified. While he was below decks he felt the ship shudder under the shock of what seemed like a heavy explosion. Buckingham immediately returned to the bridge, where to his amazement he found that no alarm had been raised, and all seemed quiet with the convoy, no soaring rockets, no starshell, no rumble of depth charges being dropped. Was he imagining things?

Unhappily, Fred Buckingham's imagination was not working overtime. The blast he had felt below decks, but had gone unnoticed on the bridge, was the shock of Adalbert Schnee's torpedo exploding in the hull of the leading ship of Column 2, the 1809-ton *Ciscar*.

Built just after the First World War, the *Ciscar* was owned by MacAndrews & Company of London, who in the inter-war years had operated a joint service with the Yeoward Line, carrying general cargo and passengers outward and fruit homeward between British ports, Spain and Morocco. On her current voyage, the *Ciscar* had been chartered to carry 1,400 tons of Government stores from Bristol to Gibraltar. She was armed with a 4-inch anti-submarine gun and nine machine-guns, manned by a team of nine DEMS gunners. In command was Captain Edward Hughes, and her total complement, including the gunners, was thirty-nine. Captain Hughes put on record the events of the night:

At 0310 BST on the 19th August, in position 49° 10'N 17° 40' W, we were struck by a torpedo in the engine-room on the port side just abaft the funnel, practically amidships. Nothing had been seen of the submarine or of the track of the torpedo, the explosion was not very loud, more of a dull thud, there was no flash or smoke and no water was thrown up, but there was a strong smell of cordite. I was standing on the starboard side of the bridge at the time; I started to run over to the port side when I found that the port side of the bridge had been blown away and debris and splinters were falling all around me. Three or four seconds later a second torpedo struck the vessel, again on the port side, this time further aft in No.4 hold which contained general cargo. The explosion was again dull, there was no flash and nothing was seen of the track of the torpedo. The 4-inch gun fitted aft was blown to one side, hatch covers and beams of No.4 were blown off, and a sailor who was walking past this hatch at the time was blown 50 feet into the air and into the water. (He was picked up later). The gunners' quarters in the tween deck of No. 4 hold were wrecked and the four gunners must have been killed instantly by the second torpedo.

After this the vessel at once started to list to port going down by the stern as she rapidly heeled over 90°, finally settling by the stern and disappearing within 45 seconds. Just before she went I told the 2nd Officer to lay off the course; he ran out of the chartroom, the gunner followed him, then the man at the wheel, and I told them to get on to the raft which was on top of the hatch near the bridge. I jumped over the top of the wheelhouse to the other side, grabbed hold of a raft, and two seconds later the vessel sank under me and I was in the water. The others had no chance to follow me and were washed over the lee side of the ship. Everyone was wearing a lifejacket fitted with a red light. These red lights are wonderful but on this occasion several failed to work.

Caught in the suction of the sinking ship, Hughes' grip on the liferaft was broken, and he found himself being dragged down into the depths of the cold, dark waters. Fighting every inch of the way, he was taken fifty to sixty feet down, before the hungry sea released its hold on him, and he shot to the surface again. He came up within ten feet of the liferaft, and swam towards it.

Captain Hughes was a competent swimmer, but the wooden raft, drawing only a foot or two of water, was being blown away from him by the strong breeze faster than he could swim. Eventually, he was forced to look around for something else to support him. Luckily, he found a wooden hatch cover, which would just take his weight and no more. Looking around him, he saw a cluster of tiny red lights bobbing on the choppy sea nearby. He was not alone in this dark, alien world.

Very soon after the *Ciscar* had sunk beneath the waves, a cheer went up from those in the water when a ship was seen approaching. She was the 800-ton British motor vessel *Stork* riding very low in the water, her main deck rails almost awash; an ideal rescue ship. As the *Stork* neared the survivors, so convinced were they that their ordeal was over, became hysterical. When their would be rescuer failed to stop, or even slow down, their disappointment was acute. Someone on the bridge of the *Stork* hailed them as she passed by, with reassuring the survivors with words to the effect that the next ship along would pick them up.

There was indeed another ship following close in the wake of the *Stork.* She was the 1810-ton *Cervantes*, the *Ciscar's* sister ship. The men in the water recognised her, and again the cheers went up. The cold, wet, and now forlorn survivors suffered another bitter disappointment. The *Cervantes* steamed past without even an acknowledgment of their predicament.

The twenty-six *Ciscar* survivors were eventually picked up by the 1354-ton *Petrel,* which had been nominated as one of three rescue ships for the convoy. The *Petrel* lowered two boats, and lay stopped for two hours while she carried out the rescue work. Captain Hughes, who had lost his red lifejacket light, and was therefore difficult to locate in the darkness, was one of the last to be pulled from the water. Commenting on the torpedoing of his ship later, he said:

On talking over the attack, four of my crew said they had seen the periscope of the submarine standing 2 feet out of the water. One man said it was stationery, another that it was moving towards the rear of the convoy, but I saw nothing myself and very much doubt these statements.

With regard to straggling, one of the Irish ships, the s.s. Lanahrone, straggled during the afternoon of the 18th, the day before the attack, and the 2nd Officer complained to me once or twice about this ship showing bright lights. She was with the convoy when we were torpedoed as I saw her when I was in the water. One thing about these Irish ships is that they all have distinctive red and white funnel markings, which could easily be seen by enemy aircraft, and the enemy would then know that the convoy is bound for Gibraltar.

The Limerick Steamship Company's ships *Clonlara* and *Lanahrone*, appeared to be reluctant participants in OG 71. As neutral seamen, sailing under a neutral flag, they wanted no part of this terrible war of attrition. Moreover, they were unused to convoy routine and their behaviour had become a matter of concern to the other ships.

During the night of the 20th, a night during which the U-boats had kept their distance, the Irish ships, (despite frequent warnings by the nearest escorting corvette, HMS *Campion*) continued to show lights from time to time. This was probably due to poor blackout arrangements in both ships rather than deliberate rule breaking intention. However, Lieutenant Commander Johnson, *Campion's* commander, eventually became so frustrated by their laxity, that when *Clonlara* again showed a light, he put a burst across her bridge with the Lewis gun. He then hailed the offending ship and told her, in no uncertain terms, that he would open fire on her in earnest unless she mended her ways. When morning came, the Commodore ordered the *Clonlara* to change her position into the centre of the convoy, where other ships would be able to keep an eye on her.

Captain Hughes reported that he had heard a loud explosion when he was in the water, which he assumed was another ship being hit. His assumption was all too correct.

Schnee had used the scatter-gun principle when firing his opening salvo of four torpedoes at the leading ships of Convoy OG 71. His theory was, that with the seven columns of slow-moving merchantmen keeping close station on one another, if he missed the first ship, then its opposite number in the next column was likely to be hit. And so it was. U-201's torpedoes completely missed the lead ship of Column 1 and sped on towards the unfortunate *Ciscar*, where two found their target. The remaining two ran across the bow of the *Ciscar*, missed the leading ship of Column 3, and headed straight for the biggest prize of all, the Commodore's ship, *Aguila*.

Although the night was quiet, leaving the *Aguila's* bridge in the danger hours before the dawn was against Captain Frith's better judgement, but he desperately needed rest. As a compromise, he took off only his uniform jacket, and stretched out on his dayroom settee. He would sleep for just one hour, and no more.

Frith was not destined to rest that night. He had no sooner closed his eyes, than the *Aguila* was rocked by two massive explosions in quick succession. The first torpedo struck in her stokehold, the second in the engine-room, only a few feet further aft.

Had the torpedoes gone home in the cargo holds, the cargo probably would have absorbed much of the blast, and although the *Aguila* must have eventually sunk, her going would have been a slow and more dignified process. Unfortunately for the British ship, Adalbert Schnee's missiles had found their target in her vast, largely empty, engine spaces and the effect of the double explosion was catastrophic, literally breaking her in two.

Captain Frith was extremely fortunate to escape from his sinking ship. Tumbling out onto the deck dazed with shock, he found himself knee-deep in water as the sea surged over the rails. Fortunately, at that precise moment a liferaft, automatically released when the forward part of the ship went down, floated past. Realising that he could do nothing to save the *Aguila*, Frith flung himself onto the raft, and floated clear just as the sea claimed the rest of his ship.

As Frith grappled for a hold on the tossing raft, he was joined by Assistant Steward Harold Hughes, who had been in the main lounge when the first torpedo struck the ship. *Aguila's* Wrens and other passengers were sleeping in this lounge, and when the lights went out and the main staircase erupted in flames, panic followed. Hughes, dragging a frightened young Wren with him, managed to escape to the deck by an emergency ladder. He lost the girl in the darkness on deck, and was himself washed overboard as the ship foundered.

The raft was taken down by the suction of the sinking ship, capsizing as it went. Frith and Hughes were thrown clear, but the suction pulled them down after the raft. After what seemed like an age, but was really only seconds, they fought their way back to the surface again, gasping for breath. The buoyant raft, breaking free of the ship, shot to the surface after them, and the two exhausted men managed to clamber back aboard. Very shortly, they were joined by Yeoman of Signals Fred Buckingham, who later made the following statement:

At 0308, I heard a violent explosion to starboard and to seaward, and ran to the bridge to the starboard side and at exactly 0310 a torpedo hit the ship on the port side abaft the bridge. Within a few seconds a second torpedo struck the ship again somewhat further aft. I gathered my CBs (Confidential Books) and a flare and ran to the starboard side of the lower bridge with the 2nd Officer. At this time the Commodore was standing in the port wing of the bridge. I tried to light the rocket when the ship broke in half and the 2nd Officer and I were carried forward beneath the rigging, in which I became caught. I released myself and on reaching the surface I found a raft quite close, and swam for it. I passed about five people floating in the water whilst I was swimming. My watch stopped at 0311½.

The men Fred Buckingham saw in the water were Able Seaman Joseph Bautenbach, Able Seaman Arthur Cracknell, Ordinary Seaman Bruno Hännile, Assistant Officers' Cook Sydney Cole, Assistant Steward David Kerr, Leading Aircraftman William Churchouse and William McCrae, a DEMS gunner from the *Ciscar* who had been blown overboard when his ship was hit. One of these survivors, 22-year-old Joseph Bautenbach, later wrote:

I can vaguely remember going over the side, after switching on the light which we all carried on our life-jackets. My one thought was to swim away as fast as I could to avoid being sucked down by the ship. Whilst I was doing this, I passed people in the water, who did not respond when I called to them. After a while, I took a breather and looked back to where the ship should have been, but she was gone. At that point I looked to the sky and thanked God I was alive. For a moment I wondered how Arthur (Cracknell) was, and also whether any of the twenty-two WRENS, who had been on board, had survived. Some of them had been singing and dancing on the deck the evening before. They were a happy lot.

Then I decided to look for something to keep me afloat. I swam towards a light that I could see bobbing about, and came upon a raft which had floated off the ship when she went down, and lo and behold! who should be on board but Arthur! He helped me aboard and we clung to each other, sobbing our hearts out. We talked about our experiences and he said that he had been on the boat deck when the torpedoes struck, and without thinking had jumped into a lifeboat which was slung on the davits beside him. When the ship split, it tore the boat in half and he fell into the water, and then the raft fell in next to him. We had recovered slightly when we noticed a figure approaching in the water; we helped him aboard and he told us he was Bill Churchouse, a Fleet Air Arm rating going to Gibraltar to join an aircraft carrier.

Captain Frith, Fred Buckingham and Harold Hughes eventually ended up on the same raft, while three others were on a smaller raft. Frith was of the opinion that the eight men were all that was left of his crew and passengers, but, unknown to him at the time, there were others.

When, early on the 19th, the peace of the warm summer's night was shattered by the savage attack on OG 71 by Walter Kell in U-204 and Hans Heidtmann in U-559, the tug *Empire Oak* was steaming in the centre of the convoy. Built to order for the Ministry of War Transport, and managed by the United Towing Company of Hull, the *Empire Oak* was a 482-ton salvage tug assigned to Gibraltar, where she was to be stationed ready to go to the aid of torpedoed ships. Commanded by Captain Fred Christian, with a crew of nineteen, including three DEMS gunners, she was armed with a 12-pounder and two Hotchkiss machine-guns.

The *Empire Oak* was called upon to help seamen in distress sooner than Captain Christian had anticipated:

As we moved ahead we came upon the lifeboats and rafts from the s.s. Alva *so we stopped and picked up 11 survivors, the s.s.*Clonlara *also picking up survivors at the same time.*

We got all the men on board without mishap, although there was a big sea running and it was a dark night. We used white cotton heaving lines to pick up these men, so that they could see them in the darkness, and they remarked later how useful this had been. The convoy kept formation and no emergency turn was made, probably because we were due for an alteration of course at 0200.

I had lost some time picking up survivors so I increased speed and altered course to catch up with the convoy. At 0300 on the 19th, as we drew near the convoy, another attack was made, and I saw the flares going up from the escorts. When we reached that position I saw a number of lights in the water which I took to be the red lights attached to lifejackets. I manoeuvred my ship towards the survivors until they were alongside and my crew could give the utmost help and we picked up 6 men from the s.s. Aguila. *The Chief Officer of the* Aguila, *who was a rather heavy man, was on a raft attending to a man with a broken thigh, but we got them both on board quite safely; the escort was also picking up survivors. We cruised around for a while but could find no more men so I continued and rejoined the convoy at daylight. That afternoon, the 19th, I signaled for a doctor to attend the man whose thigh was broken; he came on board and, after satisfying himself, said that the man would be all right and left the injured man with us.*

The *Aguila* survivors on the two rafts were picked up after one-and-a-half hours by the corvette *Wallflower*, which screened by another corvette, HMS *Campanula*, used star shell to search the sea astern of the convoy. Joseph Bautenbach commented:

Fortunately, we only had to wait a short time amid the explosions which were still going on as the convoy steamed away, before a corvette appeared which we later learned was HMS Wallflower. *We climbed up the scrambling nets which were hanging over the side, and into the arms of the Navy. We were immediately rubbed down, wrapped in a blanket, and then a sailor hove in view with what appeared to be a teapot – although what was in it was certainly not tea, it was Navy rum and it nearly blew our heads off! I have nothing but the highest praise for those Navy men who looked after us so well.*

The gallant old *Aguila*, veteran of so many voyages south to Iberia and the Canaries, had gone to her last resting place in just ninety seconds, taking with her 145 souls, including twenty-two young women. Nineteen-year-old assistant steward David Kerr, who had been assigned to look after the Wrens, was the only survivor able to shed any light on their fate. Floating in the sea, dazed with shock from the explosion that had blown him overboard, he heard cries all around him in the darkness, some of them feminine voices calling for help. Powerless to go to the aid of 'his girls', he was carried away on the swell, the anguished cries becoming fainter and fainter, until he could hear them no more. Not one of those young women, who looked forward so eagerly to their first posting abroad, survived that night. Alongside them died the Convoy Commodore, Vice-Admiral Patrick. E. Parker, DSO, RN, four of his staff, five DEMS gunners, sixty-one naval personnel sailing passenger in the *Aguila,* and fifty-two of her crew.

A dramatic finale to that night of horror came just as the first rays of the rising sun were paling the sky in the east. Walter Kell, in U-204, having caught up with the convoy again after torpedoing *Bath*, fired a fan of four torpedoes into the slow moving columns. Miraculously, the merchantmen in Kell's line of fire escaped unscathed, but the tiny corvette *Campion*, on the other side of the convoy, was suddenly confronted by four streaks of white foam racing towards her. Lieutenant-Commander Johnson was master of the situation, coolly issuing helm and engine orders bringing the corvette short round, and saving her from being blown out of the water.

While the *Empire Oak* and the *Petrel* continued to pick up survivors, *Leith* attempted to bring a semblance of order to the scattered convoy. With both the commodore ship *Aguila* and the vice commodore *Ciscar* gone, the master of the 1589-ton Ellerman's Wilson Line steamer *Spero* was requested to take over as Convoy Commodore. He agreed, and set about reforming the remaining nineteen ships into five columns. This was accomplished by noon, by which time *Empire Oak* and *Petrel* had rejoined. A count of survivors revealed that eleven from the *Alva* and six from the *Aguila* were in the *Empire Oak*, twenty-five from the *Ciscar* in the *Petrel*, nine from the *Aguila* in HMS *Wallflower* and ten from *Bath* aboard HMS *Hydrangea*.

During the daylight hours, there was a change in the U-boat pack. U-204 and U-559, having used up their torpedoes, were ordered home, their places being filled by the arrival of U-552 and U-564. U-552, two days out of St. Nazaire, was under the command of Erich Topp, while U-564, which had left Brest on the 16th, was commanded by Reinhard Suhren. Both Topp and Suhren were experienced commanders with a string of sinkings to their credit.

It had been feared that another attack would come that night, but a sudden deterioration in the weather brought heavy rain and poor visibility. A series of alterations of course were made, which it was hoped would confuse the U-boats. However, at 2200, the corvette *Zinnia*, screening on the port quarter, reported seeing a flare some miles astern, indicating a possible shadower. The flare may have been shown by U-106, which had reported to BdU that she was in contact with OG 71 at 1713.

The night passed without incident, but out in the rain-swept darkness the wolves were gathering. U-106, U-201 and U-564 were lying in wait some miles ahead, and others were battering their way through the rising seas, eager to join in the battle.

At 2258 U-201 signalled Lorient that she was in contact. Adalbert Schnee's sighting was brief, however, for during the night the convoy went through a series of no less than eight alterations of course under the direction of the master of the *Spero,* By the time daylight came on the 20th OG 71 had shaken off her pursuers. And help was on the way.

Following the sinking of the destroyer *Bath,* OG 71's escort force was left with no ships capable of high speeds – even the sloop *Leith* could manage only 16½ knots – which, in effect, meant that not one of the escorts was capable of overhauling a U-boat running on the surface. The Admiralty decided to redress this imbalance, and at noon on the 19th the destroyers *Gurkha* and *Lance* were ordered to leave Convoy WS 10, then 350 miles to the north-west, and join the beleaguered OG 71 at full speed.

HMS *Gurkha* and HMS *Lance*, Tribal-class and Weapons-class destroyers respectively, were both 35-knot ships, the senior ship being *Gurkha,* commanded by Lieutenant-Commander C.N. Lentaigne. In command of *Lance* was Lieutenant Commander Ralph Northcott RN, DSO. After leaving WS 10, the two destroyers set course to the south-east at 22 knots, with *Lance* keeping station on *Gurkha's* port beam at visibility distance. Both ships were equipped with the new HF/DF (High Frequency Direction Finder), with which they were able to take accurate bearings of U-boat radio transmissions. *Gurkha* also carried radar. They had not steamed many miles before bearings were obtained, too weak then to be of use, but after dark, as the destroyers approached the convoy, the German transmissions increased in frequency and strength. It was plainly obvious that OG 71 was being shadowed by several U-boats.

At 0320 on the 20th, *Gurkha* and *Lance* were 2 miles astern of the convoy, and overtaking rapidly. Contact was established with OG 71, and Lieutenant Commander Lentaigne, although the senior man in time served, agreed with Lieutenant Commander Hutton that he, Hutton, should continue as S.O.E, while *Gurkha* and *Lance* operated independently, acting as an anti-submarine striking force and anti-aircraft guard. This established, Lentaigne reduced speed to 12 knots and the two destroyers began to sweep astern and on both sides of the convoy at a distance of 4 miles, the intention being to surprise any U-boats that might be planning a dawn attack. Visibility was now very poor and Asdic conditions bad. HF/DF bearings were obtained indicating the presence of U-boats, but no attack developed, although the drone of at least one aircraft circling overhead was a grim reminder that the enemy was still with them in the air. In fact, six U-boats, U-106, U124, U-126, U-201, U-552 and U-564, were also in the vicinity.

There was no improvement in the visibility with the coming of daylight, and *Gurkha* and *Lance* remained screening astern of the convoy, acting independently of the other escorts. At 1110, on receipt of orders from the Admiralty, *Hydrangea* left the convoy to proceed to Gibraltar to land the survivors from *Bath*, many of whom were seriously injured. It was soon after she left that the *Focke-Wulf* was sighted.

It fell to Ordinary Seaman Vaughan, a lookout in HMS *Leith*, to be first to sight the enemy aircraft. The four-engined Condor was 7 miles off, low down on the water, and hidden from sight whenever it passed through the mist patches; it was closing on the convoy with obvious intent. *Leith* immediately opened fire with all guns that could be brought to bear. No hits were scored, but the hot reception caused the *Focke-Wulf* to sheer away. It then began to circle the convoy out of range of its guns, its radio sending a continuous series of coded signals on 352 k/cs. The wolves were being called in to attack.

Fortunately for OG 71, the Condor's radio transmissions were affected by the poor weather conditions, and were consequently garbled when received by Lorient. When, at 1400, BdU contacted the U-boats, the convoy was actually 120 miles south-south-east of the position given. Not surprisingly, the U-boats searched for their quarry without success, and just before sunset U-201, U-564 and U-106 made a rendezvous in mid-ocean to discuss tactics. Later they joined up with U-124 and U-126 to form a line of search on the surface at 13 knots.

Meanwhile, the U-boat transmissions were being closely monitored by OG 71's escort vessels, now reinforced by the arrival of another destroyer, HMS *Boreas*. HF/DF bearings taken indicated that at least five, and possibly seven, U-boats were spread out on a rough line parallel to the convoy at a distance of 15 miles. Correctly, as it turned out, Lieutenant Commander Hutton assumed that the U-boats were, as yet, ignorant of the exact position of the convoy, but had a shrewd idea of where to search. Rather than send ships in pursuit of the U-boats, Hutton and Lentaigne decided to stage a diversion. The corvette *Bluebell* was ordered to leave the convoy as soon as it was dark, to steam to the north-west for two hours, and then simulate a battle, firing starshell, dropping depth charges, and using her radio to send a bogus signal to the Admiralty. It was hoped that this disturbance would result in the U-boats racing for *Bluebell's* position, leaving the convoy to escape to the south. Having created a convincing diversion, the corvette was to make off to the east at full speed, hopefully with the U-boats in pursuit, and rejoin the convoy at dawn on the 22nd.

Shortly after midnight, starshell was seen to the north-west, followed by the thump of exploding depth charges and a great deal of excited chatter on the R/T. It was a very convincing battle, seen and heard from afar, and in the early hours of the 22nd HF/DF bearings were growing noticeably weaker and further north. The rest of the night passed peacefully, and when *Bluebell* rejoined the convoy at first light it was assumed that the ruse had worked. But those manning BdU's Operations Room at Lorient were not deceived. They guessed correctly that *Bluebell's* show was intended to mislead, and while U-75 and U-552 were ordered to investigate the starshell display, all other U-boats in the vicinity were instructed to continue searching on a southerly course.

CHAPTER FOUR

Crescendo

Friday 22 August opened quietly over OG 71. The weather was fine and pleasantly warm, the convoy then being in latitude 42° and some 150 miles due west of Vigo. At 0830, a Catalina of RAF Coastal Command appeared overhead. This was the first friendly aircraft seen in two days and her arrival was welcomed with a cheer. OG 71 was sorely in need of help from the air, however transient. Unfortunately, communication between the aircraft and the ships proved to be extremely difficult. Furthermore, the feeling of added security felt with the arrival of the flying boat was quickly dispelled when, just over an hour later, two *Focke-Wulf* Condors were sighted coming in from the north-east.

The big four-engined bombers began to circle out of range of the convoy's guns, the homing signals they were transmitting to the U-boats clearly audible to the wireless operators in the ships below. The Catalina was lightly armed, and with a top speed of 120 mph, only half that of the German planes, it was powerless to challenge them. The destroyer *Lance*, with her six 4-inch dual-purpose guns was sent to drive off the Condors, but like the birds of prey from which they were named they continued to hover near the vulnerable merchantmen.

The enemy aircraft stayed until noon, when they made one last circuit of the convoy, and then flew away. This was no great comfort to the men manning the ships of OG 71, for they knew well that it was only a matter of time before the U-boats would be with them. Fortunately for their peace of mind, they were not aware that the wolves were gathering in such force. Closing in on the convoy in answer to a call from Lorient were Helmuth Ringelmann in U-75, Jürgen Oesten in U-106, Klaus Scholtz in U-108, Erich Topp in U-552, Ottokar Paulshen in U-557 and Reinhard Suhren in U-564. Adalbert Schnee's U-201 had temporarily lost contact after being forced to dive deep by the circling

Catalina, but the position of the OG 71 was already known with some degree of accuracy by Lorient.

The convoy's sagging morale was given a welcome boost when, at 1237, the 31-knot destroyer *Wivern* came over the horizon. The Admiralty, alerted to the increased danger threatening the convoy, had sent in yet another reinforcement. OG 71's escort now consisted of four destroyers, one sloop and five corvettes. Lieutenant Commander Lentaigne rearranged his outer screen, positioning the destroyers around the convoy at a distance of 6 miles, while Hutton's corvettes were drawn closer in around the merchantmen.

The first alarm came at 1250, when HMS *Boreas* reported that the Catalina had sighted a U-boat right ahead. *Lance* and *Boreas* were sent away to search for the enemy, but no contact was made. From the reports he was now receiving, Hutton estimated that at least eight U-boats were in the vicinity, some of them very close, but other than keeping the convoy together within the double ring of escorts, there was little else he could do but to wait.

The break in the ranks of the convoy came without warning later in the afternoon, when, at 1500, the steamer *Marklyn*, sailing in ballast, hoisted two black balls and began to fall astern of the others. She signaled the Commodore by lamp indicating she had engine problems which might take some time to fix. Meanwhile she was dropping out of the convoy.

The corvette *Campanula*, which was keeping station on the convoy's starboard quarter, was ordered to stand by the *Marklyn*, and half an hour later, while the two ships were straggling astern, the ominous drone of aero-engines was heard in the north. Very soon, two He 111 bombers appeared flying high. The German pilots spotted the helpless *Marklyn* and immediately swooped on her. Second Engineer A.W. Walker, in the Irish ship *Clonlara*, was an eyewitness to the attack:

> *About 1530 I heard and felt two loud reports and shocks. I immediately went on deck to see what had happened and noticed that one ship had dropped out of the convoy and that one of the corvettes was standing by her. Suddenly two aircraft appeared, one attacked the corvette and the other attacked the damaged ship, which was the* Marklyn. *Four bombs were dropped near the corvette and five near the* Marklyn, *but none of them appeared to do any damage. All the ships in the convoy opened fire and the planes flew off and we did not see them again.*

Both the *Marklyn* and *Campanula* came out of the attack unscathed, and shortly afterwards the *Marklyn's* engineers, possibly spurred on by the bombs falling near the ship, reported to the bridge that repairs had been completed. Both ships then made speed to rejoin the convoy.

At 1636, reliable HF/DF bearings taken by several escorts indicated a submarine bearing 237° at 8 miles. *Boreas* and *Wivern* were sent to investigate, but even though conditions were ideal with a smooth sea and visibility in excess of 20 miles the destroyers were unable to make a contact . They were not chasing a ghost, however. U-564 had been discreetly shadowing the convoy for more than three hours.

Entries in *Oberleutnant* Suhren's War Diary show that he first sighted the smoke of the convoy at 1258. At the same time he also sighted an aircraft circling which he identified as a Catalina, and therefore hostile. He consequently made his approach with extreme caution, on the surface, but trimmed down so that only U-564's conning tower was showing above water. By 1500, he had the Allied ships in sight, and sent a brief signal to Lorient informing them of his contact with OG 71. He was ordered to shadow the convoy and report its position at regular intervals. Meanwhile, Lorient ordered the other members of the wolf pack to close in.

Enemy radio traffic was now intense, a sure sign that the U-boats were preparing to attack. Owing to the limited capability of the merchant ships, many of whom were ageing coal burners, the convoy's speed rarely exceeded 7 knots, and although it was heavily escorted at the moment, that situation would soon change. Both *Gurkha* and *Lance* were running low on fuel, and would have to leave sometime during the next twenty-four hours. Furthermore, the other destroyers, *Boreas* and *Wivern*, had been steaming at full speed throughout that day, and would also soon have to break away to refuel.

The outlook for Convoy OG 71 was very bleak. A signal received from the Admiralty indicated that up to nine U-boats were believed to be in the area, most of them to the west of the convoy. In support were the enemy's long-range bombers, now constantly on the horizon and waiting for an opportunity to attack. A wholesale slaughter of the helpless merchant ships looked to be a distinct possibility.

Lentaigne and Hutton, were by now seriously considering making a dash for Lisbon, which they estimated could be reached before nightfall on the 23rd. At least a third of the ships were bound for that port, and once safe in the neutral waters of the River Tagus the Gibraltar-bound ships would have a breathing space until more escorts could be called in. After consulting with the Acting Convoy Commodore, the two commanders decided to alter course for Lisbon after dark, but first the U-boats must be driven back, so that they were unaware of the diversion.

At 2100, as dusk was setting in, the escorting Catalina, which had been faithfully keeping watch overhead since early morning, was nearing the end of its endurance. The flying boat made one more low level run over the convoy, waggled its wings in farewell, and turned for home, its crew eagerly contemplating a hot meal and a soft bed after a gruelling day's work.

HF/DF bearings taken of U-boat radio transmissions indicated that the wolves – possibly eight or nine in number – were moving in from the west and, to meet the threat OG 71's destroyers, commenced an anti-submarine sweep. *Boreas, Gurkha, Lance* and *Wivern* formed up in line abreast, 3 miles apart, and with guns' crews closed up and depth charge parties standing by, set off to the west at 18 knots with their bow waves frothing. The horizon ahead of them was still light, but behind them, in the direction of the convoy, it was dark. Against this backdrop they would not be easily seen from the west, which might enable them to surprise any approaching U-boats on the surface. While they were away, HMS *Leith* and the five corvettes moved closer to the convoy, drawing a thin protective ring around the slow-steaming merchantmen.

The deployment of the destroyers by Lentaigne was a bold move, but it proved to be misguided. Admiral Sir Percy Noble, C-in-C Western Approaches, later commented:

It is considered that the Senior Officer Destroyers was incorrect in using his destroyers as a striking force in the vicinity of the convoy. Except in cases where destroyers from other Commands join a convoy for part of the trip and are specially detailed as a striking force, it is essential that all A/S escorts act under one Senior Officer...It is considered that while some offensive action must if possible be taken against shadowing U-boats with the object of trying to shake them off, and while escorts are authorised to do this by W.A.C.I. part 306, paragraph 9, Gurkha on this occasion made an error of judgement in carrying out a sweep with all destroyers at a time when U-boat attack was likely and the corvettes in company were very inexperienced...

As it transpired, unknown to Lieutenant Commander Lentaigne, U-564 was already inside his net, and stealthily approaching the convoy.

U-564, another Type VII C with an impressive record, was under the command of 25-year-old *Oberleutnant* Reinhard Johann Heinz Paul Anton

44

Suhren, known simply as 'Teddy' throughout the Service. Young in years, perhaps, Reinhard Suhren was long on experience, having learned his trade as First Watch Officer of the highly successful U-48. Under his command, U-564, although only four months out of the Blohm & Voss yard at Hamburg, had already made her mark in the attack on Convoy HX 133, sinking two 8500-ton ships and damaging another. Two days later, acting alone, Suhren sent the Icelandic ship *Helka* to the bottom. Suhren was well on his way to becoming one of Germany's top U-boat aces.

U-564's first contact with OG 71 came soon after midday. Suhren's War Diary reads:

1258	Smooth sea, clear skies, visibility over 20 miles	Five smoke clouds bearing 115° in sight. Course 120°.
1330		One aeroplane, probably a Sunderland, in sight.
1340		A U-boat in sight bearing 060°. It approaches nearer.
1450		A Sunderland in sight bearing 100°, course 130°. Turned away to port and flew off.
1455		The U-boat out of sight bearing 000°.
1500	Quadrant CG 1565	One smoke cloud bearing 100°. Soon after more smoke clouds appear, four in total. It is finally the convoy after a long search. Air Reconnaisance has again provided inadequate information.
1550		One aeroplane in sight bearing 150°, but very far away
1600	Quadrant CG 1595 Wind W'ly 1, swell SSW. Isolated clouds. Very good visibility.	Reporting continuously. Furthermore, as ordered, transmitting beacon signals for Luftwaffe. Convoy air cover in sight, two aeroplanes on same side.

On receipt of Suhren's sighting report, Lorient ordered all U-boats to 'make the utmost use of the opportunity to attack'. Uncharacteristically, they were told 'on no account to economise on torpedoes'. In fact, they were urged to use salvoes of four when attacking. Such was Dönitz's determination to stop OG 71 getting through.

The odds were in Reinhard Suhren's favour as he approached the convoy. The night was dark, with little wind and a relatively calm sea, and the destroyers were away chasing shadows. Suhren made an unhurried approach on the surface, and when he was within 1,500 metres of the ships in OG 71's starboard column, he gave the order to fire the four forward tubes simultaneously. Tubes 1, 2 and 4 responded, and three torpedoes sped towards the concentrated mass of merchant ships; however, the bow cover of Tube 3 failed to open. Reacting quickly, Suhren turned the boat short round, and fired the fourth torpedo from the stern tube.

The deep-sea tug *Empire Oak*, having been in the thick of the attack on the convoy on the night of the 19th, had on board seventeen survivors from the stricken ships *Alva* and *Aguila*. Thereafter, she had remained a state of immediate readiness with guns manned and extra lookouts posted. Captain Christian was in the starboard wing of the tug's tiny open bridge, scanning the western horizon, when out of the corner of his eye, he caught a fleeting glimpse of a feathered track racing in from two points on the starboard bow. A fraction of a second later, Christian felt the big tug stagger as one of Suhren's torpedoes exploded in her engine-room. The explosion threw up a huge column of water and debris which then fell back on the bridge, drenching Christian and the deck he was standing on.

When the sudden downpour ceased, a dazed Fred Christian watched in horror as the *Empire Oak's* funnel collapsed and fell over one side of the tug, while the mainmast went the other way; a sure sign that the torpedo had broken her back. Any doubts he might have had were confirmed when, seconds later, his ship sank under him, dragging him down with her. Christian later reported:

I was taken down with the suction but had my lifejacket on and soon came up, when I noticed about 10 ft of her bow still above water, absolutely perpendicular, and after 5 minutes this too disappeared. Ten minutes later I saw the Clonlara *torpedoed. She was the rear ship of a column and about ¾ mile away, almost abreast of the position where we were hit. She seemed to be struck by two torpedoes, as I distinctly saw, in the light of the flares that were fired from the escort, two columns of water, one on her port side and one to starboard.*

The Irish collier *Clonlara*, which in view of her tendency to show lights at night had been moved to a position in the inner ranks of the convoy, had the misfortune to be next in line for one of Reinhard Suhren's bow torpedoes. In addition to her crew of nineteen, the *Clonlara* had on board thirteen survivors from the *Alva*, who now suffered the indignity of being torpedoed for the second time in less than four days. Second Engineer A.W. Walker, of the *Clonlara*, survived the attack, and later wrote:

...we were struck by a torpedo in No.1 hold on the port side (sic), shattering the forward part of the ship. The Captain was on the bridge and ordered us to abandon ship.

The engines and dynamos had stopped and we went to boat stations. As we were getting into the boats about five minutes later we were struck by another torpedo on the starboard side in the boiler-room. The boilers blew up and I remember flying through the air and landing in the water. I went under and when I came to the surface I found myself under the stern of the ship which had settled by the bow and her propeller out of the water. The ship sank about three minutes after she was struck by the second torpedo.

I swam away as quickly as I could and saw a lifeboat about 50 yards away and swam towards it. This boat had been cast off and had drifted away from the ship. It was half full of water, but seemed otherwise to be alright. A donkeyman appeared swimming towards me so I pulled him into the boat. Then two men appeared close by so I threw them a lifebuoy each and dragged them in. We had not been able to free the oars as they were lashed down with wire and we could not get them adrift. We eventually managed to free them, but the boat was half full of water and we had nothing with which to bale it out. I started to row with one oar, but my feet gave way and I could do nothing more.

About 10 minutes later a corvette came along. We shouted to it and he answered us, but went away. This corvette, HMS Campion, *circled round and came back to us and lowered a boat which came to us and told us to pull alongside the corvette, while the boat picked up survivors from the water.*

While the *Clonlara* survivors were being taken on board by *Campion*, Captain Fred Christian and those who survived the sinking of the *Empire Oak*, were in the water nearby, still awaiting rescue. Christian later remarked:

Whilst we were in the water depth charges were dropped and the shock from these was like a kick in the stomach. The shock was much worse than when the Clonlara *was torpedoed, and she was only ¾ mile away. I cannot say how close the depth charges were to us, but it was a horrible sensation.*

Christian and his men suffered a further disappointment when Cardigan Shipping Company's *Grelhead* sailed past them, oblivious to their frantic calls for help. It was not until two hours later that the corvette *Campanula* sighted a cluster of red lifejacket lights and came to their rescue. Captain Christian wrote in his report to the Admiralty:

I did my best to save the Mate of the Aguila, *but he was very despondent, this being the second time he had been torpedoed within a few days. I myself was all right, even after 2 hours in the water, and I found a piece of wood which I told the Mate to hang on to whilst I held the other (end) so that we should not be separated. My Chief Officer was also quite near us and we three remained together. He too was very downhearted, especially when the ships passed without stopping. I kept cheering these two up, sometimes pretending to bully them so that they would not give up hope. When eventually the* Campanula *came along they told us that we must be patient as they could not pick up everyone at once. I could see some more lights at a little distance from us, and knowing I was all right and that these men might not be, I told the* Campanula *to carry on as I should be all right. They lowered a boat for these men then came back for us and threw us a line. Unfortunately the light on the lifejacket of the Mate of the* Aguila *had gone out so the rope was thrown to me, and as I tried to catch it I let go the piece of wood and the Mate drifted away. With the backlash of the rope I lost it, then I got cramp in my legs and could not swim back for the Mate. Eventually I caught hold of the rope and I called to them to pull me up, which they did, and as I reached the deck I told them about the Mate of the* Aguila, *stressing the fact that he had no light so would be difficult to find. Also, just before I parted from him I heard him give a kind of groan, and when I called out to him I received no reply. They bundled me below, of course, and the Mate was never found. My Chief Officer was also thrown a line and pulled on board. It would have been so much better if the corvette had put nets over the side, as I am sure I could have climbed up, and the Mate could at least have hung on, or even a rope ladder would have done. I believe the* Campanula *had nets and do not know why she did not use them.*

The rescue operation all but ended in disaster, as HMS *Gurkha* came racing back to join the escort screen. She was close to the convoy when a flare and a flashing light were seen on her starboard bow, and nearby a 'low dark object', which was identified in the heat of the moment as a U-boat on the surface. Lentaigne immediately altered course to ram, but at the last minute realised that the 'low dark object' was in fact the part-submerged hull of a torpedoed ship. Only by hauling the *Gurkha* round under full port helm did he avoid ploughing through the men struggling in the water.

There was a heavy loss of life from the two torpedoed ships. The tug *Empire Oak*, manned by a crew of twenty, including three DEMS gunners, also had on board eleven survivors from the *Alva*, and six from the *Aguila*. When she went down, twenty-three men went with her, fourteen of her crew, including the gunners, the six *Aguila* survivors, and three from the *Alva*. The *Clonlara* was carrying nineteen crew and thirteen survivors from the *Alva*, of which 12 crew, including Captain Joseph Reynolds, and eight survivors were lost.

Amongst all this confusion, HMS *Campion* had a narrow escape. Reinhard Suhren fired a final salvo of four torpedoes, which were seen to go streaking across the corvette's bows. Lieutenant Commander Johnson reacted instinctively, bringing *Campion* round under full port helm to present her stern to her hidden attacker.

Following the torpedoing of the *Empire Oak* and *Clonlara*, the Acting Commodore of OG 71, in the *Spero*, signalled an emergency turn to 120°, this course to be steered until 0400 on the 23rd, when the convoy would return to 150°. It was hoped that this diversion, made under the cover of darkness, might confuse the U-boats, but eventually resulted in the loss of another ship. When, at 2300, *Spero* switched on the requisite coloured lights denoting a change of course, the 2129-ton Norwegian-flag steamer *Spind*, carrying a cargo of coal and engine parts from Barry to Lisbon, failed to see the signal. The other ships altered course towards the coast, but the *Spind* carried on, and Captain Johannes Berg Jonassen soon found his ship alone on an empty sea.

After sinking the *Ciscar* and *Aguila* in the early hours of the 19th, Adalbert Schnee had taken U-201 deep to avoid the avenging depth charges of OG 71's escorts. By dawn, he was back on the surface again, shadowing the convoy at a discreet distance, and looking for an opportunity to add to his score of enemy ships. However, Lieutenant Commander Hutton had by this time positioned his escorts in an impenetrable ring around the merchantmen. Although he used every trick he had learned in his four years in U-boats, Schnee was unable to manoeuvre into a favourable position to fire his torpedoes again.

Throughout the rest of the night and the day that followed, U-201 followed tenaciously in the wake of the convoy, but late that night rain set in, the visibility deteriorated, and all contact with OG 71 was lost. Schnee reported the situation to BdU in Lorient, and was ordered to continue searching to the south.

At 1600 on the 20th, Schnee made a rendezvous with Jürgen Oesten in U-106, Ernst Bauer in U-126 and Reinhard Suhren in U-564. The meeting was without the sanction of Lorient, the four commanders were all frustrated at their inability to get to grips with OG 71. Lying stopped in hailing distance of each other, they held an impromptu council of war lasting nearly two hours. Eventually, they parted company and began sweeping to the east and south at 13 knots. They searched an empty sea for three hours, until, with darkness coming in, the organised hunt was abandoned, and the boats went their own separate ways.

In the meantime, under the cloak of darkness, and helped by the rain and failing visibility, OG 71 had disappeared into the night. It was not until well after sunrise on the 21st that the first clue to the whereabouts of the convoy reached Adalbert Schnee. At 0646, he received a brief signal from U-564 reporting a British flying boat sighted in 43° 33'N 15° 45' W, some 260 miles due west of Cape Finsterre. Assuming that any British aircraft venturing so far from home must be giving cover to a convoy, Schnee headed for the reported position at full speed.

The day revealed nothing but a few Spanish fishing boats scurrying for home, and by midnight, with not a single ship in sight, Schnee was beginning to accept that Suhren's 'British flying boat' must have been a patrolling *Focke-Wulf*. Then, fifteen minutes into 22 August, lookouts searching the horizon reported a dark shadow to the west. Within minutes, the shadow had resolved itself into the unmistakeable silhouette of a convoy escort vessel. She was on a south-easterly course, and appeared to be making full speed.

After checking round the horizon for other ships, and finding none, Schnee tucked U-201 into the wake of the hurrying warship, and followed at a safe distance. No evidence has come to light regarding the identity of the escort, but it seems highly likely that Schnee had stumbled upon the corvette *Bluebell* rejoining OG 71 after staging a mock battle to the north-west to draw off the U-boats. Inadvertently, the corvette was now leading U-201 directly towards the convoy.

Suhren was in radio contact with two of the newcomers, Helmuth Ringelmann in U-75 and Erich Topp in U-552, and homing in on his bearings, they moved in to join the chase.

The sun climbed over the eastern horizon soon after 0500 on Friday 22 August, its golden rays revealing a flawless blue sky and a glassy calm sea. In more peaceful times it would have been a perfect summer's day, a day to enjoy, but Adalbert Schnee, motoring on the surface and nervously scanning the horizon from U-201's conning tower, felt cruelly exposed. His worst fears were realised when, three hours later, with the sun well up, the lookout man on U-201's after gun platform shouted a warning. Schnee followed the man's pointing finger and was horrified to see an enemy destroyer coming up astern, her razor-sharp bows cleaving a foaming path through the calm sea. There could be no doubt that the U-boat had been seen and the enemy was intent on ramming.

Schnee hit the alarm and followed the lookouts down the ladder, slamming the conning tower hatch shut after him. By the time he landed on the deck of the control room, U-201 was under and going deep.

Leveling off at 80 metres, Schnee ordered silent routine. Isolated in their gently rolling iron coffin lying deep in the cold Atlantic, the men of U-201 were only too well aware of the danger that threatened. Those who needed to move, did so with extreme care, the others stood at their posts like waxworks dummies, the strain showing in their faces as they waited to receive what they knew must soon come.

As the enemy destroyer approached, the threshing of her twin screws was clearly audible. And then the depth charges began to rain down, the thunderous blast of their explosions hammering at U-201's flimsy pressure hull, and tossing her from side to side like a rag doll being worried by an angry dog.

The weather conditions on the surface were ideal for the unknown attacking destroyer, and for the next three hours she crossed and re-crossed over the submerged boat. Each time her Asdic told her she was near the target, a pattern of depth charges went tumbling down into the depths. The attack was unrelenting.

As they had done so on many past occasions, Adalbert Schnee and his men endured the attack stoically. Gauge glasses shattered, pipes burst spraying oil and water, and even the layer of cork insulation on the hull crumbled under the enemy's blasts. The lights flickered and went out, and the blue emergency lighting kicking in shed an unearthly glow on the strained faces of the men whose only means of escape was through complete inactivity.

The dreadful nightmare ended as abruptly as it had begun. At ten minutes before noon the depth charges suddenly ceased, and hydrophone contact with the enemy was lost. Schnee waited for another 40 minutes, and then carefully eased the boat up to periscope depth. He searched around the horizon, but there was nothing in sight. The British destroyer, either satisfied that she had sunk her quarry, or accepting that it must have escaped, had left the scene. At 1230, equally carefully, Schnee brought U-201 to the surface. The sea was still like a mirror, the horizon unlimited, but there was no sign of his attacker, or of the convoy he was seeking, not even a wisp of smoke.

But U-201 was not completely alone. At 1430, a Ju 88 reconnaisance aircraft flew in from the east, the sun glinting on her perspex gun turrets. Recognition signals were exchanged, and the pilot informed Schnee that the convoy was to the east of U-201, and only just over the horizon. Schnee altered course to intercept, but his pursuit was frustrated in the late afternoon by a patrolling Catalina that appeared out of an empty sky, and forced him to submerge in a hurry.

The Catalina followed U-201 down with four depth bombs, but these exploded harmlessly in the wake of the diving submarine. Suhren surfaced an hour later, only to find that the flying boat was still patiently quartering the skies, forcing him to dive again. It was dark before it was safe for U-201 to return to the surface.

CHAPTER FIVE

The Survivors

When Adalbert Schnee brought U-201 to the surface again some three hours later, he found that he had unwittingly crossed ahead of Convoy OG 71, the lead ships of which were just visible in the gathering dusk astern. He immediately reversed course and increased speed to intercept, angling in towards the head of the outside column.

Sailing as No.12, second ship of OG 71's port outside column, was the 1974-ton *Aldergrove*, a tall-funnelled Glasgow tramp of 1918 vintage. She was carrying a heavy load, down to her summer marks with 2,600 tons of patent fuel, brickets of small coal mixed with tar and other combustible materials, highly volatile, and highly inflammable. As an afterthought, being bound for the neutral port of Lisbon, she also had on board 10 tons of Red Cross parcels consigned to British prisoners of war in German camps.

When she ran her trials in the Clyde all those years ago, the *Aldergrove's* stout triple-expansion steam engine had produced a service speed of 9½ knots, and this she may have averaged in her heyday. Now, after 23 years pounding the road to Gibraltar and the Mediterranean, her engineers were hard pressed to maintain the convoy's designated speed of 7½ knots.

The *Aldergrove's* owners were David Alexander & Sons of Glasgow – also known as the Grove Line – and in 1941 she was the company's sole remaining representative afloat on the high seas. Grove Line had been unlucky in war, the fleet of ten vessels built up since the company was formed in 1899 being all lost in the First World War. When war broke out again in 1939, only two ships sailed under the Grove Line colours, and they both went down in the first four months of the conflict. The *Aldergrove*, ex-*Elba*, was a replacement, bought at a knock-down price from the Clydesdale Shipowners Ltd. in 1940, and a symbol of Grove Line's determination to carry on showing the flag.

It was Captain Hugh McLean's custom to visit the *Aldergrove's* bridge before midnight to write up his night orders and see the ship settled for the night, before turning in to snatch a few hours rest. But this had been an eventful day, culminating in the sinking of the *Empire Oak* and *Clonlara* at 2230 and 2300 respectively. Not surprisingly, the *Aldergrove's* Second Officer, who had the midnight to 4 watch on the bridge, was apprehensive of what might happen during these darkest hours to come. Captain McLean decided to stay with him for a while.

The first hour of the watch passed quietly, then, shortly before one o'clock on the morning of the 23rd, the *Aldergrove's* radio officer on watch reported he could hear voices in German on the radio telephone frequency. McLean went aft to the wireless room, where for a few minutes he listened in to the R/T. Neither he nor the radio officer understood German, but both were in agreement that the source was very close, and conversation sounded suspiciously like two U-boats conferring. What McLean and his operator heard was most probably Adalbert Schnee in conversation with Helmuth Ringelmann in U-75, or Erich Topp in U-552, both of whom were said to be nearby at the time.

In the wake of the furore caused by the torpedoing of the *Empire Oak* and *Clonlara*, the destroyer *Gurkha*, acting independently, conducted a sweep to port of the convoy firing starshell, hoping to flush out the attacker. Lieutenant Commander Lentaigne, in his Report of Proceedings, wrote:

2316 the RDF reported an echo bearing Green 60° (approximately 140° true). The ship was turned and a large echo straight ahead was obtained. The distance opened, so speed was increased. A flash of light was seen in this direction and the chase continued until 0014/23 when the echo was lost at 4000 yards. Shortly afterwards an A/S echo was obtained and although definitely classified as "non-sub" course was set to close as it might have been the wake of a submarine. This echo disappeared almost immediately but at 0017 got a range of 2800 yards 5 degrees on the starboard bow. This closed to 800 yards in a little over a minute. The A/S then obtained hydrophone effect, which was however soon lost.

At 0027 the RDF obtained a range at 1500 yards, red 5, which rapidly opened to 2000 yards, crossing to starboard being at 0033 Green 85 range 2200 yards. The ship was turning towards and soon the object was closed to 1800 yards. When at 0035 it disappeared almost ahead. At 0041 it reappeared at Red 10, 2700 yards by RDF but disappeared after half a minute to reappear a minute later at a range of 3100 yards and off again immediately to reappear six minutes later at 6000 yards, Red 20. In the next four minutes it closed to 2400 yards and in the following three minutes (0055) opening to 7500 yards Green 20. It was then closed and 16 minutes (0111) to 5900 yards. These latter ranges were undoubtedly one of the escorting ships or back or side echoes on the convoy.

Gurkha's RDF, an early form of radar, was a far cry from the sophisticated equipment of today, consisting of a six-inch cathode ray tube on which targets showed up as blips reminiscent of peaks on a heart monitor. From these, a trained operator was able to calculate the bearing and approximate range of an echo, but the screen gave no clue as to its identity. It may well be that at 2316 on the 22nd (0016 on the 23rd Central European Time, the time kept by the U-boats) *Gurkha's* RDF detected U-201 as she moved in to attack, but in his report Lentaigne gave no indication that his ship was in any way threatened. There again, it was a dark night, tensions were running high, and it could be that no one aboard *Gurkha* saw Schnee's torpedoes narrowly missing the destroyer.

U-201's War Diary contains an entry that may be relevant to this:

0037, 23 August: Position CG 1969 (40° 33' N 11° 34' W). Few clouds, WNW 1, no swell, visibility 6000 metres. Destroyer in sight. U-201 approaches to within 1600 metres and fires three torpedoes aimed at bridge.

Schnee claimed that two of his torpedoes missed the target, but the third scored a hit on the destroyer abaft her bridge. However, no evidence has ever come to light to substantiate his claim. Any destroyer, sloop or corvette, taking a direct hit abaft her bridge would almost certainly have broken her back and sunk, yet none of OG 71's escorts or merchant ships reported being attacked, and certainly no ship was sunk.

After spending only a few minutes in the *Aldergrove's* wireless-room, Captain McLean hurried back to the bridge, where the Second Officer reported to him that he could hear a strange whirring noise on the port beam. McLean followed the officer out onto the port wing of the bridge, where they both stood and listened. The Second Officer was of the opinion that the noise came from one of the escorting corvettes, but McLean was not convinced and, as it transpired, with good cause. What the two men were hearing was U-201's high-revving diesels as she approached the convoy.

Since his abortive attempt at sinking the elusive destroyer – possibly the *Gurkha* -Adalbert Schnee had been stalking the convoy for one and a half hours, uncertain whether the dark shadows he was seeing on the horizon really were ships, or just figments of his overtaxed imagination.

At 0200 on the 23rd (0100 convoy time), Schnee was at last close enough to OG 71 to be able to make out the silhouettes of the merchant ships. There were no escorts in sight, so he decided it was safe to remain on the surface. At 0214, he ran his sighting binoculars along the massed columns of slow-moving ships, and settled on the most likely target, an oil tanker of about 8000 tons. She was slightly overlapping a freighter of about 5000 tons in the next column, giving Schnee the perfect target. He fired a spread of four torpedoes.

Schnee's '8000-ton tanker' was in fact the 1974-ton *Aldergrove*, his 'freighter of about 5000 tons' General Steam Navigation Company's 787-ton motor vessel *Stork*. The latter ship's holds and decks were stacked with a lethal cargo of cased petrol. Seen in the dark from U-201's conning tower, no more than 12 feet above sea level, these relatively small ships may have looked a lot bigger, and *Oberleutnant* Schnee can be forgiven for his generous over estimation of his targets. This was in fact a common trait in U-boat commanders.

Captain Hugh McLean was in the port wing of *Aldergrove's* bridge, sweeping the horizon with his binoculars, looking for the U-boat he was convinced was somewhere out there in the darkness. He saw no submarine, but he did spot the track of the torpedo racing towards the stern of his ship. Without hesitation he ordered the helm hard to port. The *Aldergrove*, although she was making no more than 7½ knots, did everything that was asked of her, swinging her stern to starboard, so that the enemy torpedo missed by inches, carrying on to hit the unfortunate *Stork* in the next column.

The *Stork* erupted in a spectacular display of flames and smoke as her cargo of cased petrol exploded, but on the bridge of the *Aldergrove* McLean had little time to contemplate the awful fate of his near neighbour. Only a few seconds after the first torpedo had been seen tracking across her stern, Schnee's second torpedo struck the *Aldergrove* between her No 3 hold and the engine-room. The German commander – as was his intention – had hit the merchant ship in her most vulnerable spot. The *Aldergrove* was already breaking her back as Captain McLean sent his men to the boats. He wrote in his report to the Admiralty:

I think the torpedo must have penetrated the ship's side, and then exploded, as the sound of the explosion was not loud, no doubt killed by exploding amongst the patent fuel cargo. The sea at the time was smooth with a moderate NE swell, wind was NE force 3, weather was fine and clear, visibility dark but good. We were making 7½ knots and course 120°. The watertight doors were closed, with the exception of the one leading to the funnel, which was open.

The *Aldergrove's* main engine raced briefly, indicating that her propeller shaft was broken, and then suddenly stopped, shut down by the engineer on watch. Looking aft, McLean saw a great gush of patent fuel blocks surging skywards, accompanied by a cloud of thick black smoke or dust. The *Aldergrove* was shuddering and groaning like a wounded beast, and McLean needed no telling that his ship was finished. He brought her final voyage to an end by ringing 'Finished with Engines' on the engine-room telegraph.

McLean's next duty was to let the other ships know that he had been torpedoed, but when he went out into the starboard wing to fire the emergency rockets, he found that the port fires – long-burning matches – were damp and would not ignite. Rather than waste time – for there was no time to waste – McLean reached for the whistle lanyard, intending to sound two sets of six short blasts the signal for 'enemy submarine on the port side'. He pulled, and the lanyard came away in his hand, broken by the explosion or rusted away by the harsh salt air. In the general confusion, no W/T message was sent out.

When she was struck, the *Aldergrove* first listed heavily to port, then as the sea poured into her holds, she heaved herself upright, and began a dignified descent to the bottom on an even keel. McLean sent the Second Officer and the Helmsman of the watch to clear away the lifeboats, which in these unpredictable days were kept swung out at sea, bowsed into the ship's side by patent slips. Once these were released by a blow with an axe, the boats were ready for lowering. By the time this was done the *Aldergrove* was so low in the water that her crew had only to step off her boat deck into the boats and cast off.

The *Aldergrove* had gone down just six minutes after Adalbert Schnne's torpedo ripped open her hull, but her going was relatively calm; no fuss, no casualties, no drama.

The same could not be said of the little *Stork*. Commanded by a redoubtable Welshman, Captain Evan Atterbury Morris Williams, she was just one of the many small ships that kept open the Army's lifeline to

Gibraltar. Manned by a crew of phlegmatic British seamen, who took the horrendous risks of this sea war in their stride, she had sailed voyage after voyage always coming through unscathed. This time it was different.

When the *Stork* erupted into the night sky, and the petrol leaking overboard set fire to the sea around her, *Gurkha* and *Boreas* raced down each flank of the convoy firing starshell and sweeping the sea with their searchlights. This demonstration of aggressive defence came too late. After firing her stern tube into the convoy, U-201 had disappeared into the night. Luckily, Schnee's last torpedo did not find a target.

Meanwhile, the corvette HMS *Campion* had approached the fiercely burning *Stork* from the weather side, in the hope that there might be some survivors to be snatched from the inferno. Lieutenant Commander Johnson moved in as close as he could without putting his own ship in danger, and then dropped a rescue boat manned by five picked men. The coxswain of the 16ft dinghy, 19-year-old Leading Seaman Geoff Drummond, took the boat right in to the edge of the burning sea surrounding the remains of the *Stork*, and began a patient search for survivors. He was aware that he had little time to waste, for his own ship, stopped and exposed to the enemy in the light of the leaping flames, was in great danger.

It seemed to Drummond that it was impossible for anyone to be still alive beyond the flames, but he continued to search. Then, when he was about to return to *Campion* empty-handed, three men appeared through a gap in leaping flames. One, the *Stork's* carpenter, Stanley Smart, a giant of a man, was swimming on his back, clutching the Second Mate under one arm, and the Second Engineer in the other. The engineer was badly injured, having fractured both feet when diving out of a porthole when his cabin burst into flames. These three men were the only ones to survive the torpedoing of the *Stork*.

One of the survivors, Second Mate H.L. Wolley, recounted his story of the attack on reaching Gibraltar:

I was flung on the wheelhouse deck by the explosion. I got up and looking out of the starboard door saw that the ship was aflame from stem to stern, which was to be expected considering the nature of her cargo. Captain Williams and the machine-gunner were standing on the starboard wing, seemingly unable to move and enveloped with flames. I turned to go to the port wing, which was the weather side, tripped and once more fell to the deck. I managed to struggle clear of the wreckage which had fallen on me and joined Smart and the helmsman on the port wing. I followed them into the water. The explosion had flung burning oil to windward and it was floating down on us. The ship, which still had way on her, was laying a stream which edged us away to windward. She sank as we swam a few yards away from her. I managed to make my way clear and got to windward of the blazing inferno. I was joined by Smart. The man at the wheel we never saw again.

Smart, from whom I had been separated, had been attracted by my whistle. When he came up he relieved me of it, and we took turns to blow, this being his suggestion. It was louder than his own, and also there was a danger of my dropping it, as having received a blow on the left eye, I was suffering from concussion. I was content to float on my back, kicking my feet to keep us up to windward, at Smart's suggestion. We heard shouts and soon after we were joined by Mr. Maxwell. He was suffering from a broken foot, though he did not know it at the time, and it was giving him some trouble. Smart tried massaging it and kept us going by his cheerful talk, his suggestions, and his efforts to keep us together. We saw a flare from a lifeboat of the ship which had been torpedoed just previously to our own. We tried to swim to it and attract the attention of the people in it by our shouts and whistles. I had an electric torch attached to my life-jacket, which I flashed now and again. Smart, whose own was not working, visualising a long stay in the water, had suggested we treat it economically. It proved to be one of the factors which saved our lives, as the corvette which picked us up was directed to us by its small red blink. We were picked up at 3.40 am after nearly 2½ hours in the water. I was all in, and felt sure if it had not been for Smart's company in the water, I should have given up the ghost long before.

Captain T.C. Stone, master of the *Starling*, another of General Steam's ships sailing in OG 71, said of Stanley Smart:

From the story told afterwards in Gibraltar by the second mate and the second engineer, it seems certain that the second engineer owed his life to Smart's courage and to a large extent the second mate. Smart was standing on the weather side of the bridge when it happened, and only by jumping overboard on that side were they able to get away, the second engineer managed somehow to get through a porthole, but as one, if not both, of his legs were broken he could not get away from the fire. Smart towed him through a lane of fire until they were able to get on some sort of raft. In this he also greatly assisted the second mate. Later the flames spread to the raft, making it necessary to abandon it.

Here to my mind is the bravest thing of all. Knowing he could not help himself, the second engineer wanted to be left, but Smart just dragged him off the raft and towed him away from the fire again, also assisting the second mate. It was some time before they were rescued by a corvette, but I am told Smart was still quite fit when rescued and I believe made himself very useful there. Without a doubt the second engineer owes his life to Smart's courage, and to a great extent the second mate does also.

Stanley Smart was undoubtedly a man of great bravery and resilience. Of his arrival alongside *Campion*, Lieutenant Commander Johnson had to say: 'Out of the darkness came an enormous voice, "Good old Navy – this is the 5th time, get my rum ready! I loves Navy rum!" and over the side came the carpenter, Smart, 22½ stones with the 3rd mate under his arm, followed by the 2nd engineer with a broken leg.'

The rescue of the three men was one of the few rewarding moments in the long ordeal of OG 71. Unfortunately for Captain Williams and the remaining eighteen crew members of the *Stork*, there could be no miraculous deliverance for them. They died with their ship.

It was not until all the excitement had died down, and the *Stork* was no more than a red glow on the horizon astern, that the *Aldergrove's* boats were found. The two boats, with thirty-two men on board, had been burning red flares for two hours before HMS *Campanula* came across them. Some of the *Aldergrove's* survivors were injured, and it took some time to get them aboard the corvette, where they joined survivors from several other ships already picked up by *Campanula*. Given that the *Aldergrove* took only six minutes to sink, it is much to the credit of Captain Hugh McLean that only one man, Seaman Gunner Campbell, lost his life in the sinking.

An unnatural peace now descended on the convoy, unnatural in the sense that it was known that the U-boats had not gone away, but any relief, however transitory, was more than welcome. In the escorts, the situation was approaching critical. Lieutenant Commander Lentaigne later reported:

After three days almost continuously on the bridge, the reaction of all officers was slower than usual. To think at all became increasingly difficult. Even the Medical Officer had been continuously assisting with cyphering and plotting and had not been to bed. Moreover, the three-day battle had proved a considerable strain on the communication department, and towards the end of the night this was beginning to tell.

In the merchant ships, all of them sitting ducks on the millpond of an unusually benign Atlantic, the level of stress was even higher. Seven of their number and one destroyer had already gone. It must have occurred to those manning these remaining ships, that even with their large escort force – now an unprecedented eleven warships to fifteen merchantmen – they were still not safe from the German torpedoes.

On the other hand, the U-boats were also feeling the effects of this prolonged running battle. Their crews, confined in their iron coffins, were constantly on the alert for retaliation, and the boats, pushed to their ultimate limits, were beginning to reveal their weaknesses. Schnee's U-201 was reporting her main compressor out of order and requesting permission to return to base. Permission was granted, and Schnee, satisfied that he made a very significant contribution to the attack on OG 71, set course for Brest. Meanwhile, U-552 was experiencing major problems with her diesel engines.

On the afternoon of the 22nd U-552's port diesel clutch had failed, and an hour later the starboard clutch began to slip. Limping along on one unreliable engine, Erich Topp reported his predicament to Lorient and was ordered to take U-552 to the north to await allocation to another attack area. There followed an anxious wait while U-552's engineers worked on the clutches. The port engine proved beyond repair at sea, but shortly before 1900 Topp was able to get under way again, making 9 knots on the starboard diesel. He was tempted to ignore BdU's orders and go after the convoy, but by this time U-552 was some 30 miles astern of the British ships, and darkness was closing in.

Heading out into the Atlantic before turning north for her new hunting ground, U-552 was 14 miles west of OG 71 when, early on the morning of the 23rd, by pure chance, she came across the Norwegian ship *Spind*.

Jacob Salvesen's 2129-ton *Spind* was fourteen days out of Barry Dock carrying 3000 tons of best Welsh coal and coke for Lisbon and on her summer marks – if not below – but in this war many blind eyes were being turned to Sam Plimsoll's lines. After inadvertently parting company with the convoy during the night, Captain Johannes Jonassen had made no attempt to rejoin OG 71, reasoning that being less than twenty-four hours steaming from his destination there was little point in making the effort. He was soon to regret this decision.

Unknown to Jonassen, his ship had already been under attack during the night. Reinhard Suhren, in U-564, claimed that at 0235 he had fired no less than four single torpedoes at the *Spind*. He reported a direct hit with at least one torpedo, but he must have been mistaken in this, for at daylight the Norwegian ship was still unharmed.

When he saw the enemy steamer, deep-loaded, completely unprotected, and breasting the long swells at the speed of a horse-drawn cart, *Oberleutnant* Erich Topp could hardly believe his luck. This was a target most U-boat commanders could only dream of. Yet when, with the newly risen sun behind him, Topp closed the gap on the *Spind* and fired a spread of two torpedoes, he missed the apparently helpless merchantman completely, both torpedoes porpoising to the surface. The ageing collier seemed to bear a charmed life – or, more likely, she was so slow that the U-boats were allowing too much deflection when aiming their torpedoes.

It was a few minutes before 6 o'clock, and with most of her crew still in their bunks, the *Spind* had not yet come to life. First Mate Erling Johannesen had the watch on the bridge, and neither he nor his lookout man saw the tracks of U-552's torpedoes. The first indication of trouble came when Johannesen heard the fast beat of the U-boat's single diesel engine somewhere out on the starboard beam. He was scanning the horizon through his binoculars when Topp's first 88 mm shell came whistling over to explode just off the *Spind's* bow, throwing up a tall column of dirty water.

Having wasted two of his precious torpedoes, Erich Topp had taken a careful look around the horizon, and satisfied that no enemy warships were in sight, decided to use his more economical deck gun to sink this unescorted steamer. His well-drilled six-man gun's crew had a rate of fire of eighteen rounds a minute, and soon a hail of high explosive was dropping around and on the *Spind*. Chief Engineer Karl Halvorsen, asleep on the settee in his cabin, was rudely awoken when a shell smashed through the ship's side, roared over his head, and exploded in the adjacent cabin. Its occupant, Second Engineer Severin Aasheim, was fortunately on watch in the engine-room at the time.

Captain Jonassen had meanwhile reached the bridge in time to experience the full ferocity of the enemy's gunfire – in addition to her 88mm, U-552 had opened up with her 20mm canon and heavy machine guns, and was raking the *Spind* from stem to stern. The Norwegian's gun's crew, led by their American seaman gunner Robert McLennand, had managed to return fire with her 4-inch, but after a few rounds were forced to abandon the gun. By this time, the *Spind's* accommodation and bunker hatch were on fire, and Jonassen decided it was time to abandon ship.

U-552's gunners were still laying down heavy fire, and with shells bursting aboard and bullets ricocheting off the steel decks, lowering the lifeboats was an extremely hazardous operation. Second Mate Eivind Olsen was seriously injured by machine-gun fire while attempting to lower the starboard boat, and when the port boat was put in the water U-552 motored around to that side and continued to rake the ship. The eighteen men crammed into the boat were forced to take cover below the gunwales as the bullets whistled over their heads.

It was not clear whether Erich Topp's gunners were deliberately targeting the *Spind's* boat, but at that moment the situation was resolved when the destroyer *Boreas* appeared on the scene. She had seen the flash of gunfire from 14 miles away, and raced in at 25 knots to investigate. Sighting U-552 on the surface, she opened up with her 4.7s, and Topp was obliged to break off his attack and take cover underwater. Before submerging completely, he fired another torpedo at the Norwegian ship, hoping to put her down before the destroyer could intervene. This was not Erich Topp's day, for this third torpedo also failed to find the target.

Boreas went after the fleeing U-boat, but, because of the close proximity of the *Spind's* lifeboats and some men in the water, the destroyer had to content herself with dropping a single depth charge. She then approached the burning ship and lowered a boat to take off the injured Second Mate who, with a bullet in his lung, was dangling on the end of a lifeline suspended from the starboard lifeboat davits. Twenty-four other survivors were then picked up from two lifeboats, one of which was holed by machine-gun fire and leaking badly.

Campanula had now arrived to assist in the rescue, and when all survivors were safely on board the destroyer, the corvette dropped a full pattern of depth charges, more as a warning to a potential enemy than anything else. U-552 had by now vacated the scene of her botched attack. Twelve hours later, when she was well away from the area, Topp sent the following report to Lorient: 'Have sunk steamer Spind (2129 grt) from the convoy by gunfire.'

Boreas put men aboard the *Spind* to investigate the possibility of saving her, but they found her cargo well alight, and when her ready-use ammunition began to explode, she was again abandoned. The burning ship was deemed to be a hazard to other shipping, and *Boreas* speeded her demise with a well-aimed salvo of 4.7s. The *Spind*, veteran of two world wars and countless tramping voyages, sank in less than five minutes. *Campanula* landed her crew in Gibraltar, where the only casualty, Second Mate Eivind Olsen, was admitted to the Colonial Hospital. The others were looked after by the Norwegian Consul.

Not all of the survivors landed in Gibraltar by HMS *Campanula* received such consideration. Captain McLean, of the Aldergrove, reported:

When we arrived at Gibraltar we were received by Mr Tamplin of the Ministry of War Transport. He took us to the Shipping Office – some of the men had to walk through the streets in bare feet – and it was arranged for some of the men to go to the Sailors' Home and some of us to the Victoria Hotel. He stated that he had no funds at his disposal and could not do anything else for us. I complained to Captain Hawkins RN about this treatment. Whilst I was ashore I noticed in the local Gazette that £250 had just been subscribed for a fund for Distressed Merchant Seamen, to enable them to buy necessary clothing. There were about 134 survivors at Gibraltar, and clothing was very costly and very scarce.

The accommodation and food at the Victoria Hotel were very bad. The wash basin in my room was filthy and there was no soap. After spending 20 minutes cleaning the basin, the water stopped running. We complained about the poor accommodation at the Victoria Hotel and were later found accommodation in the Grand Hotel, where we were able to at least get a salt water bath. The food here was also very poor.

Captain McLean and his men were unwilling guests at Gibraltar for three and a half weeks before being given a sea passage home. It was a passage they would rather not have accepted, had they known how it would end.

CHAPTER SIX

Port of Refuge

OG 71 had sailed from British waters confident in the knowledge that its safe passage to Gibraltar was assured. Twenty-two merchantmen strong, and with an escort of unprecedented strength for these early days of the war, it was glibly predicted that the enemy, for all his ruthless efficiency, would not dare to challenge such a show of force. The optimists, ashore and afloat, were wrong, of course.

By the time the first pale streaks of approaching dawn appeared in the east on the morning of 23 August, the convoy had sailed into the Gates of Hell and out through the other side. The onslaught by Dönitz's U-boats had been fierce and unrelenting, resulting in eight merchantmen and their precious cargoes, along with the Norwegian destroyer *Bath*, being consigned to the bottom of the Atlantic. With them had gone 313 souls, British merchant seamen, Norwegians in exile, and saddest of all, twenty-two young women, innocents setting forth on the first great adventure of their lives.

As daylight approached, OG 71 closed its battered ranks and continued its disputed passage to Gibraltar. Guarding the remaining fourteen ships were the destroyers *Gurkha* and *Lance*, the sloop *Leith* and the corvettes *Wallflower* and *Zinnia*. The other escorts were scattered far and wide, *Boreas* standing by the crippled *Spind*, *Campion* and *Campanula* picking up survivors from the *Stork* and *Aldergrove*, while *Bluebell* was somewhere astern, presumably hunting U-boats. At this juncture, in the half-light between night and day, the convoy was at its most vulnerable. Anticipating that the U-boats were gathering their strength for an attack in force, Commander Lentaigne decided to create another diversion. He took *Gurkha* out of the screen, and raced northwards at 27 knots until she was 13 miles off the convoy. There he staged a mock battle, dropping depth charges, firing rockets and Very lights, before beginning a star shell search to the north and north-west.

It was all very realistic, giving the impression that the convoy was far to the north of its actual position, but it failed to fool the U-boats. At 0420, as *Gurkha* was heeling round to port under full helm to return to the convoy, the corvette *Zinnia* was torpedoed.

Reinhard Suhren, having wasted four valuable torpedoes in an attempt to sink the *Spind* earlier that morning, had pushed U-564 to her absolute limits for more than two hours, and was at last back in contact with the convoy. It was a calm morning, with only a low swell disturbing the surface of the sea. Visibility was good, and as he closed in on the convoy's port side Suhren was able to discern the outline of a ship on his starboard bow. This was the port outrider of OG 71's close escort, HMS *Zinnia*.

Zinnia was a Flower Class corvette of 925 tons, completed and commissioned at Smith's Dockyard on the River Tees only five months earlier. In command was 35-year-old Lieutenant Commander Charles Cuthbertson RNR, DSC. An ex-merchant seaman of considerable experience Cuthbertson had been with the sea since leaving school, firstly in the training ship HMS *Worcester*, then as an officer with the prestigious Union Castle Line sailing to the Cape. He held a foreign-going Masters Certificate, and on the outbreak of war in 1939 had been serving as second officer/navigator in the 20,141-ton passenger liner *Caernarvon Castle*, from where he was called for active service with the Royal Navy.

At Cuthbertson's side on the bridge of the *Zinnia* was his First Lieutenant, Australian-born Lieutenant Harold Chesterman RNR, 24 years old and another merchant seaman reservist. Chesterman was also *Worcester* trained, held a foreign-going Masters Certificate, and had sailed with Shaw Savill Line before being called to the colours in 1939. *Zinnia* was in the hands of very professional seamen.

While *Gurkha* was away creating a diversion, Lieutenant Commander Hutton, for reasons not recorded, ordered *Zinnia*, then on the port bow of the convoy, to change places with *Wallflower* on the port quarter. This was not a complicated manoeuvre, but its execution inevitably lowered the degree of vigilance in both corvettes. It was thus that U-564, still on the surface, was able to approach within 500 yards or so of *Zinnia* without being seen.

Crouching low over his waterproofed sighting binoculars, Suhren took slow and careful aim, firing three single shots from his bow tubes. Then, without waiting to observe the results of his attack, he cleared the conning tower, and took U-564 quickly below the surface.

Steering a broad zig-zag pattern at 14 knots, *Zinnia* was on full alert, with all hands at their action stations. Her small open bridge was crowded,

Chesterman was at Cuthbertson's side, behind them the helmsman and yeoman of signals, and in each wing a lookout with binoculars. In the Asdic House abaft the bridge, the operator was sweeping 80 degrees either side of the convoy's course. Conscious of the vulnerability of his ship, and with the disaster that had overtaken *Bath* in mind, Cuthbertson had wisely ordered all depth charges to be set to safe.

Shortly after 0400, Cuthbertson handed over the con to his Number One and went aft to the Asdic House. Chesterman moved to the starboard side of the bridge, peering into the darkness. His orders were to take up a position within 800 yards of the outer ships of the convoy, and then turn onto a parallel course. At 0421, when he was just able to make out the shadowy shapes of the merchantmen, he ordered the helmsman to apply ten degrees of port helm.

Zinnia was swinging to port, when one of Reinhard Suhren's torpedoes slammed into her port side aft of the bridge. Lieutenant Commander Cuthbertson later reported:

…Ship swinging rapidly to port under 10 degrees of wheel, when a violent explosion and blinding flash followed by escaping steam occurred on the port side abreast of the funnel.

I was stepping out of the Bridge Asdic House and facing the funnel and about 25 feet from the explosion. The Asdic House collapsed and parts of the ship were thrown in the air. She immediately heeled over on to her starboard beam ends and in five seconds had capsized through 120 degrees. The blast did not hurt me and the capsizing hurled me into the water on the starboard side abreast of the bridge. Looking upwards I saw the deck of the ship coming over on top of me, when she broke in two about the funnel, and a swirl of water took me down. When I came to the surface again my lungs and stomach were filled with fuel oil, and I was partially blinded. The time now was about twelve seconds after the explosion. I could see the bows rising vertically out of the water, they disappeared within a few seconds. HMS Zinnia had sunk in 15 to 20 seconds. There was no wreckage…

…About the time the bows submerged, five severe underwater explosions were felt, these were exceedingly painful. This would appear to have been the bulkheads giving way, furnace explosions or possibly torpedoes or depth charges exploding at about 750 yards distant…

Lieutenant Chesterman, who was on the compass platform, and intent on handling the ship, was blown off his feet by the blast, and seconds later *Zinnia* capsized. He suddenly found himself in the water and choking on the black, viscous oil gushing out from the ruptured fuel tanks.

The corvette had gone down so fast that not only had there been no time to launch boats, but the lashings on the Carley floats had not been cut. Both lifeboats and floats sank with the ship, leaving those who had survived the blast – and their numbers were woefully small – with only their lifejackets to keep them afloat. They had neither whistles nor lights to advertise their presence in the water. And to add to their terrible predicament, the other escorts took the explosions to be all part of *Gurkha's* staged diversion. No one was dashing to the aid of the survivors.

The thick oil was everywhere, severely hampering all movements by the men in the water. Lieutenant Commander Cuthbertson's commented, 'I endeavoured to blow up my Service Inflatable Lifebelt, but found this to be impossible. I could not even remove the Barr and Stroud 1900A glasses, which remained hanging round my neck...' His report continued:

> *I heard many cries for help in the water, and estimated there were about 40 men floating. I could do nothing to help them. The water was thick with oil fuel, and it was all I could do to keep my balance in the swell, and my nose and mouth above the oil. I remained afloat 40 minutes before finding the trunk of a body which had been blasted and was buoyant, this kept me afloat for the remaining 30 minutes...*

After swimming aimlessly around for some time, Lieutenant Chesterman found refuge on an equally bizarre piece of flotsam. He came across one of *Zinnia's* smoke floats, one of the few pieces of wreckage that remained to mark the corvette's sudden end. The canister was not big enough for Chesterman to climb aboard, so he clung to it, holding on literally by the tips of his fingers as it bobbed up and down on the swell. Time ceased to have any meaning, as coughing and choking he tried in vain to clear the oil from his lungs. He held on to his steel canister, hugging it tighter than he would any lover. And all the time there was the nagging thought at the back of his mind that these floats were programmed to sink after so long in the water. How long, he could not remember.

Finally, with his fingers bleeding and his ribs rubbed sore by the constant movement of the heavy float against his body, Chesterman began to accept that there would be no rescue for him. He was only too aware that the

Zinnia had gone down so quickly that no SOS had been sent, nor had distress flares been sent up. He was alone in this dark sea without the slightest hope of rescue. It occurred to him that it might be better to end it all now, rather than die a slow, lingering death. He released his hold on the smoke float, and allowed himself to sink.

Twenty-four year old Chesterman had sunk only a few feet into the cold depths of the Atlantic when he realised how little of his life he had lived. And then a vision of his wife's face floated before his eyes, and the will to live returned stronger than ever. He kicked his way to the surface, and again swam to the smoke float, his island of hope in this sea of despair. His grip on the canister was more tenacious than ever. Harold Chesterman was determined to live.

When realisation finally dawned on the other escorts that *Zinnia* had been sunk, a frantic search for survivors was begun. This was not easy, for no one knew the exact position of the sinking, no wreckage was visible, and those left struggling in the water were without lifejacket lights, whistles, or any other means to signal for help.

One of *Zinnia's* fellow Flower-class corvettes, HMS *Campanula*, was first on the scene, her commander, Lieutenant Commander R.V.E. Case RNVR, following his nose to the patch of black oil that was *Zinnia's* only grave marker. The cries of the men in the water were pitiful, and Case's first, and overwhelming instinct was to heave to and drop a boat to go to their aid. But his orders were quite explicit, and they were that he should at no time put his own ship at risk to pick up survivors. Momentarily, Case fought a battle with his conscience, but there was no doubt in his mind that the U-boat that had sunk the *Zinnia* was still close by, watching and waiting. Eventually, he came to terms with the situation by throwing over scrambling nets, and steaming slowly amongst the survivors, attempting to haul them alongside the ship with heaving lines. It was a brave try, but doomed to failure. The heaving lines were slippery with oil, and the men in the water, cold and exhausted, were unable to hang on to them. *Campanula* left them struggling in her wake.

Among those in the oil-covered water hurling curses after *Campanula's* disappearing stern was *Zinnia's* captain, Lieutenant Commander Charles Cuthbertson. After over an hour in the water he was coated with thick fuel oil and partially blinded, but he was still clinging to his macabre lifebelt, the bloated body of one of his dead crew members. Nearby, but unseen, was Cuthbertson's Number One, Lieutenant Harold Chesterman, barely conscious, his bruised arms still locked around the smoke float, which as yet showed no signs of sinking.

And that was how *Campion* found them. Her captain, Lieutenant Commander Johnson, was also aware of Standing Orders regarding survivors in the water, but he was unable to turn his back on them. He ordered the cutter into the water.

Once again, 19-year-old Leading Seaman Geoffrey Drummond was at the tiller of *Campion's* rescue boat. With a crew of four, he took the 16ft boat into the night with the cries of the stricken men in his ears and the stench of fuel oil in his nostrils. Three men were hauled out of the water, one of whom died on the way back to *Campion*. Drummond then left two of his crew behind to make more room in the boat, and went back into the oil, where men were still fighting for their lives. Eight more *Zinnias* were snatched from the sea, among them Lieutenant Commander Charles Cuthbertson, exhausted to the point of near death when he was hauled over the gunwale, but with his precious binoculars still slung around his neck.

Finally, Drummond was satisfied that no one else remained alive in the water, and was about to return to the ship, when he heard a faint cry for help. He turned the boat around, and soon a strange object came into view. It was *Zinnia's* smoke float, with Lieutenant Chesterman still clinging to it.

In all, Leading Seaman Drummond and his crew saved twelve men from a lingering death in the water. Once aboard *Campion*, the survivors, suffering dreadfully from the oil they had swallowed, were treated with every care. The corvette carried no doctor, but led by Sick Bay Attendant Thompson, her crew cleaned the oil from the survivors bodies, dressed their wounds, splinted fractures, and wrapped them in blankets. Prominent among the helpers was survivor Stanley Smart, the *Stork's* carpenter, a tower of strength in all ways. It was he who took personal care of Lieutenant Commander Cuthbertson, who was covered in oil, passing blood and oil from both ends, and partially blinded. Smart stripped Cuthbertson, wiped him down with paraffin to remove the oil, and then cleaned out his clogged eyes with petrol, before putting him to bed. He gave the same treatment to Lieutenant Chesterman. Second Officer Wolley, who following the sinking of the *Stork* owed his life to Stanley Smart, said of the 20-stone carpenter:

Smart won the hearts of all aboard the corvette. A huge man, the immersion in the water seemed to have affected him not in the least and soon after

70

he was giving a hand on deck to launch the corvette's boat to rescue more survivors from another escort (HMS Zinnia). In fact, he was ordered out of the boat, being fully prepared to man it though his only garment was a blanket. He soon lost that too, giving it to one of the survivors who needed it more than he did. I was below at the time, but the captain of the corvette has written a report of the splendid work which Smart performed on his ship. In fact, to end the story of his bravery and cheerful courage, the next morning found him acting as anaesthetist to the doctor who boarded. It was only when he could perform no other work or acts to aid those who were on board that he thought of himself and finally very nearly collapsed through exhaustion, having been up for a long period and going through what he did with no sleep.

Years later, Lieutenant Commander Johnson wrote:

...I could not stand the bleating in the water so against orders I stopped and dropped one boat and hooked in sixteen, including Cuthbertson C.O. and Chesterman No.1...

...All this while I had gout, starting each night with my foot in a bundle and ending bare footed. I had great trouble with Cuthbertson and Chesterman because they recorded that Case had allowed their ships company to drown but even more when Case ran me in for disobeying orders, which was strictly correct; but one had a choice of just letting survivors drown and not going near or stopping to pick them up and remain a sitting target while doing so...As we were not torpedoed nothing was said. I wonder what would have happened if we had been?

Through her commander's humane decision to disobey orders, *Campion* had unwittingly become the centre of OG 71's rescue operations. She now had on board survivors from the *Alva, Clonlara, Stork* and *Zinnia,* many of whom were injured, and SBA Thompson was unable to cope. At 0830, after a request for medical assistance by Lieutenant Commander Johnson, *Gurkha* sent across her surgeon. Later in the morning, although he was still very weak from his long struggle in the oil-covered sea, Lieutenant Commander Cuthbertson read the burial service over the bodies of several of his men retrieved from the water. Meanwhile, the search for survivors from the *Zinnia* went on. HMS *Wallflower* found three more and pulled them from the water before the oil killed them, and *Campaula* picked up two, one of whom was badly injured. Of *Zinnia's* crew of eighty-five, only seventeen had survived her sinking.

At 0915, the destroyer *Vidette* joined to reinforce the escort, but three hours later the advantage was lost when *Gurkha* and *Lance*, both dangerously low on fuel, left the convoy for Gibraltar to refuel.

London was by now seriously concerned for the safety of the remaining ships in OG 71. At 1632, *Leith* received the following signal:

> All ships of OG 71 are to be escorted to Tagus and instructed to proceed Lisbon.

Within the hour a further signal was decoded:

> Escorts are to carry out anti-submarine sweep over an arc 320 degrees to 260 degrees from Cape Roca. Escorts are to detach from convoy as soon as it reaches territorial waters. Escorts should continue hunt until prudent limit of endurance, returning to Gibraltar to refuel. Request maximum air cooperation.

At 2150 *Leith* replied:

> Campanula, Wallflower, Campion *have been sent to Gibraltar with injured and survivors.* Wivern, Boreas, Vidette, Leith *and* Bluebell *carrying out sweep. OG 71 entering Tagus.*

The bedraggled remnants of Convoy OG 71 arrived at the pilot station in Cascais Bay, near the mouth of the River Tagus, just after 2000. Portuguese pilots were embarked, and the fourteen surviving merchantmen, grateful for the darkness that hid their shame, began their passage up river. The ships were salt-stained and battle-scarred, their crews weary after six days and nights stood to their action stations, tense and fearful, awaiting the crash of the unseen enemy torpedo designed to tear the bowels out of their ship. Eight of their number had been sunk, along with two of the escorting warships and the loss of over 400 lives. That this could have happened while they were being protected by such a powerful force of destroyers and corvettes, supported much of the time by aircraft, was difficult to comprehend.

Anchoring off the port of Lisbon in the early hours of 24 August was for the men of OG 71 like arriving in another world, a world where blackouts, rationing and all the other rigours of war had no place. Even at this ungodly hour the town was a blaze of light, and there was a heady, almost exotic scent on the air as the ships came in one by one and were brought up to an anchor. Magically, the horrors of the past week were pushed aside, and as the dawn approached the talk in the messrooms was all of the prospects of a run ashore.

General Steam's *Petrel* was first into the anchorage. She had cargo to discharge in Lisbon, and she also had survivors on board, namely Captain Edward Hughes and twenty-five crew members from the *Ciscar*, sunk by Adalbert Schnee's U-201 on the 19th. Early next morning, which was a Sunday, the master of the *Petrel*, Captain John Klemp, anxious to be rid of the passengers who were making a large hole in his voyage stores, went ashore to request permission for his survivors to land. He had anticipated that this would be a simple matter of presenting a list of names to the port authorities, but it was not to be. In the first place, it was Sunday, and, war or no war, no Portuguese official was prepared to do business on the Holy Day. It was late on Monday the 25th, and then only after much argument and form filling, that Captain Hughes and his men were allowed ashore. They landed dressed in an assortment of clothes borrowed from the crew of the *Petrel*, having lost everything when their ship went down. Given all they had been through, they were, not surprisingly, bitterly disappointed at their casual treatment at the hands of the Portuguese.

The unexpected arrival of a British convoy in the River Tagus caused a flurry of interest in neutral Lisbon. German spies, of which there were many in the port, observed and reported, while newspaper correspondents arrived hot foot with notebooks in hand. British Embassy officials made no effort to protect the *Ciscar* survivors, in fact, a press conference was arranged, at which all the masters of the surviving merchant ships were in attendance and free to answer questions put by reporters. The *Daily Telegraph*'s special correspondent in Lisbon filed a colourful report which appeared in paper on the 26th:

14 SHIPS BEAT U-BOATS AND PLANES: RUNNING FIGHT OFF FRENCH COAST: FALSE GERMAN CLAIMS

After facing repeated bombing and submarine attacks fourteen ships of a British convoy of twenty-one arrived in Lisbon to prove the falsity of German claims, for all of them were sunk by the Berlin radio, together with a destroyer, a corvette and another escort vessel…

The report admitted that seven merchant ships had been sunk, but denied the sinking of the escorts. In fact, the *Telegraph*'s correspondent gave such an up-beat version of the running battle for OG 71 that it could have been construed as a major victory for the Allies. It must have delighted the Ministry of Information in London, hence its immediate approval for publication.

In reality, the assault on Convoy OG 71 resulted in a very convincing victory for Admiral Dönitz. Although protected by an unusually strong escort force, eight merchantmen, 36 percent of the convoy, had been sunk, along with two of the ships guarding them. And all this without loss or damage to any German U-boat or aircraft.

There had been no lack of commitment on the part of merchantmen or escorts, but quite obviously something had gone horribly wrong. One of the weak links appears to have been in the divided command of the escort force. Commander Lentaigne, in the destroyer *Gurkha*, was by virtue of rank Senior Officer Escort, but it seems that with Lentaigne's agreement Lieutenant Commander Hutton, in the sloop *Leith*, continued to control the close escort of corvettes.

While it is beyond doubt that confusion in the disposition of the escorts contributed heavily to the rout of OG 71, it must be remembered that those manning the ships, naval and merchant, had been operating under tremendous strain for a considerable period. Some of them, especially those on the bridge, had not closed their eyes for several days. In the case of the escorts, by Commander Lentaigne's admission, his crews were worn out by the continuing battle. It was perhaps fortunate for OG 71 that the protection offered by the neutral waters of Portugal was close at hand, otherwise the destruction of the convoy might have been complete.

Among those who witnessed the arrival in Lisbon of the battered remains of Convoy OG 71 were the men of a passage crew sent out by Irish Shipping Ltd. of Dublin to bring home their newly acquired ship the ex-Greek flag *Vassilios Destounis*. When they were told that they were to go north in a British convoy, they flatly refused to sail. The *Vassilios Destounis*, soon to become the *Irish Poplar*, eventually sailed home alone, and arrived in Ireland without as much as a scratch on her new paintwork.

The bands were playing and cheering crowds lined the quaysides when the U-boats returned to Brest. Walter Kell was first to arrive, bringing U-204 into the Penfeld River late on the 24th with victory pennants snapping in the breeze. Kell, who dealt the first blow to OG 71 when he sent the Norwegian destroyer *Bath* to the bottom with such grievous loss of life, also claimed to have sunk two merchant ships. He was followed by Adalbert Schnee, who eased U-201 into her berth in the Rade-Abri a little after sunset on the 25th. Schnee was undoubtedly the hero of the hour, claiming to have sunk six ships with a total tonnage of 37,000 gross. U-564 arrived to an equally tumultuous welcome forty-eight hours later. Teddy Suhren had reported eight merchant men sunk and four others damaged.

And so it went on, the other boats dribbling in, but all receiving an ecstatic welcome. Their claims were wildly exaggerated, of course, but Germany was hungry for victories at sea, and they were believed. The German High Command in Berlin was so elated with the action that it issued a press statement claiming that the U-boats had sunk twenty-one merchant ships and three escorts, with another five ships damaged. Before the last boat had docked, the *Befehlshaber der U-boote* himself, Admiral Dönitz, had arrived in Brest and the Iron Crosses First Class were being handed out.

Had the German claims been true, they would have amounted to the complete annihilation of OG 71, but it could not be denied that the U-boats had brought off a coup of major proportions. Not only had they destroyed eight merchantmen and two escorts, but for the first time in this war they had forced a British convoy to abandon its voyage and seek refuge in neutral waters. For the Royal Navy it was the ultimate humiliation.

The arrival in Gibraltar on the night of 24 August of the corvettes *Campanula* and *Campion*, their decks packed with survivors, received scant attention. The virtual disowning of the *Aldergrove's* men by the local authorities, as described by Captain McLean, was typical. Even the *Zinnia's* pathetic band of seventeen – all that was left of the corvette's crew of eighty-three – were virtually ignored. Lieutenant-Commander Cuthbertson, although still a very sick man, refused hospital treatment, and was flown home to report to the Admiralty. This left his Number One, Lieutenant Harold Chesterman to see to the welfare of the others. As a mere lieutenant RNR without a ship his task was not an easy one, but in spite of the apathy of the local shore establishment, he managed to get the fit men into a rest camp, and the sick and injured into Gibraltar Hospital. It was here that the battle for OG 71 claimed its last victim, when Sub Lieutenant J.S. Millar RNVR died despite the efforts of the doctors and nurses to save him. Chesterman was grateful to the commander of the cruiser *Manchester*, then in port, who offered to arrange the burial of young Millar with full military honours. He was laid to rest in the North Front Cemetery with all the remaining *Zinnias* at his graveside.

When the remnants of OG 71's Gibraltar-bound ships reached the port attempts were made to determine exactly what happened to the Wrens that the Queen Alexandra's nursing sister the *Aguila* carried. Most of them were said to have been asleep below decks, either in the lounge or in their cabins. As U-201's torpedoes struck on that side, the consensus of opinion was that the girls were killed outright by the explosions. However, there were reports that women's voices were heard in the water after the ship sank, so perhaps some lived on or an hour or two, only to drown or die of exposure. It was claimed that one Wren – just one – was picked up by the *Empire Oak*, but she was not among the survivors when the tug was torpedoed later. The fate of these twenty-two brave young women must for ever be a matter of conjecture.

Leading Aircraft Mechanic William Churchouse, one of the few to survive the sinking of the *Aguila*, arrived in Gibraltar in HMS *Wallflower* on 26 August. Churchouse, who was on his way to join the aircraft carrier *Ark Royal*, spent a few days recovering from his ordeal before joining his ship, which was then escorting supply convoys through to beleaguered Malta. The carrier sailed into the history books when she was sunk a few miles east of Gibraltar by U-81 on 13 November, and Churchouse, for the second time in two months, found himself abandoning ship. He was snatched from the water by the destroyer *Legion*, and enjoyed another short period of 'survivor's leave' in Gibraltar before securing a passage home in the small escort carrier *Audacity*, sailing in Convoy HG 76. He later recalled:

We sailed on or about the 15th of December to join a homeward bound convoy and after two or three days at sea we received a signal to say that there were several U-boats in our vicinity, so the Escort Commander decided to detach the Audacity *on the evening of the 21st and for the* Marigold *to escort us. We had not left the convoy long when at approximately 2130 we were torpedoed...*

This time, Churchouse left his sinking ship in a lifeboat, but that too sank under him, and once again he found himself in the water. He was picked up by HMS *Marigold,* and eventually reached Liverpool on Christmas Eve 1941 wondering if he was ever meant to complete a voyage.

There was speculation – and it has remained speculation – that OG 71 was sacrificed to draw the U-boats away from another more important convoy, which was southbound in the Atlantic at the same time.

Early in 1941, the British Army of the Nile under General Wavell had advanced 500 miles westwards across the desert, driving the Italians before it. General Graziani's army, nine divisions strong, was completely routed, and 130,000 prisoners, 400 tanks and 1,290 guns were captured. By early February, most of Cyrenaica was in British hands, and Egypt and the Suez Canal were safe. Then General Erwin Rommel arrived in North Africa.

By the beginning of April Rommel had assembled his armoured Panzer divisions, and began his counter-attack. The British, their supply lines stretched beyond the safe limits, lacked sufficient armour and men, and were soon on the retreat. By the end of the month, they had been pushed back to within 50 miles of the Egyptian border, leaving only the Australians holding out in the port of Tobruk 80 miles behind the lines. If Egypt and the vital Suez Canal were to be saved, Wavell urgently needed more men, more guns, more tanks.

Wavell's supply line to Britain was through the WS convoys, known as 'Winston Specials'. They were made up of fast ex-passenger liners converted to troopships and fast cargo liners carrying supplies. They sailed to the Middle East via the Cape of Good Hope under heavy escort. In order to meet the needs of the Desert Army, in the spring of 1941 the Winston Specials were stepped up to one a month, each carrying up to 40,000 troops and their equipment.

WS 10X sailed from Liverpool on 15 August 1941, two days after OG 71, and consisted of P & O's *Strathmore* and *Strathnaver*, Orient Line's *Orion*, Blue Star's *Brisbane Star*, Port Line's *Port Jackson* and Royal Mail's *Palma*, 96,000 tons of Britain's finest shipping. The convoy was escorted initially by the heavy cruiser *Dorsetshire*, the light cruiser *Heemskerk* and the destroyers *Whitehall*, *Witch*, *Gurkha*, *Lance*, *Piorun* and *Issac Sweers*.

This vital, but highly vulnerable, troop convoy was routed from the North Channel to 22° West before altering south, thereby giving the hostile coast of Biscay a wide berth of some 900 miles. At his distance, the troopers were out of range of the Ju 88s stationed at Mérignac, and on the extreme range of the *Focke-Wulfs*. This was, in fact, the original route designated for OG 71, but with the two convoys at sea at the same time and steaming south on parallel courses, one had to make way for the other. While WS 10X was considered of vital importance, OG 71 was, after all, only a motley collection of smallish tramps carrying mundane cargoes, and the inevitable followed. OG 71 was pushed 200 miles further in towards Biscay, and suffered the consequences, while the Winston Special ships sailed on unmolested. Intentional or not, OG 71 ended up drawing the fire away from WS 10X.

77

PART TWO

HG73 Gibraltar–Liverpool

CHAPTER SEVEN

North Again

In that late summer of 1941 the U-boats were reaping a rich harvest in the Atlantic. Twenty-six Allied ships totalling 78,000 tons gross had gone in August, and that total had already been surpassed by the middle of September. The deteriorating situation is perhaps best summed up by the brutal savaging of Convoy SL 87.

SL 87 left Freetown, bound for Liverpool, on 14 September 1941. It was a small convoy, consisting of thirteen merchant ships escorted by a sloop, a corvette, two armed trawlers, and a Free French minesweeper. This nondescript collection of escorts had no experience of working together, and were more suited to guarding a coastal convoy than this assembly of deep-sea traders. Presumably it was hoped they would muddle through on the passage north, which in the event was exactly what they did not do.

When passing 300 miles west of the Canary Islands on the 22nd, SL 87 had the misfortune to run into a gathering of Dönitz's best. Lying in wait across SL 87's course were Günther Müller-Stöckheim in U-67, Karl-Friedrich Merten in U-68, Werner Winter in U-103 and Günter Hessler in U-107. In a mêlée that lasted some forty hours, seven of the twelve merchantmen were sunk, taking with them in the region of 50,000 tons of produce from Africa and the East. The escorts could do little more than rescue those who had survived the enemy's torpedoes.

As a direct result of the heavy sinkings in those months, Lisbon had become a clearing house for temporarily unemployed Allied seamen. The survivors – in the case of the British, designated as Distressed British Seamen (DBS) – were kicking their heels in the port until they could find a ship willing to take them home. Amongst them was 22-year-old Radio Officer George Monk.

George Monk had sailed out of Liverpool as Second Radio Officer in the Harrison Line ship *Auditor,* bound for the Cape with a full general cargo. Six hundred miles north-west of the Cape Verde Islands, and sailing alone, she had the gross misfortune to meet up with Reinhard Hardegen in U-123, who sank her with one well placed torpedo.

By the grace of God, and with a little help from a well-disciplined crew, only one man, a DEMS gunner, lost his life when the *Auditor* went down. The remaining seventy-four crew members got away in three boats, which after an epic voyage of 13½ days, fetched up in Tarafal Bay in the Cape Verdes. The survivors eventually reached Lisbon, where they joined the growing band of beached seamen.

The port of Lisbon, with its tree-lined avenues, roadside cafes and shops packed with every conceivable luxury, seemed like the end of the rainbow to the war-battered seamen decanted onto its shores. But behind this welcoming façade lurked a centre of international espionage, crawling with the spies of every nation, most of them hostile to Britain. A similar situation prevailed further north in Oporto, as revealed by Chief Officer Jack Stow of General Steam's motor vessel *Starling*. The *Starling* had diverted from OG 71 to rescue the crew of a Swedish ship sunk by a *Focke Wulf*. Stow commented:

We arrived safely in Oporto with the rescued crew. At this time Portugal was of course neutral and when we were ashore we rubbed shoulders with Germans and all other nationalities. We were not allowed to wear any uniform or badge showing who we were. I recall being in a nightclub and someone pointed out a table where one of the leading Nazis in the city was sitting. Later we sailed up the River Douro in our ship's dinghy and picnicked on the private estate of the German Ambassador. Needless to say, he did not know that a bunch of British sailors were on the grounds.

For a while, George Monk enjoyed the unscheduled holiday in Lisbon as much as anyone, but after a few weeks of inactivity, for him at least, the delights of Portugal paled. Without a ship, and on reduced pay, presumably as a reward for surviving the German torpedoes, he began to agitate for a passage home. There were promises of 'the next ship going north', or 'a seat on the next available aircraft', but as summer turned to autumn there was no move to repatriate him. Eventually, the young radio officer decided to storm the residence of the British Consul in Lisbon and demand action. His temerity paid off, and within a few days he had the offer of working his passage home as radio officer of the 1600-ton Danish steamer *Ebro*. He accepted the offer without hesitation.

The *Ebro* had been through the holocaust of Convoy OG 71, after which her Danish radio officer had packed his bags and disappeared down the gangway, never to return. Being under the control of the Ministry of War Transport, the *Ebro* was classed as a British ship, and as such was unable to sail without a radio officer on board. With her cargo of cork for Preston already loaded and her hatches battened down, she had been lying idle in her berth for over a week when, on the afternoon of 16 September, George Monk was welcomed aboard. One hour later, with all her papers in order, the *Ebro* received her port clearance, and she cast off her moorings and put to sea, under orders to sail to Gibraltar to join a north-bound convoy. Keeping close into the coast to take advantage of the shelter of neutral waters, and making her best speed of 12 knots, she rounded Cape St. Vincent at 0300 on the 17 September, and headed in for the Straits.

The Rock of Gibraltar, a brooding symbol of Britain's dominance of the Mediterranean Sea since 1704, had, in 1941, resumed the role it played in Nelson's day. As from June 1940, following Italy's entry into the war and the ignominious surrender of the French fleet, access to the Mediterranean for Allied merchant ships was largely restricted to the occasional fast convoy attempting to fight its way through to Malta under heavy escort. Gibraltar's main role had become as an assembly point for convoys of ships trading between Iberian ports and Britain.

One such convoy lay anchored in the shadow of the Rock on 17 September 1941. Convoy HG 73 consisted of twenty-four ships, eight of which, the *Petrel, Lapwing, Starling, Spero, Empire Stream, Cervantes, Lanahrone* and *Switzerland*, had come out with OG 71 only a few weeks earlier. They had survived that convoy, and were now loaded and ready to run the gauntlet of the U-boats and *Focke-Wulf*s all over again. The commodore ship for HG 73 was Yeoward's *Avoceta*, sister-ship to the ill-fated *Aguila*. She was commanded by Captain Harold Martin, and carried the Convoy Commodore, Rear Admiral Sir Kenelm Creighton, KBE, MVO, RNR.

HG 73's escort for the voyage home was assembled in the inner harbour, and was made up of the destroyers *Duncan, Farndale and Vimy*, the sloop *Fowey*, and the Flower-class corvettes, *Begonia, Gentian, Hibiscus, Jasmine, Larkspur, Myosotis, Periwinkle* and *Stonecrop*. HMS *Fowey*, a Bridgewater-class sloop commanded by Lieutenant Commander Robert Aubrey, RN, was the senior ship. A late addition to this already exceptionally strong escort force was the Pegasus-class fighter catapult ship (FCS) HMS

Springbank under the command of Captain Goodwin. Built in 1926 for Bank Line of London, and taken into service with the Royal Navy in 1940 as an A/A ship, the *Springbank* carried eight 4-inch guns in four high-angle turrets and eight 2-pounder pom-poms. In March 1941, she was fitted with a rocket propelled catapult, on which was mounted a two-seater Fairey Fulmar fighter of 804 Squadron Fleet Air Arm. The Fulmar was verging on the obsolescent as a fighter but, powered by a Rolls Royce Merlin, it had a top speed of 266 mph, and mounted eight .303-inch machine-guns. This latter addition to the *Springbank's* armament was – or so it was hoped – the answer to the U-boats' eyes in the sky, the long-range *Focke-Wulf* Condors. The theory was that on the approach of an enemy aircraft the Fulmar would be launched to chase away the intruder. However, launching the Fulmar was essentially a one-way operation; the plane being unable to return to the ship. If there was a friendly shore nearby, so long as he had sufficient fuel, the pilot could land at a convenient airfield. Failing that, the only alternatives were to bale out and hope to be picked up, or ditch alongside the ship. The weather in the North Atlantic being habitually bad, the risks involved with both the latter were very great. Nevertheless, the mere presence of the Fighter Catapult Ship was a boost to the morale of the men in the merchant ships, particularly those who had been involved in OG 71.

Early in the afternoon of 17 September, wisps of steam could be seen rising from the forecastles of the ships in Gibraltar Bay, and the clanking of anchor chains being hove home echoed back from the Rock. At around 1500, HMS *Fowey* appeared from behind the breakwaters of the inner harbour, followed by the destroyers and the line of sturdy, rust-stained corvettes. Flags signals flew from *Fowey's* yard arms and her signal lamps clattered, urging the tardy merchantmen to hasten their preparations for sailing. All of which did not escape the watchful eyes of German and Spanish agents ashore in Algeciras, on the other side of Gibraltar Bay. Before the first Allied ship left the anchorage, the Abwehr station in Madrid was fully informed of the composition of Convoy HG 73, and within the hour, details of the sailing had reached Admiral Dönitz in Lorient.

There were few in the ships who were not aware that they were under surveillance by the enemy, but there was precious little that could be done about it. In an attempt to confuse the watchers, HMS *Springbank* left the bay first, making a great show of setting course to the east as though she were heading for Malta. Captain Goodwin had orders to reverse course after dark and rejoin the convoy, which was then forming up into two lines abreast, and steaming west into the Straits under the protection of *Fowey* and the corvettes. Once clear of Tarifa, where the Straits widen out into the Atlantic, Rear Admiral Creighton gave the order to form up into seven columns, the Commodore's ship *Avoceta* taking the lead at the head of Column 5.

As with the *Aguila*, the *Avoceta* offered a degree of comfort no ordinary cargo ship could match, and not surprisingly, she was much sought after as commodore ship. With Rear Admiral Creighton on board, she had sailed out of Liverpool on 18 August at the head of Convoy OG 72, arriving in Gibraltar on 1 September after an uneventful passage. There she picked up a number of survivors from the ships sunk in OG 71, who had been waiting patiently for a ship to carry them home. They included Captain Frith of the *Aguila* and Captain McLean of the *Aldergrove*. She then doubled back to Lisbon, where she loaded a cargo of cork and sardines, along with 573 bags of mail, and a large number of refugees. The latter were variously described as, 'mostly foreign women and children married to British citizens once living in France', 'wives, children and relatives of Free French men who had escaped from France and joined the forces of England', and 'European women, with their young children, who had married men of British nationality'. It is difficult to discern through the fog of war who these passengers really were, but it is on record that they boarded the *Avoceta* in Lisbon, after crossing through Spain and Portugal with the help of the Spanish Underground. With her cargo holds and passenger accommodation filled to capacity, the *Avoceta* had returned to Gibraltar to await a northbound convoy.

The church bells were calling the faithful to prayer when, three days earlier, on Sunday 14 September, U-201 had sailed out of Brest again. She was given the usual rousing send-off from her berth by the band from the local Wehrmacht barracks, and *Oberleutnant* Adalbert Schnee stood proud in his conning tower with his newly acquired Knight's Cross dangling from a ribbon at his throat. Although Schnee was grateful to be at last free of the restrictions of the shore, his wind-tanned face showed the premature lines of a man pushed beyond reasonable limits.

U-201 had returned to Brest on 25 August after eleven hectic days, during which she was involved in the attack on Convoy OG 71, sinking four ships, including the *Aguila*. The patrol had been cut short when the submarine's main air compressor had failed, leaving her unable to submerge safely. The return to base, much of the time on the surface and dangerously exposed to attack from the air, had been a frightening nightmare for Adalbert Schnee and his men. At the very least, they had looked forward to a month in port in which to wind down and, perhaps, even snatch a few days home leave. But it was not to be. With a fresh coat of paint and a new compressor fitted, U-201 was back at sea in less than three weeks.

On the morning of 20 September Schnee was to the north-east of the Azores, and on the lookout for likely targets, when he received a radio message from Johann Mohr in U-124. Mohr had sighted the 27-ship Liverpool to Gibraltar convoy OG 74, which was then 600 miles to the west of Land's End, and heading south in longitude 22 West. He invited Adalbert Schnee to join him.

What Mohr omitted to mention was that OG 74's escort included the escort carrier HMS *Audacity*. An ex-German cargo ship captured in 1940, the *Audacity* carried six Grumman Martlet fighters, two of which were in the air patrolling over the convoy throughout the daylight hours. As U-201 approached the convoy, she was spotted by one of the Martlets, which alerted the senior escort, the sloop *Deptford*. Joined by the corvette *Arbutus*, *Deptford* immediately attacked. U-201 was forced to crash dive, and pounded by depth charges, Schnee hastily retired from the vicinity of OG 74.

Maintaining a safe distance off the convoy, Schnee witnessed commotion, just before midnight, when U-124 attacked, sinking two merchantmen in quick succession. Another twenty-four hours passed before U-201 was in position to join in, and when she was Schnee made good use of his torpedoes, sending three ships to the bottom in the space of half an hour. This brought the total sunk by the two U-boats to 8629 tons. By the time the last ship had disappeared beneath the waves OG 74 was nearing the Western Approaches, and U-201 and U-124 had withdrawn. They then made off to the south, trailing their coats along the now familiar UK-Gibraltar convoy route.

Urged on by the east-going current in the Straits, the *Ebro* was only 14 miles from Gibraltar when, at around 1700 on the 17th, she met HG 73 heading westwards into the Atlantic. The convoy was steaming in two orderly columns, with its escort substantially reinforced by the arrival of the destroyers *Duncan, Farndale and Vimy*. HMS *Farndale*, a Blankney-class destroyer of 1050 tons commanded by Commander Stephen Carlill, RN, had taken over as Senior Officer Escort.

The convoy made an impressive sight as it steamed majestically westwards, and it occurred to Radio Officer George Monk, standing watch on the bridge of the Danish ship, that the sensible thing to do would be to tag on behind. However, *Ebro's* master continued to the east. Monk was not surprised when, as they were entering Gibraltar Bay, a naval launch came racing out with orders for the *Ebro* to turn about and join HG 73.

The *Ebro* had a good turn of speed for a cargo ship, usually averaging 12 knots, but returning to the west she was stemming the current, and it was dusk before she caught up with the rear ships of HG 73. The convoy was now steaming in eight columns of three ships, and the *Ebro* was ordered to join Column 5, which was led by the Commodore's ship *Avoceta*. She was thus the back marker of the convoy, and in a highly vulnerable position. There were few on board her who slept easy that night.

Early next morning HMS *Springbank,* having performed her somewhat futile charade to divert attention from the sailing of HG 73, rejoined, and took up a position at the head of the convoy, between Columns 4 and 5. HG 73's formidable defensive screen was complete, and soon to be tested.

The convoy was then off Cape St. Vincent, and it was not long before the inevitable Focke Wulf Condor appeared on the horizon. The aircraft came within 2 miles of the outer ships of the convoy, and then began to circle in long, lazy sweeps carefully choreographed to keep it out of range of the convoy's guns. It was a dreadfully familiar routine to those who had sailed the convoy lanes, usually the frightening prelude to an attack by the U-boats the plane was then homing in. But this time HG 73 had the ability to hit back.

With her bow-wave frothing as she increased speed, *Springbank* sheered away from the convoy and opened fire on the intruder with her eight 4-inch AA guns, peppering the sky around the German plane with puffs of black smoke laced with shrapnel. As she neared the Focke Wulf, her 2-pounder pom-poms joined in, sending arcs of tracer skywards. In the face of this unexpected reception the enemy pilot jettisoned his bombs and hastily retired out of range. He must have been even more unhappy when, a few minutes later, with a loud bang and a cloud of white smoke, the *Springbank's* Fulmar, piloted by Petty Officer Shaw, was catapulted off from her foredeck.

The chase was on, and with the Fulmar close on her tail, the Focke Wulf dropped low on the water and fled for the horizon. The Fulmar was the faster plane, if only marginally, and Petty Officer Shaw went in for the kill, closing the gap remorselessly. Unfortunately, when the moment came for him to open fire, Sod's Law intervened. The Fulmar's guns jammed after only one short burst. The Condor, flying so low that her propellers were furrowing the water, slowly drew away to the north. Half an hour later, the

Fulmar was back over her parent ship, where Shaw reported the failure of his guns. There was too much of a chop on the sea for a successful ditching, so the Fleet Air Arm pilot opted to make for Gibraltar. 'And that,' remarked Rear Admiral Crieghton, 'was the end of our air protection.' However, HMS *Springbank's* substantial AA barrage, followed by the appearance of a British fighter aircraft, had been quite enough to scare off the *Focke Wulf*, though the enemy plane had served its main purpose. While it circled out of range, it had been radioing details of HG 73, its position, course and estimated speed, and the strength of the naval escort.

Ironically, the convoy might have escaped the attentions of Dönitz's U-boats, had it not been for Hitler's unwelcome interference in the war on Allied shipping. At the end of August, infuriated by the successful campaign being waged by the Royal Navy and RAF against shipping supplying Rommel in North Africa, the Führer had ordered a number of U-boats to be diverted from the North Atlantic into the Mediterranean. Dönitz, who felt that he had at last established a stranglehold on Allied shipping in the Atlantic, was furious, but he was overruled.

U-371, commanded by *Oberleutnant* Heinrich Driver, had been chosen to lead the incursion into the Mediterranean, and it so happened that she was southbound, and in the vicinity of HG 73 when the Condor spotted the convoy. With U-371 was the Italian submarine *Luigi Torelli* (*Capitano di Corvetta* Antonio de Giacomo), and possibly two other Italian boats, also on their way into the Mediterranean. Acting on the Condor's signals, U-371 and the *Torelli* steered for HG 73, sighting the convoy at 1900 on the 19th in a position 410 miles due west of the Straits. Heinrich Driver was under orders from Dönitz not to engage in any protracted operations in the Atlantic, so he contented himself with shadowing the convoy, reporting to Lorient.

The Italian boats, which were ideally placed to mount an attack were likewise ordered to keep their distance. Although they were under his wing, Dönitz did not hold Italian submariners in high esteem, describing them as 'not sufficiently hard and tough for this type of warfare' and that 'their way of thinking is too sluggish and according to rule to allow them to adapt themselves clearly and simply too the changing conditions of war. Their personal conduct is not sufficiently disciplined and in the face of the enemy not calm enough'.

Later that day, the lone *Focke Wulf* was back, flying up and down the starboard side of the convoy, occasionally sweeping across ahead and astern, but taking care not to stray within range of the escorts' guns. *Springbank*

Crew of Norwegian destroyer *Bath* relaxing before joining OG 71. (*G. Drummond.*)

Yeoward Line's 3255-ton *Aguila*, commodore ship of Convoy OG 71. (*Allen Collection.*)

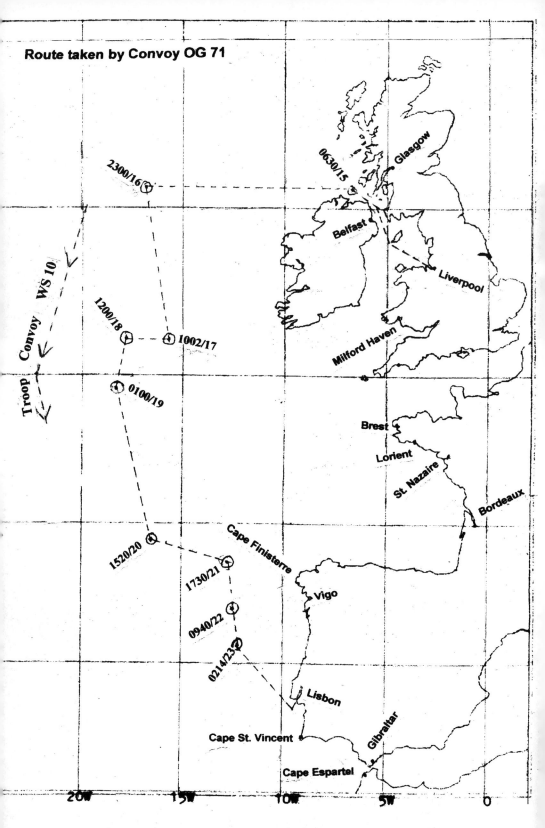

Route taken by Convoy OG 71.

General Steam Navigation's *Lapwing*, one of the short-sea traders that formed the core of the Gibraltar convoys. (*Library of Contemporary History, Stuggart.*)

Flower-class corvette HMS *Campion* (Lieutenant Commander A. Johnson). (*G. Drummond.*)

Focke-Wulf FW 200 'Condor' - 'the scourge of the Atlantic'. (*Source unknown.*)

U-201 sails from Lorient with pennants flying. (*Post Scriptum.*)

The Auditor's No.1 lifeboat made a landfall at Tarafal Bay. (*G. Monk.*)

Tarafal Bay, Cape Verde Islands. (*G. Monk.*)

Lieutenant Commander Cuthbertson (right) on the bridge of HMS *Zinnia* with his Number One Lieutenant Harold Chesterman, RNR. (*G. Drummond.*)

Campion's dinghy, with Leading Seaman Drummond at the tiller, sets out to rescue Zinnia's survivors.

Second Radio Officer George Monk, s.s. Auditor. (*G. Monk.*)

19-year-old Leading Seaman Geoffrey Drummond, HMS *Campion* 1941. (*G. Drummond.*)

Lieutenant Commander Charles George Cuthbertson, RNR, DSC. (*G. Drummond.*)

Oberleutnant Adalbert Schnee, U-201. (*Post Scriptum.*)

John P. Cox, RN, HMS Z. *Campion*
(*G. Drummond.*)

Geoffrey Drummond today.
(*G. Drummond.*)

broke away to engage, forcing the big aircraft to keep its distance. After circling aimlessly for more than two hours, the German pilot gave up and flew away to the north-east.

The night that followed was quiet, the Portuguese Trades blowing light and sweeping the horizon clear of mist. It was very dark, with only the occasional brief glimmer of light from an inadequately curtained doorway betraying the presence of this small armada of ships making its way north at an almost leisurely 7½ knots. The heavily-laden merchantmen rolled easily in the long Atlantic swell, each keeping station on the other as they strove to hold to the orderly lines that constituted part of the defence of the convoy. HMS *Duncan* led the way, zig-zagging ahead of the convoy, her Asdics pinging and RDF probing the darkness from bow to bow. *Farndale* and *Vimy* were astern carrying out a similar sweep, while *Fowey* and the corvettes guarded the flanks

The Admiralty had obviously learned the lessons of OG 71, and HG 73 was routed far out into the Atlantic, with orders not to alter in for the north-western approaches to the British Isles until reaching longitude 24½° West. It was hoped that this wide deviation would stretch the marauding *Focke Wulfs* beyond their safe limits, but there was a price to be paid. In more peaceful days, most of the merchant ships, regular Mediterranean traders, would have expected to make the voyage to Gibraltar in just over six days. HG 73's allotted route, taking it deep into the Atlantic before approaching Britain through the North Channel, would prolong the passage to at least thirteen days, and every extra day spent at sea was another day exposed to danger.

HG 73's escort was reinforced next afternoon by the arrival of the destroyer *Wild Swan* from Gibraltar. Soon after her arrival, the usual Condor hove in sight, making a tentative approach from seaward. So long as the enemy plane stayed out of range of the convoy's guns it was able to circle unmolested, but this pilot made the mistake of straying too close, and was greeted by a fusilade of shells. The plane immediately flew away to the north, but she had done the job she was sent to do, keeping BdU and the U-boats up to date on the position of the convoy.

In the early hours of next morning, the 21st, *Duncan* and *Farndale* were detached for other convoy work, leaving HG 73 with only two 1917-vintage destroyers *Vimy* and *Wild Swan* with the screen. At that time, no one in the convoy was aware that its movements were being closely monitored and reported on by U-371 and the Italian boats. It was only later in the day, when *Vimy* had dropped back and was sweeping astern of the convoy that the shadowers were discovered. A 'definite sub' contact was obtained, and the destroyer attacked with depth charges. The *Luigi Torelli* was unfortunate enough to be within range of *Vimy's* charges, and the Italian submarine was badly damaged, and forced to retire. U-371 and the other Italian boats, now known to be the *Leonardo da Vinci* (*Capitano di Corvetta* Ferdinando Calda), and the *Alessandro Malaspina* (*Tenente di Vascello* Giuliano Prini), were also ordered to break off operations on HG 73.

Despite the discovery of U-boats in the vicinity, the convoy's escort force was further depleted when, next day, *Vimy* and *Wild Swan* left. They were replaced later in the day by HMS *Highlander*, a Havant-class destroyer commanded by Commander W.A. Dallmeyer, RN. The *Highlander*, commissioned in 1940, mounted three 4.7-inch guns and had a speed of 36 knots, but as the only destroyer in HG 73's screen, she had a vast area of sea to cover.

By now, HG 73, was in longitude 22° W, and nearly 600 miles WSW of Cape Finisterre, and having got thus far unharmed, it must have been presumed that the convoy was relatively safe – for the time being, at least. This was not so. Following their successful strike against Convoy OG 74, U-124 and U-201 had received orders from BdU to 'proceed further to the south at economical cruising speed in order to be in a position to operate on the northbound convoy reported by the Italian boats.' However, by the time Mohr and Schnee reached the position given, HG 73 was nowhere to be seen, and Air Reconnaissance had lost contact.

At 1000 next morning, the 23rd, contrary to Admiral Dönitz's expectations, HG 73 was rediscovered by Ferdinando Calda in the *Leonardo da Vinci*. Calda tucked himself in behind the convoy, reporting to BdU at four-hourly intervals. His signals brought U-124 and U-201, which had been returning to the north empty-handed, hurrying back at full speed.

Before the German boats came within reach, a *Focke Wulf Condor* was circling the convoy, reporting its position at 1345 on the 24th to be in 44° 09'N 21° 45" W, 540 miles WNW of Finisterre. This aircraft also reported two ships of the convoy sinking and one on fire. It was later claimed that the Italian submarine *Alessandro Malaspina* was responsible, but as she disappeared shortly afterwards, it could not be established if she actually fired any torpedoes. To this day it is not known what happened to her, but whether the Italian fired or not is irrelevant, for HG 73 was still very much intact when the day ended. No ships had been sunk, no ship was on fire.

Meanwhile, Mohr and Schnee had been joined by Rolf Mützelburg in U-203. The three boats took cross bearings of the aircraft over the convoy, and began to close in. Johann Mohr was first to make contact, at 0353 on the 25th reporting HG 73 to be in position 45° 21' N 24° 15' W, and on a course of 315°.

The convoy was making steady progress to the north-west at 7 knots, steaming in eight columns abreast, with *Highlander* scouting ahead with long probing sweeps, while *Fowey* covered the rear of the convoy in a similar manner. *Springbank*, now minus her fighter aircraft, had dropped back to a position astern of the lead ships in Columns 5 and 6. The eight corvettes, *Hibiscus, Periwinkle, Jasmine, Begonia, Myosotis, Stonecrop, Larkspur* and *Gentian*, were guarding the flanks, four either side. The weather remained reasonable, with a SW'ly wind force 3–4, scattered cloud, and isolated rain squalls, although a falling barometer indicated that there was a deterioration coming. Nevertheless, Liverpool was only six days away, and having come thus far without any serious threat emerging, there was a cautious air of optimism in the merchant ships. Those in the escort ships, listening in to a babble of R/T chatter between U-boats close by, probably reserved their judgement on this. It would have been obvious to them that the wolves were gathering around HG 73. They were not to know, however, that the wolf pack hastily assembled by Lorient was small in number.

At that time, thanks largely to Hitler's mad insistence on sending boats into the Mediterranean, Admiral Dönitz's forces in the Atlantic were hard pressed to meet the demands placed on them. While the heavily escorted HG 73 sedately made its way north, five other Allied convoys were at sea in the same waters. The 'Winston Special' WS 11X, fifteen supply ships and troop carriers under heavy escort, had sailed from the Clyde on the 17th, and was on its way south to the Cape. ON 17 and ON 19, sailing from Liverpool on the 18th and 21st respectively, were heading west across the Atlantic to Halifax: OS 6, having left Liverpool on the 12th was making its slow way south to Freetown, while SL 87 was northbound from Freetown. The North Atlantic was not exactly Piccadilly Circus on a busy Saturday night, but there were certainly a great number of Allied wakes criss-crossing its grey waters. The U-boats were spoiled for choice.

The Italian boats having gone on their way into the Mediterranean, all Admiral Dönitz could muster to challenge the passage of HG 73 was four U-boats. U-124, U-201 and U-203 were already in contact on the 25th, and U-205, under the command of Franz-Georg Reschke, was on the way in. The first three were boats with an impressive record of sinkings, Mohr's U-124 being the most outstanding. The Type IXB, a long-range boat scaling

1430 tons submerged and with a speed of 18½ knots on the surface, had twenty-two ships totalling 97,000 tons to her credit. U-205, on the other hand, was on her second war patrol, and was yet to taste success. Given the opportunity, Franz-Georg Reschke intended to alter that, with the help of HG 73.

CHAPTER EIGHT

The Wolves Attack

The pre-dawn hours of 25 September were dark, wet and miserable. It was the North Atlantic at its equinoctial worst, heavily overcast, moonless, and with banks of icy rain sweeping in from time to time, blotting out the horizon. Visibility was reduced to a matter of yards. Seamen fortunate enough to be tucked up in their warm beds at home have bad dreams about nights like this.

In the conning tower of U-124, *Kapitänleutnant* Johann Mohr, the rain streaming off his oilskins, wiped the lenses of his binoculars, and peered into the darkness again, silently cursing his luck. U-124, with her superior turn of speed, had been the first of the wolfpack to sight Convoy HG 73, albeit that Mohr had only a brief glimpse of a slow-moving cluster of dark shadows on the water, before losing them again in the rain.

U-124 was Johann Mohr's first command, his promotion to the rank of *kapitänleutnant* at the tender age of 25 being an indication of the scale of the losses currently being suffered by the U-boat Arm. Taking over the Type IXB on 8 September 1941, Mohr's baptism of fire followed swiftly. Twelve days into his command, in company with Adalbert Schnee in U-201, he had gone against the southbound convoy OG 74, and had not been found wanting. On 20 September, with one fan of three torpedoes, Mohr sank two British steamers, and narrowly missed another. Now, only five days later, he was closing with the enemy again.

Johann Mohr was not alone in being handed the burden of command at an early age. Captain Stanley Evans, commanding the steamer *Empire Stream*, bringing up the rear of HG 73's third column, was 27 years old, with the ink barely dry on his Master's Certificate. Less than two weeks earlier, he had been serving as Chief Officer in another ship, and wrestling with the complexities of cargo stowage and crew management, with the prospect of years in the same rank ahead of him.

Traditionally, promotion in British merchant ships was painfully slow, particularly so on the bridge. The long crawl from indentured apprentice to Master, even with the necessary certificates of competency, usually took a minimum of twenty years, and it was rare for a suitably qualified officer to reach command before he was in his forties. The war had changed all that, as hundreds of officers were lost with their ships month by month. Admiral Dönitz had exacerbated the situation by giving instructions to his U-boat commanders to, whenever possible, take prisoner the Master and Senior Officers of ships falling to their torpedoes. This act of kidnap on the high seas – for that is what it was – had paid rich dividends for Dönitz; the men being snatched from the lifeboats, particularly captains, being irreplaceable at short notice. In the autumn of 1941, the British merchant fleet was running dangerously short of men who could command, and it had been Stanley Evans' good fortune to be in the right place at the right time.

Evans' first command, the 2922-ton *Empire Stream*, was a wartime replacement ship, built early in 1941 for the Ministry of War Transport, and put under the management of J.S. Stranaghan & Company of Cardiff. She was a forerunner of the modern ore carrier, with wide hatchways, unencumbered by cargo gear, and engine-room and much of her accommodation placed right aft. Seen from a distance, she might easily have been mistaken for an oil tanker, and it was this similarity that was to prove her downfall.

The *Empire Stream* was manned by a crew of twenty-nine plus four DEMS gunners. The latter manned and maintained her armament consisting of an ancient 4-inch, two Hotchkiss light machine-guns, two stripped Lewis guns, and an assortment of anti-aircraft rockets. Also on board were two Spanish stowaways, who had revealed themselves shortly after sailing from Huelva. Captain Evans had made every effort to land these men in Gibraltar, but the authorities there would have no truck with them. And so the Spaniards remained on board to run the gauntlet of U-boats and *Focke-Wulf*s in the hope of starting a new life in a Britain currently being pounded into ruin by German bombers.

In her holds, the *Empire Stream* carried a cargo of 3,370 tons of potash, loaded in the Spanish port of Huelva for Dundee. Potash is an inert cargo, but it has its dangers in wartime, being heavy enough to send a ship to the bottom in minutes, should she be torpedoed. And, given that the *Empire Stream* was in a very exposed position at the rear of Column 3, the possibility of such a happening had never been far from the newly-promoted Captain Evans' thoughts. Since sailing from Gibraltar he had been rarely away from the bridge, snatching a few hours sleep on the chartroom settee at night, and only when he felt it was safe to do so. This night, was no exception. The visibility was indifferent at best, poor in the rain squalls, and keeping station on the other ships was a laborious exercise, requiring constant vigilance and fine judgement. The regulation distance between columns was 5 cables, half a mile of clear water, while 2 cables separated the ships in line ahead. Space enough on a fine, clear day perhaps, but on this black, rain-swept night, with a heavy swell coming in from the west, the danger of collision was very real. Evans decided to remain on the bridge after midnight to lend support to the Officer of the Watch.

Midnight came and went, and the eight columns of ships, except for the occasional heart-stopping near-collision, moved quietly through the night in good order. By 3 o'clock on the morning of the 25th, the rain squalls had become less frequent, and visibility was up to 4 miles. At this juncture, Captain Evans, his tongue furred by too many mugs of steaming hot coffee, his eyes gritty from constant peering into the darkness, decided that he must sleep for a few hours if he were to face the new day. Taking one last look around the horizon, and satisfied that all was well, he left the watch to the Second Officer, and bedded down on the chartroom settee.

There was no sleep that night for Johann Mohr either. Motoring on the surface at 14 knots, U-124 was at last in sight of HG 73; just a few vague shadows on the horizon ahead, which Mohr recognised as the back-markers of the convoy.

Remaining on the surface, Mohr approached the ships warily, keeping an eye on one small vessel that was zig-zagging lazily in the wake of the convoy. By its size and outline, this appeared to be one of the convoy's escorts – a corvette, perhaps. It was, in fact, the sloop *Fowey* with Lieutenant Commander Aubrey doing his rounds of the escort screen.

After a long night on full alert, it is possible that the men on *Fowey's* bridge – or on the nearby merchant ships – were not as vigilant as they might have been. Certainly, no one saw the long, menacing shape of U-124 as she silently infiltrated the ranks of the convoy, passing between Columns 3 and 4.

Johann Mohr had good cause to feel that the gods were on his side that night. The rear ship of the column to port had her funnel and accommodation right aft, and was almost certainly a loaded tanker. She was a prize worthy of Mohr's long night spent in U-124's conning tower.

The sky was lightening in the east by the time Mohr had manoeuvred into a favourable position on the *Empire Stream's* starboard quarter. At 0548, he had the funnel of the enemy 'tanker' in the crosshairs of his surface attack sight. He aimed for the engine-room, the most vulnerable part of the ship, and fired two torpedoes.

Mohr had overestimated the speed of his target, and instead of laying the *Empire Stream's* engine-room open to the sea, one of his torpedoes went home in her deep tank, immediately forward of her bridge. The other passed ahead of the ship, and narrowly missed another ship two columns away to port, General Steam's 1348-ton *Lapwing*, sailing as rear ship of Column 1.

Captain Evans, sleeping the sleep of the exhausted in the *Empire Stream's* chartroom, had a very rude awakening. He later wrote:

The explosion was terrific, largely due to the torpedo striking the deep tank, and a large column of water was thrown up over the bridge. The Mate, who was on the bridge at the time, was blown onto the lower deck and his face was covered with black powder. There was a strong smell of cordite.

When I regained consciousness I found myself in the middle of the wheelhouse, having been blown over the chart room table and through the doorway (the door of which had been blown away) into the wheelhouse. The man at the wheel was blown out of the wheelhouse and was later found with a portion of the wheel still in his hand. He was badly cut by glass.

Although still in shock, Evans soon realised that the *Empire Stream* was already sinking. His first thought was to stop the ship to avoid the boats being swamped when they were lowered. Picking his way through the smouldering debris in the wheelhouse, he grasped the handle of the engine-room telegraph, and rang it to stop. There was no ring of acknowledgement from below. With some difficulty, Evans made his way down onto the main deck and went aft to the engine-room top. Below was all silence and darkness. The engines had already been stopped, the engine-room abandoned.

The *Empire Stream* was now noticeably by the head, and developing a heavy starboard list as the sea poured into her hull. Evans gave the order to abandon ship, aware that this was not going to be a copybook operation. The wind was in the west, and increasing in strength, the sea rough, and swell beginning to heave. With the ship dead in the water, nothing could be done to make a lee, but the *Empire Stream's* crew were tramp ship men, often ill-disciplined, but fine practical seamen. Overcoming all the difficulties, they put both lifeboats in the water without damaging them.

Evans and his Chief Engineer, having checked to see that no one was left behind, were the last to leave the ship, shinning down a ladder into the port boat, which was rising and falling dangerously alongside. As the boats cast off, the doomed ship suddenly lurched heavily to starboard, fouling the starboard boat and capsizing it. Evans watched helpless as his men were thrown into the water.

From the time Mohr's torpedo hit, the *Empire Stream* had taken no more than five minutes to sink, and in the opinion of Captain Evans, she would have gone sooner if she had been hit anywhere but in her deep tank. The watertight bulkheads of the tank had held long enough to allow the boats to be launched.

The *Empire Stream* went down bow-first, the sea mercifully muffling the dreadful cacophony of groans and crashes as her cargo shifted and her boilers broke free of their mountings. Then, there was silence, and only a patch of disturbed water and floating wreckage marked her grave.

The remaining lifeboat pulled clear of the sinking ship, and stood off waiting for the turbulence to die down, Captain Evans then went back in amongst the wreckage to search for survivors from the capsized starboard boat. As they approached, a small cluster of tiny red lights bobbing on the waves became visible. The *Empire Stream* was one of the first British ships to be supplied with the new Eastcote Lights, small battery-powered red lights fitted to lifejackets, and in those pre-dawn hours they proved their worth. By the time the sun came up, Evans had twenty-seven survivors on board, and the boat was so low in the water that the sea was lopping over the gunwales.

Two survivors, the *Empire Stream's* boatswain and one of her stewards, were unconscious when pulled from the water. There was very little Evans could do for them, other than to lay them in the bottom of the boat. Unfortunately, both men died within just over an hour of being rescued. Their bodies were committed to the deep with as much dignity as the crowded, half-swamped lifeboat would allow.

A head count of those left in the boat revealed four crew members missing, including Third Officer David Harries and two of the DEMS gunners. There was also no trace of the two Spanish stowaways, and Evans presumed that all six men had been lost with the ship, possibly when the starboard lifeboat capsized.

When the quiet of that early September morning was rudely shattered by the thunder of Johann Mohr's torpedo blasting open the *Empire Stream's* hull, the Convoy Commodore, Rear Admiral Creighton acted quickly, taking the convoy through a series of emergency turns designed to confuse the enemy. HG 73's escort, on the other hand, already in some disarray, was taken completely by surprise. *Highlander* was out on the port side of the convoy searching for the steamer *Danos,* missing from her station at the head of Column 2. At the same time, *Fowey* was also to the west, nearing the extremity of the port leg of her zig-zag. The weather was calm, but the visibility indifferent, down to 1½ miles most of the time, and several of the corvettes were experiencing difficulty with their primitive radars, and had wandered away from the convoy.

Lieutenant Commander Aubrey was of the firm opinion that the attack had come from the port side, and on his instigation *Highlander* fired star shell to port, while he took *Fowey* out on to the port quarter of the convoy to engage the U-boat. The corvettes *Myosotis* and *Stonecrop* also began to sweep up the port side. It was not until the *Lapwing*, rear ship of the port wing column, broke radio silence to report she had seen a torpedo break surface, passing from starboard to port, that the mistake was realised. By this time U-124 had disappeared into the shadows of the western horizon.

After drifting in the wake of the receding convoy for another two hours, the twenty-four men who survived the sinking of the *Empire Stream* were picked up by the corvette HMS *Begonia*. They were landed at Milford Haven three days later. So ended Captain Stanley Evans' first command.

Thursday 25 September dawned fine and clear, the sea an innocent blue rippled by a light south-westerly breeze, all the horrors of the previous night fading with the rising sun. But that the enemy was still there was confirmed by *Springbank* reporting on R/T that she had sighted a U-boat on the surface. A great flurry of activity followed, with *Highlander* and *Fowey* making high-speed dashes to challenge an enemy that failed to materialise. It turned out that *Springbank* had picked up some hydrophone effect that could have been a submarine below the surface, and equally could have been a shoal of fish.

The convoy quickly settled down to normal daytime routine again, with hot food and the prospect of a few hours sleep putting new life into men who had had precious little of either during the night. But the euphoria was short-lived. Early in the afternoon the ominous drone of aircraft engines was heard, and HG 73's resident *Focke-Wulf* was back, circling the convoy out of range, and transmitting continuous homing signals. There would be no more relaxation in the ships.

One of the recipients of the *Focke-Wulf*'s signals was U-201. Hurrying south after using his torpedoes to good effect on Convoy OG 74, Adalbert Schnee had overshot the northbound HG 73. When reports began to come in of U-124's opening attack, U-201 was already 160 miles to the south and east of the convoy. Acting on a fix given by BdU, Schnee had turned around and raced north at full speed on the surface.

At noon on the 25th, Mohr signalled that he had lost the convoy in the rain, and when, at 1545, U-201 reached the last reported position of HG 73, she also found the horizon empty. Schnee continued to the north, and was by now in contact with Rolf Mützelburg in U-203, who was also searching for the convoy.

As the afternoon progressed, and Schnee continued to the north, he became increasingly anxious than the night would be on him before he found the enemy. Then, at 1740, with twilight approaching, to his great relief mastheads were sighted on the horizon. Schnee informed Mützelburg and Mohr of his discovery, adding that he would shadow the convoy until twilight, and then move in to attack.

Luck was not on Adalbert Schnee's side that evening, for as he settled down confidently to creep up on the rear ships of HG 73, Commander Dallmeyer decided to take *Highlander* astern of the convoy and carry out a sweep before darkness closed in. When she was some 8 miles astern, the destroyer's WT/DF operators, keeping watch on 1107 kcs, picked up transmissions coming from an unknown source bearing dead astern. As the transmissions were coded, and no British ships were known to be in the area, Dallmeyer assumed he must have found a U-boat. The indications are that it was Schnee attempting to contact Mohr and Mützelburg.

Highlander made a high-speed dash back along the bearing, but U-201 was long gone, creeping away under the cover of a passing rain squall. Dallmeyer searched up to 12 miles, but there were no more radio transmissions to guide him, and after about an hour he reversed course to rejoin the convoy.

Steaming hard, *Highlander* finally caught up with the rear ships of HG 73, and at 2330 was abeam of the starboard column, intending to resume her station ahead of the convoy. Before she could do so, the night sky to port was suddenly lit up by two brilliant flashes. Heavy explosions followed, and then the white distress rockets went soaring into the sky.

Silent and unseen, U-203 had come in from the west to strike a devastating blow at the convoy. Suddenly confronted by the massed ranks of HG 73, a flotilla of dark shadows gliding slowly through the night, Rolf Mützelburg aimed for the middle of the convoy, and fired a spread of four torpedoes from his bow tubes.

The unfortunate occupant of the centre of the port column of HG 73 was the 1374-ton MacAndrews' steamer *Cortes*. A First World War wartime replacement ship built in 1919 as the *War Waveney*, the *Cortes*, loaded with a full cargo of potash, sank like the proverbial stone when one of Mützelburg's torpedoes slammed into her port side and exploded in her engine-room. She took with her Captain Donald McRae, his six passengers, and thirty-one crew members. When the ship stationed directly astern of the *Cortes*, General Steam's 1348-ton *Lapwing*, commanded by Captain Thomas Hyam, searched for survivors, she found only four men still alive in the water. They were 41-year-old Radio Officer George Alan, an Arab fireman, and two Filipino ratings.

Mützelburg had fired his salvo of four from a position off the port quarter of the *Cortes*, and the remaining three torpedoes ran diagonally through the convoy, narrowly missing the ships in Columns 2, 3 and 4, before finding a target in Column 5. This was the Norwegian steamer *Varangberg*, which was at the time romping ahead of her station. Her poor position-keeping put her right in the path of one of Mützelburg's torpedoes.

The 2842-ton *Varangberg*, owned by A/S Malmfart of Oslo, and commanded by Captain Edward Stenersen, was considered by those who sailed in her to be a lucky ship. Having escaped from Norway ahead of the invading Germans in March 1940, she had been taken under the wing of the Ministry of War Transport in London, and assumed her place in the ranks of Allied ships supplying Britain with the essentials of war. In December of that year, she was attacked by a U-boat when sailing alone to the west of Ireland, but escaped unharmed. Six weeks later, in February 1941, she was in Convoy SLS 64, bound from Freetown to Liverpool unescorted, when the German heavy cruiser *Admiral Hipper* appeared over the horizon and opened up on the defenceless ships with her 8-inch guns. In the space of thirty minutes, the *Hipper* disposed of seven ships and 50,000 tons of cargo. On this occasion, the *Varangberg* was spared by virtue of her slow speed. She had straggled so far behind the convoy that she was out of sight when the *Hipper* pounced.

The *Varangberg* met her end at 2335 on the night of 26 September 1941, when two of Rolf Mützelburg's randomly fired torpedoes caught up with her. One torpedo exploded in the region of her forward hold, and the other hit forward of the bridge. Loaded with 4,100 tons of ore from the Moroccan port of Melilla, the Norwegian ship went down so fast that no attempt could be made to launch the boats.

Fortunately, six wooden liferafts floated off the *Varangberg* as she went down, but there were very few left alive to take refuge on them. Third Mate Emil Parelius, pulled under by the suction of the sinking ship, fought his way to the surface and found himself alone on a dark and hostile sea. For over an hour he swam around, and was near to despairing when he found one of the drifting rafts, and was helped on board by its sole occupant, Ordinary Seaman John Joanne, who had been at the helm of the *Varangberg* when she was torpedoed. First Engineer Hans Hansen, also dragged under when the ship sank, came to the surface close to the wreckage of the *Varangberg's* wooden chart house, to which Captain Stenersen was clinging. Stenersen was badly injured, and Hansen helped him climb onto the wreckage, but did not board himself for fear of capsizing the flimsy platform. The engineer, who was also injured, eventually managed to find and board another liferaft. When one of HG 73's escorting corvettes found him some hours later, Hansen was so exhausted that he had to be lifted aboard by his rescuers.

Only three others of the *Varangberg's* crew of twenty-six survived the sinking. They were Third Engineer Birger Hansen, Steward Rangvald Bordvik and Stoker Sverre Jensen, all of whom were asleep when their ship was hit, but managed to board one of the liferafts.

First Engineer Karl Halvorsen, who had a miraculous escape when the *Spind* was sunk in the attack on Convoy OG 71 a month earlier, was a passenger in the *Varangberg*. This time, his luck deserted him. He died with the *Varangberg*.

On a dark night with poor visibility, which this was, even a well-experienced U-boat commander would have considered himself extremely fortunate if only one of a spread of four torpedoes fired found a target. In this case, the result of Rolf Mützelburg's salvo exceeded all expectations. Not only did three of his torpedoes register hits, but the fourth, spreading out as it sped through the water, also went home. And Mützelburg's final victim proved to be HG 73's commodore ship *Avoceta*, then leading the convoy at the head of Column 5. Her end was sudden and violent, a near-mirror image of the sinking of her sister ship *Aguila* a month earlier.

Captain Harold Martin, when interviewed by the Admiralty, stated:

At 2336 BST on 25th September, when in position 47° 57′ N 24° 05′ W we were struck by a torpedo on the port side close to the engine room abreast the mizzen mast. It was a very loud explosion, the ship shuddered violently and heeled over to port.

The engine room was filled with water immediately and when I rang down to the engine room for the engines to be stopped I found they had already stopped on their own accord. The ship sank stern first within 2 minutes of being torpedoed. The bow reared up and the vessel slid down and sank.

Able Seaman Joe Bautenbach, one of the survivors of the *Aguila* taking passage in the *Avoceta,* reported:

Arthur [Able Seaman Arthur Cracknell, also a survivor of the Aguila sinking] *and I had decided that although we had a cabin, we were afraid to sleep in it and would stay on deck with our lifejackets on and sleep in our deck chairs. This action saved our lives…Arthur and I managed to get to the rails and hang on as the bow of the ship came up out of the water. Looking around, we could see people coming out of cabins onto the deck, but some of them could not hold on and slipped down the deck into the burning hold.*

When I realised that the water was receding from us because the bow was now nearly vertical, we both went over the side hand in hand, and hit the water so hard that I can't remember what happened after that until we were aboard a corvette, which had saved us. This turned out to be HMS Periwinkle.

Third Radio Officer Grahame Morris, who was only 19 at the time, remembered that night many years later:

The ship was already starting to go down by the stern, and as the bow reared up in the air, we found the boat gear jammed. During the next few minutes it was, literally, every man for himself and as I swung myself Tarzan fashion back down to the promenade deck below me, I found myself being sucked down into the water with the ship as she started to sink quickly in a near vertical position. After what seemed an age, I popped back up to the surface due to the fact that I was already wearing my full, waistcoat-type, Kapok-filled lifejacket, was a fairly strong swimmer and had, most importantly, the natural will to survive.

From the moment the torpedo struck until I found myself floating on the surface must have been no more than a few minutes before the ship was gone! It was later confirmed at an enquiry held in Liverpool on 3rd October 1941 that s.s. Avoceta sank in two minutes in position 47 deg 57 min N 24 deg 5 min W.

Finding myself alone in the water after seeing my ship disappear beneath the waves, I took stock and looked around for anything that might help me stay afloat for however long it might be before help arrived. Strangely, I just did not consider the probability that help may not be forthcoming. Most ships carried liferafts, in addition to lifeboats, and as these were kept loose on deck they were in effect self-launching. Avoceta had three of these rafts, two were for'ard and there was a larger one aft.

It is surprising how well one can see in the darkness and I was able to spot and get hold of a large chunk of solid cork from our cargo which had been blown out of the ship in the explosion. This helped me considerably and I now felt even more confident of survival. Some time later I saw a raft a distance away and decided to swim for it. As I drew closer I could make out figures lying on the raft who appeared to be in a bad way. So, with no help available, I made the difficult solo effort, my uniform was soaking wet and as heavy as lead and I was tired after my swim, to haul myself up on it. Once on the raft I, too, lay down to recover, and we all managed to hang on for two or three hours, when I saw the bow of a ship edging slowly and cautiously towards the raft. At that moment I had no idea if it was friend or foe, but it turned out to be one of our escorting corvettes which had been ordered to drop back and search for survivors. She was HMS Jasmine, commanded by Lt. Commander C.D.B. Coventry RNR and was a most welcome sight. As she came alongside the raft no time was lost in climbing the scrambling nets they had put over the side and when I reached the top I found myself being hauled quickly and unceremoniously over the rail by willing hands and was then treated to an extra large tot of rum! I have since learned that Rear Admiral Creighton, our Master, Captain Harold Martin, Captain Frith of Aguila, our Chief Officer, Malcolm Robertson and AB Les Swinbourne were rescued in a similar way by another searching corvette HMS Periwinkle.

Captain Martin wrote of his experience:

We managed to get the forward port boat away, but this was capsized when the sea hit it, with two men in it, and I do not know what became of them.

Several liferafts floated off and I managed to swim to one of them. I was on this raft for 2½ hours before being picked up by HMS Periwinkle. HMS Jasmine was also searching for survivors, and took one girl aged about 23 from the water after she had been swimming for 2½ hours without a lifebelt. I think there would have been more survivors, but whilst the corvettes were searching among the wreckage two torpedoes were fired at them, and they received orders to keep at a safe distance, and to return at daylight. It was not light until about 0800 and when they returned, there was no sign of further survivors.

The MacAndrews' steamer *Cervantes*, commanded by Captain Henry Fraser, sailing as rear ship of Column 5, joined in the rescue, turning back to go to the aid of the *Avoceta*. After a long search, Fraser eventually pulled three survivors from the water. During the search the *Cervantes* had fallen well astern of the other ships, and darkness was setting in before she rejoined the convoy.

The corvette *Larkspur*, commanded by Lieutenant S.C.B. Hickman, RNR, was keeping station on HG 73's port beam when Rolf Mützelburg's torpedoes turned the orderly procession of ships into a rout. *Larkspur* immediately fired star shell, lighting up the sky to port, but this revealed nothing. Nevertheless, Hickman decided to investigate further, taking the corvette out in a wide sweep to port. Again, there was no sign of the elusive enemy.

As she was hurrying back to rejoin the convoy half an hour or so later, one of *Larkspur's* lookouts reported broken water astern. Binoculars showed this to be fluorescence of a bow wave, and silhouetted against this faint light was the conning tower of a U-boat. U-203 was leaving the scene of the mayhem she had created as fast as her twin diesels would take her.

Lieutenant Hickman turned *Larkspur* short about and followed in the wake of the fleeing submarine, but though a brilliant workhorse of the convoy circuit, she was not built for speed. *Larkspur's* 4-cycle, triple-expansion steam engine gave of its best, but it was not enough. The U-boat had a full knot and a half advantage, and she was fast pulling away when Hickman gave the order to fire a single star shell. This was a mistake. The star shell failed to function, but the flash from *Larkspur's* 4-inch alerted Mützelburg to the danger, and he blew main ballast and dived.

U-203 was only 600 yards ahead of the pursuing corvette when the sea closed over her conning tower. As she went down *Larkspur's* Asdic immediately locked on to her. Hickman was tempted to ram, but the danger was that the collision would put his own ship out of action. He decided to attack with depth charges, dropping a pattern of ten charges over the diving U-boat. He followed this up with another pattern of ten, then one of six.

When the upheaval of the sea caused by the multiple explosions had subsided, contact had been lost. Hickman searched the area for another twenty minutes but his Asdics failed to regain contact. He assumed the U-boat had escaped unharmed, which proved to be true. U-203 sustained no damage, but she had used up all her torpedoes, and Rolf Mützelburg decided to retire from the attack on HG 73 and head for home.

CHAPTER NINE

The Long Way Home

After opening the attack on HG 73, when before dawn on 25 September he sank the *Empire Stream*, Johann Mohr took U-124 away to the west at full speed to avoid the wrath of the convoy's escorts. For the rest of that morning Mohr discreetly shadowed the convoy, taking advantage of the passing rain squalls to hide his presence from the enemy ships. But, as the day wore on, and the rain cleared away, it became more and more difficult to keep at a safe distance. He was forced to drop further and further astern, until finally, around noon, he lost contact with the convoy altogether.

Mohr was now down to his last three torpedoes, and he took advantage of the visibility to stop and reload his tubes. He was back again in contact with HG 73 soon after midnight, using the chaos caused by Rolf Mützelburg's devastating attack to approach the convoy unseen. He manoeuvred U-124 into a favourable position on HG 73's port quarter, and then began stalking the convoy, biding his time until a suitable target presented itself.

Hickman's *Larkspur* raised the alarm at 0034 on the 26th, breaking radio silence on R/T to report the sighting of a U-boat on the surface to port. In his determination to use every single one of his remaining torpedoes to good account, Mohr had made the mistake of approaching too close.

Highlander, which had been scouting ahead of the convoy, immediately executed a 180-degree turn, and raced back, firing snowflake as she came. Unfortunately, at that crucial moment, a heavy rain squall swept in, reducing visibility to less than half a mile, and the destroyer's illumination was wasted.

Once more hidden by the rain, Johann Mohr continued to creep up on the convoy, poised to attack.

Leading the port outside column of HG 73 was the 1354-ton steamer *Petrel*, one of four General Steam Navigation Company's ships with the convoy. The *Petrel*, under the command of Captain John Klemp, was on passage from Oporto to Bristol, via Gibraltar, with 275 tons of cork and 130 tons of general, much of the latter consisting of port wine and sherry in the familiar oak casks. She had a total complement of thirty-one on board, made up of twenty-seven crew, three DEMS gunners, and one passenger. The passenger was a Mr. Roy Wearne, a representative of Gonzales Byas, wine exporters of Oporto, presumably on board to keep an eye on his company's valuable cargo. Amongst the *Petrel's* crew was Stanley Smart, ex-carpenter of the cased petrol carrier *Stork,* lost in OG 71. After spending some time in hospital in Gibraltar, Smart was still suffering from burns received when he risked his own life to save two of the *Stork's* officers, yet he had signed on the *Petrel* to work his passage home.

Following the shock of the sudden sinking of the *Empire Stream* on the morning of the 25th, Captain Klemp had not relaxed his vigilance, keeping his crew on their toes. When, late that night, two heavy explosions were heard close on the starboard side announcing the end of the *Varangberg* and *Avoceta*, his precautions seemed justified. Sensing imminent danger, Kemp ordered his men to stand by on deck wearing lifejackets.

Although the loss of two more ships was a severe setback, HG 73 was still forging ahead at a good 7 knots, and the optimistic view in the ships was that if they could survive the next seventy-two hours, then they were home and dry. When, by 0100 on the morning of the 26th, there had been no more alarms, and the convoy was all quiet, Captain Klemp, judged it quite safe for him to leave the bridge for a short while. He went below, but he not been in his cabin for many minutes when Johann Mohr fired one of his precious torpedoes at close range, scoring a direct hit on the port side of the *Petrel's* engine-room.

Kemp heard only a muffled thud as the torpedo went home, and at first he thought one of the escorts had dropped a depth charge close by. Then the *Petrel* shook violently, and the stink of explosives was in the air. She had been hit, and hit hard. Kemp rushed out of his cabin, but when he reached the deck a shower of falling debris forced him back.

When the debris stopped raining down, Klemp clambered over the pile of wreckage blocking his cabin door and reached the deck, which by now was slanting alarmingly to port. The *Petrel's* poop deck was already under water, and the ship's only lifeboats, stowed on that deck, were no longer visible. It was abundantly clear to Klemp that his ship, sinking fast by the stern, had only minutes to live. He called out for the liferafts to be slipped, and for every man to fend for himself.

Captain Klemp was last man off, going over the rail when most of the after deck was under water. He swam to a raft drifting nearby, and as he hauled himself aboard he saw the *Petrel's* bows suddenly rear up out of the water. And then she was gone.

Klemp found himself on a half-submerged raft with nine of his crew, including Chief Officer Baxter, Second Officer A.V. Bruce, Third Officer I. Phillips, the Radio Officer, and three able seamen. When this raft threatened to sink altogether, they transferred to another raft, which was also partly waterlogged. Other men were in the water around the raft, their red lifejacket lights performing a macabre fire dance as they bobbed up and down on the swell.

When the thunder rumbled and sky glowed red over HG 73 as Johann Mohr's torpedo brought to an end the long career of the *Petrel*, the convoy's escorts raced in to deal with an invisible enemy. *Fowey* was nearest at hand, and Lieutenant Commander Aubrey moved in quickly to cut off the U-boat. Unfortunately, as *Fowey* charged in the *Lapwing* decided to go to the aid of her sister ship. As the sloop approached, Captain Hyam had his helm hard over, swinging the *Lapwing* through 180 degrees, and crossing the *Fowey's* bows. A collision was avoided only by both ships taking prompt evasive action.

Aubrey took the *Fowey* out on to the port quarter of the convoy, where he caught a brief glimpse of U-124 as she motored away at full speed into the darkness. He reported the sighting to *Highlander*, and Commander Dallmeyer, despite his dwindling fuel supply – he was down to his last 14 tons of diesel – raced in firing snowflake. Dallmeyer's efforts were in vain, for U-124 was by then well out of harm's way.

HG 73, then 750 miles due west of the U-boats' headquarters in Lorient, was still three days steaming from home waters and was now reduced to nineteen merchantmen, and the convoy was about to lose its most effective escort vessel. *Highlander* was on the last dregs of her fuel, and not wishing to be left drifting without power in these hostile waters, Commander Dallmeyer had no other choice but to break away and head for the nearest Channel port. The Admiralty, informed of the situation, had signalled Lieutenant Commander Aubrey that the destroyer *Wolverine* was raising steam, and would leave Gladstone Dock later that morning. *Wolverine*, was a 31-knot destroyer of 1920 vintage commanded by Captain J.M. Rowland. Her orders were to take the risky passage through the minefields of the St. George's Channel, and proceed south at her full speed to meet up with HG 73. At best, she could not hope to join the convoy until late afternoon on the 27th, and as a depression was moving in from the Atlantic with reported gale-force westerly winds and rough seas, the rendezvous might be even later.

When *Wolverine* sailed from the Mersey, HG 73 was already in heavy weather, with the visibility down to 2 miles in rain. This left the loaded merchant ships struggling to hold their stations, while the escorts, particularly the tiny corvettes, were labouring heavily, with their decks constantly awash. In consolation, the U-boats, which had been patiently stalking the convoy, had all lost contact in the fury of the gale.

The *Petrel's* sister ship, General Steam's *Lapwing*, rear ship of Column 1, had been a close witness to the sinking of both the *Cortes* and *Petrel*. Although she herself was obviously in danger, and perhaps already in the sights of one of the attacking U-boats, the *Lapwing's* master, Captain Thomas Hyam stopped his ship and sent away a boat to look for survivors.

The *Lapwing*, which was on a voyage from Lisbon, via Gibraltar, to Glasgow with 750 tons of pyrites and cork, had herself already had a narrow escape. When U-124 opened the attack on HG 73 on the morning of the 25th, one of Mohr's torpedoes broke surface after missing the *Empire Stream*, and was seen by those on the bridge of the *Lapwing* to be heading straight for their ship. Being in Column 1, with no ships outside her to collide with, Captain Hyam was able to use full port helm to sheer away. The torpedo narrowly missed the *Lapwing*, crossing her bow from starboard to port. Hyam broke radio silence to warn of the attack and give the approximate bearing of the U-boat, only to have his vigilance rewarded with a reprimand from the Commodore for using his radio.

Lapwing's boat was manned by Chief Officer J.B. Woodhouse and eight men, who challenged wind and sea to search for survivors in the darkness. Their task was made all the more hazardous by the huge bales of cork from the *Petrel's* cargo which were being tossed from wave to wave, any one of which could easily smash their frail craft.

When he saw the rescue boat approaching, although he and his fellow survivors on the waterlogged raft were in a precarious position, Captain Klemp shouted to Woodhouse to pick up the men from the water first. Woodhouse agreed, returning some time later with a total of twenty survivors on board, seventeen from the *Petrel* and three from the *Cortes*. The boat was now so crowded that there was no room on board for the ten men clinging to the raft. An attempt was made to tow the raft, but by now Woodhouse's boat's crew was exhausted, and it was agreed that they should first put the seventeen *Petrel* survivors aboard the *Lapwing*, then return for Klemp and the others.

The boat turned about and was soon swallowed up by the darkness. When the creak of oars in the rowlocks had receded into the distance, those left on the raft felt very alone, the slap of the waves on the sides of the raft reminding them that they were at the mercy of a very hostile sea.

More than three hours went by, at the end of which Captain Klemp and his men were slowly beginning to come to terms with the awful prospect that they had been abandoned. Then, at about 0430, with the first grey streaks of the coming dawn showing in the east, the welcome sound of oars in rowlocks was heard again, and the *Lapwing's* boat reappeared. Minutes later, the *Petrel* survivors, cold and wet, were clambering over the boat's gunwales.

With Klemp and his men safe on board, Woodhouse once more set course to return to the *Lapwing*, now under a grey dawn with an overcast sky and a fresh north-westerly wind piling up a short, rough sea. It was a long hard pull, and it was after 0530 before the ship came in sight. She was circling slowly, awaiting their return. Ten minutes later, the boat was within 50 yards of the *Lapwing*, when Johann Mohr intervened.

Mohr's torpedo hit the small ship in her port side, penetrating her bunker hatch before exploding. The men in the lifeboat watched in horror as their potential refuge was literally blown apart, hatch boards, tarpaulins, lumps of best Welsh coal and other wreckage being hurled high in the air.

When he had recovered from the shock of seeing his own ship sunk, Woodhouse called on his men to row for the wreckage in the hope that they could pick up any survivors from the water. But having been rowing almost continuously for four hours under the most appalling weather conditions, the men at the oars were at the end of their tether. They did their best, but only five survivors were found, three of whom were from the *Cortes*. Captain Thomas Hyam, twenty of his crew, and five DEMS gunners had perished. With them went the *Stork's* indefatigable Stanley Gilbert Smart, his voyaging over forever.

A little later, a corvette approached to within 60 yards of the boat, and it seemed that rescue was at hand, but then the rain came slashing down again. With great difficulty, for the boat was rolling heavily, the survivors stepped the mast, and hoisted the yellow distress flag. Then they burned a number of red flares, but they were hidden from sight in the rain, and there was no response from the corvette. Soon she was out of sight altogether.

Chief Officer Woodhouse and Captain Klemp now conferred, and it was decided to stream a sea anchor and wait out the day in the hope that rescue would eventually come. The sea anchor brought the boat's head up into the wind and sea and stopped the sickening rolling, but the survivors were still lashed by the spray coming off the tops of the waves. There was no escaping the weather.

At about 0730, another corvette came within 2 miles of the boat, but although red flares were again burned, the naval ship appeared not to see them. Shortly afterwards, another raft carrying three men was sighted, but this soon drifted away. Then, at about 1100, a small boat drifted close, and was seen to contain five men. These men, who proved to be survivors from the *Petrel*, eventually rowed across to the *Lapwing's* boat, and were taken aboard. They explained that their boat had been dropped, unmanned, by the first corvette. It seemed likely that the commander of the corvette, unable to stop, had hoped that the boat would save some lives, which it did.

Having transferred all food and water from the corvette's boat to their own, Klemp and Woodhouse decided to remain drifting to the sea anchor until next day. The boat now had a total of twenty-two men on board, men who were cold, wet, suffering the agonies of seasickness, and rapidly losing hope. One of them, Fireman Weeden of the *Petrel*, was badly injured. Both his ankles were broken, and he had severe internal injuries. As the day went on, the horizon around the boat remained empty, except for the white-topped seas that marched relentlessly by. No rescue came, and night fell.

Next morning, the wind had dropped considerably, but was still quite fresh from the north-west. Klemp and Woodhouse were both of the opinion that nothing could be gained by waiting any longer for help to come, and all in the boat agreed that they should try to reach land. With the wind still in the north-west, there was no point in attempting to go north, so it was decided to run before the wind in the hope of coming ashore in the vicinity of Cape Finisterre, which lay 650 miles to the south-east. The sea anchor was hove in, the sails hoisted, and they set off.

With the boat under sail, Klemp and Woodhouse addressed the problem of how to eke out the meagre supply of food and water over what promised to be a long voyage. At best, even with the wind right aft, the boat being heavily laden, a maximum speed of 2 to 2½knots was all they could expect – not allowing for any calms or a shift of wind. In all, the boat's lockers contained twelve tins of condensed milk, twenty-four tins of evaporated milk, and a small supply of ship's biscuits. Much of the corned beef taken from the corvette's lifeboat had been spoiled by salt water. The drinking water was in three wooden breakers, or casks, one of which proved to be half-empty. It was estimated that it would take between fifteen and twenty days to reach the land. With the higher figure in mind, Klemp and Woodhouse set the daily ration per man at one ship's biscuit thinly spread with condensed or evaporated milk, and one dipper of water (equivalent to three fluid ounces)

The survivors steered a south-easterly course for four days, during which Fireman Weeden died of his injuries, and was buried at sea. This tragedy apart, progress was encouraging, but on the evening of the fourth day under sail the wind came round ahead, and the boat lost all headway. At the best of times, it is almost impossible to sail a heavy wooden ship's boat within less than eight points of the wind – in other words, to make any progress at all the wind must be on the beam, or abaft the beam. Furthermore, by this time, all twenty-one men in the boat were suffering from exhaustion and exposure, and there could be no question of shipping the oars. After several hours lying hove to, Klemp and Woodhouse reluctantly decided to go about and run before the south-easterly wind, now hoping to make a landing somewhere on the south-west coast of Ireland.

Even with the wind aft, the seas were constantly breaking over the gunwales, and frequent bailing was needed to prevent the boat becoming waterlogged. Conditions on board slowly became worse, and within a few days two more men had died. Those who remained refused to lose heart, and slowly, painfully slowly, the boat inched its way north until, on 9 October, Klemp & Woodhouse calculated that they should be nearing the land. Roy Wearne, the *Petrel's* wine merchant passenger, had been keeping a diary:

In the afternoon of the 13th day we were all scanning the horizon for the sight of a ship or plane, or even land, when a large cormorant flew by. I remarked to the helmsman that land could not be far away, even if only bare rocks, as seldom, if ever, I believe do these birds fly far from their homes. That night we were hove to, owing to the rough seas, and about 1 a.m. we had a very heavy rainstorm. We cut a hole in the canvas covering us and caught the rain water, passing round the tins we filled so that all had as much water as they could drink, which was a great relief after so many days of thirst, but, at the same time, we had all become soaked and it did not seem possible to get warm, in marked contrast to when we were soaked with sea water which, although cold, did not seem to chill us to the bone as the rain water did.

The next morning (October 10th) a lighthouse was sighted and the excitement was great. The cover was rolled back, we all had to see it. One man, a born pessimist, said he thought it was Ushant. I asked the captain and he replied that he was certain it was not Ushant. He knew its light well and, in any case, belligerent countries were not showing lights, and therefore it must be a neutral country and most likely Eire.

Although they were not aware of it at the time, the survivors had sailed past much of Ireland, and were in sight of Slyne Head, a rocky promontory jutting out into the Atlantic north of Galway Bay.

Roy Wearne's narrative continues:

We immediately sent up flares but received no answer or signal. A big sea was running and the wind freshening, so we shortened sail as we were nearing the lighthouse too fast to be safe, and therefore ran slowly on until dawn. What a glorious sight it was to see land! But the wind was rising and the waves becoming mountainous. It was decided to run to starboard of the lighthouse and try to get under the lee of the land and find a landing place. The captain went up in the bows in order to direct the helmsman, as rocks were plentiful. In the meantime I had got the tins and handed water around to all, since it did not seem to matter how much we had.

Captain Klemp takes up the story:

We passed within a mile of Slyne Head lighthouse and burned flares. There was a terrific sea at the time and we were running before it. We tried to weather the next point, but we were unable to do so.

I then sighted a beach and tried to run between the rocks and the beach. I told the men to put their lifejackets on, and gave each of them a tin of condensed milk, in case any of them should strike a very lonely part of the beach.

Suddenly I saw two fishing boats on the beach, and thought that if they could get in, so could I. The fishermen came running down to the beach and directed us through the rocks and up on to the beach. We then learned that we were at Keeraunmore, in Galway, Ireland.

Roy Wearne's description of the landing is in marked contrast to John Klemp's modest report:

...There were rocks to the right and left and also in front of us. The captain remained in the bow, shouting instructions to the helmsman. If we struck it would mean another swim for us all, and possibly severe injuries on the rocks. We could see someone running down the beach towards us. Swiftly we moved on. We had put tins of Ideal milk in our pockets because we had a long walk ahead of us to the nearest town. Suddenly there was a crunching sound and we were running up the beach.

Willing hands helped the exhausted survivors as they staggered ashore, where they were met by the rescuers' wives bearing jugs of scalding hot tea. For men who had been without a hot drink for fourteen days this was nectar indeed. Once revived, they made their way to the top of the beach, where the locals had two ancient motor cars waiting to take them to the hospital at Clifden, the nearest town. There was not enough room in the cars for all of them, so Captain Klemp, Chief Officer Woodhouse and Roy Wearne volunteered to follow behind on foot. They had not progressed far when Woodhouse collapsed. It was then discovered that the chief officer had a severe leg injury, which he had kept from them throughout the long arduous boat voyage. Klemp and Wearne carried him to a nearby cottage, where an elderly Irish lady plied them with hot drinks, and made them comfortable until help arrived. They were later taken into Clifden and put up at the Railway Hotel, where the manager and his wife were, appropriately, the local representatives of the Shipwrecked Mariners Society.

Roy Wearne wrote in his diary:

I shared a room with the captain. We awoke often during the night and talked and drank all the water we could lay our hands on, for we had an insatiable thirst. But it was marvellous to be able to stretch out at full length on a soft bed...The next morning we received a message to the effect that the Philippino was dying. We hurried out of bed and into our clothes and went to the hospital, but were too late as the poor fellow had passed away. He was buried the following afternoon. All the village turned out and the villagers did him the homage of carrying the coffin on their shoulders the whole way to the cemetery...

It is indicative of the strength of the bond between seamen of all nations that the simple fisherfolk of Connemara, who had no part in this war, should pay tribute to a total stranger who had died thousands of miles away from his homeland.

Roy Wearne continued:

On Monday we left for Galway having to leave behind six men in hospital. On Tuesday morning we left by train for Dublin. When we reached Dublin the British authorities would not allow us to travel the next day, our feet were so swollen and painful. Klemp and I went out to buy some more things, and then returned to Jury's Hotel to rest our feet. We then caught the bus to Kingstown to board the boat early next morning. The organisation and kindness of the General Steam Navigation Company was amazing – everything had been arranged for us. When we arrived in Holyhead we were taken off the boat first, then straight through the Customs, etc., so that we should not have to stand too long. Carriages were reserved for us on the train, but only four of us went through to London, where we were met by our various relations and friends, and so home.

On her 900-mile voyage, the *Lapwing*'s lifeboat had been navigated by Chief Officer Woodhouse using an uncorrected boat's compass and a makeshift chart he had drawn up from memory on a scrap of paper. None of the survivors had any previous experience in handling a small boat, but under Captain John Klemp's guidance they brought their craft through rough seas to a safe landing on the West Coast of Ireland. It is worth considering, however, that had the course made good by the boat been just a few more degrees to port, they would probably have missed Ireland altogether, and sailed on northwards into an empty sea, almost certainly to die a cold and lonely death beyond the Arctic Circle.

CHAPTER TEN

To the Bitter End

When a very grey dawn broke over the Atlantic on 26 September, the remaining ships of Convoy HG 73 were labouring in heavy seas, their decks swept by raging torrents of green water with every agonised roll. The convoy had maintained a semblance of order, but was plainly in disarray, and until HMS *Wolverine* put in an appearance, it remained in some danger. *Fowey,* the eight corvettes and *Springbank* would put up a fight, but they were no substitute for destroyers. Not one of them could ever hope to exceed 16 knots, even with their boiler safety valves screwed hard down.

This picture of vulnerability was complete when, in mid-afternoon, the drone of unsynchronised BMW engines announced the arrival of the day's enemy-in-the-sky. The grey-painted Condor approached cautiously, and then began its slow, monotonous circling out of range of the frustrated British gunners. All the while, the plane's W/T Operator was calling in the U-boats.

Johann Mohr's U-124, a Type IX B, with an advantage of 1½ knots on the others, was first to arrive, but she was down to her last torpedo. Elated by his success so far, Mohr intended to use this to good effect.

Mohr regained contact with HG 73 at 1525 on the 26th, and tucked himself in behind the rear ships while he waited out the daylight hours. Visibility was around 2 miles, and the rough, breaking seas provided perfect cover for the trimmed down U-boat. She was soon joined by U-201, U-203 and at this point Dönitz called in U-205.

U-205, a new Type VII C, under the command of 33-year-old Franz-Georg Reschke, was on her first operational patrol, having sailed from Lorient on 1 July. Following a period of fruitless patrolling off South-East Greenland with the Brandenburg wolf pack, Reschke was on his way to the Mediterranean when BdU directed him to operate against HG 73.

Having been at sea for over two months without a chance to hit the enemy, Reschke was, to say the least, a man with a purpose.

Viewed from the air, it must have been a strange sight this assembly of unsuspecting merchantmen battling their way north through heavy seas. *Fowey* was in the lead, while the corvettes rolled their gunwales under as they struggled to keep station on the fringes. Behind, the four grey wolves followed at a discreet distance, betrayed only by their feathered wakes as they ploughed half-submerged through the rough sea. And as the convoy had no air support, it was a sight the ships remained in ignorance of the U-boats.

The London-registered *Cervantes*, commanded by Captain Henry Fraser, was leading Column 5, and with 500 tons of potash stowed low down in her holds was rolling stiffly in the swell. She had begun the voyage as No.53, with only the Danish ship *Ebro* astern of her; then had come the dreadful night of the 25th, when the two ships ahead of her, the Commodore's *Avoceta* and the Norwegian ore carrier *Varangberg* were sunk by Rolf Mützelburg in U-203. Captain Fraser had gone to the aid of the *Avoceta*, snatching four survivors, two of them women, from the water, and these were still on board taking passage to Liverpool, along with three others from the *Ciscar*, lost with OG 71. This brought the *Cervantes'* total complement to forty-two.

The U-boats kept their distance until, at around 2000, the long twilight turned to night; then under the cover of darkness they increased speed and began to overtake the convoy, U-124 in the lead. There was no moon, and Mohr confidently took his boat into the heart of the convoy, moving up between columns 5 and 6 without being seen. Soon after midnight, he was nearing the head of the convoy, no more than a dark shadow on the sea keeping pace with ships on either side.

Captain Henry Fraser was on the bridge of the *Cervantes*, where he had been for much of the day. He was desperately tired, but heartened by the improving weather. The wind was still blowing strong, but showing signs of easing, while the sky had cleared and the visibility was good. As midnight approached, Fraser went into the chartroom to write up his night orders, but as he took up his pen Johann Mohr fired his last remaining torpedo.

The *Cervantes* was hit on the starboard side, just abaft the mainmast, the torpedo exploding in her No.4 hold. The blast of Mohr's torpedo threw her over to port, but she righted herself quickly as the sea poured into the partly empty hold. Captain Fraser, deafened by the blast, staggered into the wheelhouse. When his hearing returned, he realised that the regular beat of the *Cervantes'* engine had stopped. There was only the eerie keening of the wind and the slap of the waves against the hull as the ship drifted slowly to a halt.

It was evident from the increasing and alarming tilt of the deck that the *Cervantes* was settling by the stern. She sank quickly, but on an even keel, and therefore giving her men the chance to save themselves. There was no time to lower the boats, but fortunately Fraser had anticipated such an eventuality, and had one boat cleared away and lying loose in the chocks, so that it would float off as the ship went down. While the majority of the *Cervantes'* crew took to the liferafts, Fraser and fifteen others piled into this boat which duly floated off as the ship sank under them. Within half an hour, they were picked up by General Steam's *Starling*, commanded by Captain C.T. Stone, which was in the rear of Column 4. Chief Officer Jack Stow, of the *Starling* wrote in his report:

A boat had got away and came alongside. In it were crew members and 2 women who had been rescued the night before from the Commodore's ship. They were torpedoed two nights running. It was a difficult job getting people on board up the pilot ladder. There was a heavy swell and the ship was rolling in the trough. The women were in bad shape, one was a married woman who had lost her husband and two children in the first attack. The other was a 15-year-old girl who was the only surviving member of her family. The girl was semi-conscious and I had the job of getting her up the ladder and carrying her up to the boat deck to the Captain's cabin. She was a heavy weight and with a rolling ship and a pitch black night it wasn't easy.

Although the *Cervantes* sank very quickly, she lost only six men out of her total complement of forty-four. They were an assistant steward, a fireman and a sailor, two DEMS gunners and one of the *Ciscar* survivors. Captain Fraser was generous in his praise for Captain Stone and the crew of the *Starling*, the prompt action of whom undoubtedly avoided a much greater loss of life.

HG 73, now down to eighteen merchantmen, was beginning to lose its cohesion, the danger to the remaining ships increasing by the minute. This prompted Lieutenant Commander Aubrey to contact the Admiralty, requesting permission for the convoy to enter British waters through the St. George's Channel, rather than via the North Channel. This would involve passing through the extensive minefields that blocked the southern route but, in Aubrey's opinion, the risks would be fully justified because it would reduce the time the ships were at the mercy of the U-boats. The Admiralty agreed, and the convoy altered course to pass south of Ireland.

Due to the disruption of the convoy, the Norwegian-flag ship *Siremalm* now found herself occupying the unenviable position at the rear of the outside port column. The 2468-ton *Siremalm*, owned by A.I. Langfeldt of Kristiansand, and commanded by Captain Haakon Svendsen, was aguably the most valuable ship remaining with the convoy. Like her fellow Norwegian, the *Varangberg*, now on the bottom of the Atlantic, the *Siremalm* was also loaded with 4000 tons of iron ore, a cargo vital to Britain's war effort.

Only six months earlier, Svendsen's ship had narrowly escaped destruction at the hands of Admiral Dönitz's U-boat Arm. In the early hours of the morning of 23 March, while on passage unescorted from Reykjavik to Halifax, the *Siremalm* had been attacked by U-110, commanded by Julius Lemp, of *Athenia* fame. Luckily for the *Siremalm* Lemp's first torpedo failed to explode, doing no more damage than denting her shell plating protecting the boiler room. Lemp fired a second torpedo, but this missed. He then ordered his gun's crew to open fire on the Norwegian, but in the heat of the moment the gunners omitted to remove the watertight plug from the barrel of the 105mm. The gun blew up when fired, and three of the crew were injured. And if this was not disaster enough, it was found that splinters from the shattered gun barrel had damaged pipelines on the submarine's foredeck, severely limiting U-110's ability to dive. Julius Lemp was forced to break off his abortive attack and return to Lorient. Meanwhile, the *Siremalm* escaped into the darkness. Six months later, sailing in HG 73, her run of good luck was to come to a sudden end.

Just after 0100 on the morning of 27 September, U-201, having crept up unseen on the convoy's port side, was preparing to attack. Adalbert Schnee reported seeing 'Two targets on the starboard side. One freighter of 5000 tons overlapping a large escort vessel.' Schnee, conscious that the opportunities for inflicting more damage on this convoy were dwindling by the hour, used a full spread of four torpedoes from his bow tubes.

The 'freighter of 5000 tons' in Adalbert Schnee's sights was the 2468-ton *Siremalm*, and the 'large escort vessel' behind her HMS *Springbank*, which was then filling an empty space in Column 2.

With a deadweight cargo of 4000 tons of iron ore aboard, the *Siremalm* was sailing low in the water, her main deck rails no more than a few feet above the sea. The ore was distributed two thirds in the lower holds and one third in the tween decks to minimise heavy rolling in a seaway, but as it stowed at only 14 cubic feet to the ton, the Norwegian ship's cargo spaces were more than half empty. When one – or perhaps two – of Schnee's torpedoes blasted open her hull, the sea poured in to fill the void. Her buoyancy was lost, and she sank like the proverbial stone, taking with her Captain Haakon Svendsen and his crew of twenty-six. Amongst them was Stoker Gunvald Olsen, who had survived the sinking of the *Spind* in Convoy OG 71 in August, and was working his passage home.

The fighter catapult ship HMS *Springbank,* now minus her only aircraft, but still a formidable AA ship, had throughout the voyage north occupied various positions in the ranks of the convoy. At 5,155 tons gross, with a tall naval-style bridge topped by a High Angle Director, the *Springbank* had a distinctive silhouette. Furthermore, she was ballasted with empty oil drums to keep her afloat should she be torpedoed, and unlike the merchantmen around her, she rode high out of the water. To say that the *Springbank* stuck out like a sore thumb, even on this dark stormy night, was an understatement.

Schnee's fan of four torpedoes, aimed and fired under conditions that were less than ideal, produced spectacular results. Two had ended the *Siremalm's* 35-year-old career in as long as it takes to swat a fly, and the other two, skirting the sinking Norwegian's stern by a few feet, ploughed into the slab-sided *Springbank* with devastating effect. Ordinary Seaman John Bales, many years later, remembered the horror of the night:

It was 12.20 on the morning of the 27th, pitch dark and blowing a gale, that we got hit with two torpedoes both on the port side and after a few minutes the old girl started to list over. I was still manning 'X' gun and firing away when the order to abandon ship was given. I did a rather silly thing on the spur of the moment and nipped down below to try and rescue a camera I had bought in Gibraltar, the water was pouring in and I had to fight my way out of the ship against waves of water inside. Eventually I got back onto the upper deck and by then a destroyer had come alongside to try and rescue the crew. The weather was so bad that we lost a lot of people by mistiming their jump and falling between the two ships and others by not timing their jump onto the deck of the destroyer and getting killed by the force of the impact against the ship. This is how I lost my best friend 'Lofty'.

Jim Hingston, serving aboard the corvette HMS *Jasmine,* John Bales' rescuing 'destroyer', wrote:

On the fateful night Jasmine *was taken alongside her* [Springbank] *in very heavy seas, and in total darkness. The construction of the ship was fully tested and her builders have every reason to be proud of her. The port side took a very severe bashing. Eight officers and fifty-nine ratings jumped from her decks to* Jasmine, *many were injured…*

*…*Jasmine *got away from* Springbank *in spite of all the sea could throw against her. All this rescue work was carried out at 'full ahead' and 'full astern', and all wheel orders were hard over each way. The 'full ahead' to get away was answered magnificently by the engine room department and praise is due to them. I myself was shut in a dark compartment, but at least I knew what was happening. Down below the information must have been very vague, and the 'black gang' must have had a bad tossing about with the two ships lurching and banging together.*

John Bales abandoned *Springbank* by a different route:

Seeing what was taking place I decided that I would take my chance and swim for it and so I went down aft and shinned down a rope that had a Carley float at the bottom, in that were far too many people and not enough room for me, they were all pushing and shoving so I let go and started to swim for it. I couldn't understand why I wasn't getting away from the ship as I had no desire to be sucked down with it and then rumbled that the wind was making the ship bear down on me. Then I swam around the stern of the ship only to be greeted with the full force of the gale. One minute it seemed that you were at the bottom of a large basin looking up and then you were taken up high and the white water from the crest would come over you and swamp you.

I swam around for ages with nothing in sight and then a sub passed within 20 yards of me on the surface. He was gone in no time and in any case they never stopped to pick up survivors. Suddenly I saw a barrel floating in the water and thought it could help but no. I tried to get hold of it and span it but it was impossible and with the next wave it clouted me on the head, then a bit of luck came my way. I saw a Carley float in the distance and made for that only to find just one single person on it and another dead in the bottom, everybody must have been washed overboard. The sole occupant helped me aboard as I was completely exhausted and then we saw a merchant ship, the s.s. Starling *and they manoeuvred to pick us up. They lowered a scramble net over the side for us to climb up but we were too exhausted to climb up, and so we just hung on as they pulled the whole net in.*

Chief Officer Jack Stow was in charge of rescue operations on the deck of the *Starling*:

The events were somewhat tragic, liferafts, Carley floats and just plain swimmers floating in lifejackets were all around us. At one point I had two hanging on to a rope near the stern.

I was only able to hang on to the rope but just at that moment another small ship also looking for survivors loomed out of the darkness heading right for us. Captain Stone was forced to go ahead on the engines to avoid him and I lost my two men in the propeller, or the wash of it. I thought a lot about that for a long time. There were, however, many others to get aboard. Some would get alongside in their rafts only to capsize when laying alongside of us. With our ship rolling in the swell it turned them over and not many survived. I saw many float away without a sound. Some we got aboard and had to pump water out of them and others were injured...On our little ship, the Starling, *we had 109 survivors. Our normal crew was only about 15 men with only two lifeboats. You can imagine the problem with food and shelter and still several days from port...*

So overcrowded was the accommodation of the *Starling* that for the remainder of the voyage Captain Stone and his officers slept on mattresses in the chartroom. But there must have been precious little sleep for Captain Stone, for in the midst of all the other troubles, he found he had a mutiny on his hands.

The *Starling's* firemen were Lascars, and were so frightened by the attack on the convoy that they refused to go below to fire the boilers. Stone had to resort to calling for volunteers from the survivors he had on board. The response was immediate and gratifying. These men, who had only just escaped death, had no intention of drifting engineless and at the mercy of the U-boats that still hovered on the fringes of the convoy. The volunteers formed watches, went below, and from then on the *Starling's* engines were never short of steam.

On board *Jasmine*, there was similar overcrowding, her mess decks swamped by traumatised survivors, many of whom were injured. The corvette carried no doctor, the wounded being cared for by Sick Bay

Attendant Dunmore and Steward Twiddy, who did magnificent work with improvised splints and bandages. Despite their efforts, one of the *Springbank* survivors died during the night, and it was the sad duty of Lieutenant Commander Coventry to read the burial service over his body as it was committed to the deep.

Other survivors from *Springbank* were picked up by the corvettes *Hibiscus* and *Periwinkle*, but of auxiliary's total complement of 233 men, thirty-two had lost their lives. In hindsight, it seems that the ship may have been abandoned prematurely, as her holds were packed with empty 40-gallon oil drums and it was unlikely that she would sink quickly. It is not clear who gave the order to abandon ship, but it is thought not to have been Captain Goodwin. In the event, the drums served *Springbank* well. She was still afloat 18 hours later. *Jasmine* attempted to sink her with depth charges, and when this failed, she used her 4-inch to set her on fire. HMS *Springbank* finally surrendered to the sea as night fell on the 27th September.

The crash of Adalbert Schnee's torpedoes going home and the flames lighting up the sky from the two stricken ships galvanised HG 73's escorts into action. *Fowey*, with Lieutenant Commander Aubrey on the bridge, led the attack, with the two corvettes *Jasmine* and *Stonecrop* hard on her heels. Schnee saw them coming, and wasted no time in running for cover. He remained on the surface as long as he dared, crash-diving when he had put as much distance as possible between himself and the pursuing escorts.

U-201 escaped without damage, but it was well after sunrise before Schnee deemed it safe to return to periscope depth. A quick sweep with the periscope showed the horizon to be empty all around, and he returned to the surface. The weather was again deteriorating, and Schnee set off after the convoy, with the cold spray lashing at the conning tower as U-201's corkscrewed her way through the rising seas.

Shortly after noon, a flying boat was sighted to the south, circling low down, clearly searching. The British convoy was no longer alone, for the new arrival was a Catalina of RAF Coastal Command. The high-winged, two-engined Catalina, with her .50 calibre machine-guns and depth bombs, presented a serious threat to U-boats and *Focke-Wulfs* alike. Schnee broke radio silence to send brief messages to Lorient and Air Reconnaisance, warning them of the new danger.

During the afternoon the weather worsened further, and by 1600 the seas were running high, with vicious rain squalls sweeping in from time to time seriously affecting the visibility. Lashed by spray and rain, their muscles aching through bracing themselves against the violent movement of the boat, the men in U-201's exposed conning tower were living a nightmare.

At 1655, after spending some time under water to avoid the attentions of the Catalina, Schnee returned to the surface, and was rewarded by the sight of a pall of smoke on the horizon. HG 73 was within his grasp. He at again contacted BdU, and was ordered to close the convoy and attack.

HG 73, now regrouped in six columns with Aubrey's escorts forming a tight screen around it, was only 300 miles west-south-west of Ireland and on course for the St. George's Channel. *Fowey* was zig-zagging ahead, *Gentian* was covering the stern, while the other corvettes protected the flanks. Dusk began to fall at around 1900, but by then the rain had cleared, and a bright moon was high in a sky of broken cloud. Lieutenant Commander Aubrey was aware from a report by the Catalina that at least one U-boat was in still contact with the convoy, and there might be others. The night, probably the U-boats' last opportunity to attack, would not be an easy one.

In the new formation, the 3103-ton steamer *Margareta* had taken up station as the second ship of Column 4. As such, she was well protected by the ships around her, and the escort screen outside them. Having survived for ten days, during which the convoy had steamed 1,500 miles, much of the time under attack by U-boats and *Focke-Wulf*s, the *Margareta's* master, Captain Holger Pihlgren, might have been forgiven for assuming that she would survive to deliver her Glasgow-bound cargo. As the Admiralty had agreed to take HG 73 in through the St. George's Channel, less than forty-eight hours would see them in British waters, protected by the destroyers of the Home Fleet and under the umbrella of the RAF.

The *Margareta* was sailing under the Red Ensign, but she was not actually a British ship. Built in 1939 at W. Gray's yard in West Hartlepool as the *Atlantic* for W.H. Cockerline of Hull, she had been sold on the stocks to Paul Eklöf of Finland, renamed *Margareta*, and registered in Helsinki. When the Finnish Government threw in its lot with Germany in 1940, the *Margareta* was lying in Gibraltar, and was promptly seized by the Royal Navy as a prize. Captain Pihlgren and his crew of thirty-three, all Finnish were more than willing to serve under the British flag, and the ship was transferred to the Ministry of War Transport, to be managed by MacAndrews of London. It was an amicable arrangement all round.

During the remaining hours of daylight Adalbert Schnee held U-201 well back out of sight of the escorts, then when twilight fell he began to creep closer. By the time it was fully dark the individual ships of the convoy were clearly visible in the bright moonlight, and with the dark horizon behind him, Schnee sighted on what he described as 'a 5000-ton freighter' and fired a single torpedo.

Captain Pihlgren was in the *Margareta's* chartroom when a dull thud announced the arrival of Schnee's torpedo. He immediately rushed out into the wing of the bridge, and was in time to see a column of dirty water accompanied by a blinding flash shoot skywards from the port side of No. 4 hatch.

Pihlgren's first thought, illogical though it may seem, was to run for his cabin to retrieve and throw overboard the secret code books which he kept locked in his safe. He risked his life in vain, for when he reached his cabin he found nothing but smouldering wreckage. The code books were in there somewhere, but they would be of no use to an enemy.

The *Margareta* was by now listing heavily to port and quite obviously sinking. Returning to the deck, Pihlgren ordered the boats to be lowered. With the crippled ship rolling heavily in the rough sea, launching the lifeboats called for expert seamanship and judgement, but was successfully achieved. All thirty-four crew abandoned ship, three men who had jumped into the water being retrieved quickly. Soon after the boats cleared the ship's side, the *Margareta* broke in two and sank. She had lasted exactly six minutes after being torpedoed. Captain Holger Pihlgren and his men were picked up half an hour later by the corvette *Hibiscus*.

Lieutenant Commander J.M. Rowland, urging HMS *Wolverine* south at 31 knots, had the frustrating experience of witnessing the final attack on HG 73 from 40 miles distant. The destroyer was already making her maximum speed, and Rowland could do nothing more than set course for the star shell bursts lighting up the sky over the beleaguered convoy. *Wolverine* finally joined at 0010 on the 28th as Lieutenant Commander Aubrey was attempting to round up the remaining merchant ships, and rearrange his defensive screen around them. The convoy, which had sailed from Gibraltar twenty-five ships strong eleven days earlier, was now down to sixteen. It had also lost a very valuable escort vessel, the fighter-equipped AA ship HMS *Springbank*.

HG 73 was now nearing home waters, and with the arrival of the *Wolverine*, the threat from the enemy was diminishing – that was until the Focke-Wulfs arrived.

The first of the Condors, dubbed by Winston Churchill 'the scourge of the Atlantic' was sighted at 1015 that morning, and attempts were made to lure the aircraft within range of the convoy's guns using a signal lamp. The message flashed, in plain language and in German, obviously puzzled the Condor's pilot. The plane did eventually approach to within 4 miles, but sheered away when the corvettes opened fire.

Later in the morning, the Condor was joined by two more of its kind, and the three reconnaissance bombers settled down to circling the convoy at a safe distance. All three planes were sending continuous homing signals, and reporting the convoy's course and speed. It came as no surprise, therefore, when, during the afternoon, the Admiralty warned Lieutenant Commander Aubrey to expect six or seven U-boats after dark.

There were, in fact, only four U-boats in the vicinity of HG 73; Johann Mohr's U-124, Adalbert Schnee's U-201, Rolf Mützelburg's U-203, and Franz-Georg Rescheke's U-205. The first three had already used up all their torpedoes, so were no real threat; only Rescheke's U-205 was in a position to attack, and she was not yet in sight of the convoy. Dönitz became aware of the situation, and ordered Mohr and Schnee to break off and return to base, while U-203 was detailed to continue to shadow the convoy and guide Reschke in.

Nothing was heard of U-205 during the night, and at dawn on the 29th Dönitz abandoned operations against HG 73. The convoy entered the St. George's Channel through a gap in the minefields on the 30th, and arrived in the Mersey on 1 October.

It may be that OG 71 and HG 73 were relatively insignificant convoys in the vast arena of the Battle of the Atlantic, composed of elderly salt-stained little ships carrying humdrum cargoes. In hindsight, it is hard to justify the large number of escorts defending these convoys, and even harder to excuse the heavy losses suffered.

The outward convoy, OG 71, consisting of twenty-two merchantmen, had a close escort of a destroyer, a sloop and six corvettes, and at one time had as many as four destroyers in attendance. The ships also had air cover of sorts for much of the passage, although ship to air communication was minimal. It is fortunate that Dönitz's U-boats were busy elsewhere, and that only six boats were deployed against OG 71. Even so, these consistently outwitted and outfought the escorts, who spent much of their time chasing shadows, and never once inflicted the slightest damage on the U-boats. Commander Lentaigne's men fought until they were exhausted, but they were outclassed. As for the merchant ships, pathetically vulnerable and harassed beyond endurance, their behaviour was commendable. They kept doggedly to their stations under fire, only one ship breaking ranks, namely the Norwegian steamer *Spind*, which through a misunderstanding failed to alter course on the night of the 22nd, and lost touch with the others.

The running fight for OG 71 had turned into a humiliating defeat for the Royal Navy. Eight merchant ships and two escort vessels were lost, and the remaining ships were forced to find sanctuary in the neutral waters of the River Tagus. This ignominious retreat earned OG 71 the distinction of being the only British convoy in the Second World War that failed to reach its destination.

The primary cause of OG 71's savage mauling appears to have been the decision to alter south in 18 degrees West after leaving British waters, instead of continuing on out into the Atlantic for another 100 miles or so, as was customary. This may, or may not have been a deliberate ploy to draw enemy away from the southbound troop convoy WS10X. But, whether by intention or by chance, this brought the Gibraltar convoy within easy reach of KG 40's base at Bordeaux-Mérignac, and also handy to the U-boat bases in Brittany, with the inevitable result.

The northbound HG 73, if anything, fared even worse than OG 71. Its twenty-five merchant ships, nine of which had survived the voyage out with OG 71, were again under heavy escort, being covered by three destroyers, a sloop, eight corvettes and a fighter catapult ship mounting ten anti-aircraft guns.

When HG 73 emerged from the Straits of Gibraltar the U-boats, as before, were heavily committed in deeper waters. U-371 and the three Italian boats made contact in passing, but only four other boats could be mustered to mount a serious attack on the convoy. Of these, U-205, failed to engage, but the others – just three U-boats – broke through the 12-ship defensive screen time and time again, sinking eight merchantmen and the fighter catapult ship HMS *Springbank*. On the enemy side, only the Italian submarine Luigi Torelli was damaged in the engagement.

With the mauling of Convoy HG 73, for the second time in a month the Royal Navy had been found wanting. So concerned was Admiral Sir Percy Noble, C-in-C Western Approaches, that he held a Board of Enquiry in Liverpool a few days after the sorry remnants of HG 73 arrived. This solved nothing, for the only conclusion the Board reached was that the poor performance of the escorting ships early-type radars was 'one of the contributory factors' leading to the heavy losses suffered by the convoy.

It may well be that OG 71 and HG 73 were relatively unimportant convoys. They were not part of the lifeline stretching across the Atlantic to the Americans that sustained Britain in her lone struggle to halt the advance of Hitler's armies, but the Royal Navy's inability to defend them revealed a serious weakness. In these two convoys alone twenty ships were sunk, and nearly 700 souls lost. In retaliation the two dozen or so escorts involved were powerless to inflict more than minimal damage on the attacking U-boats. This was defeat on a catastrophic scale, and raised the curtain on a year, 1942, when the Battle of the Atlantic reached its climax, with Britain losing nearly 8 million tons of merchant shipping.

PART THREE

HG76 Gibraltar–Liverpool Retribution

CHAPTER ELEVEN

The Turn of the Tide

As 1941 moved towards its close, the struggle for control of the UK-Gibraltar convoy route continued unabated. The British ships on this run, unlike those crossing the Atlantic, were at the mercy of two ruthless enemies; the U-boats, now hunting in packs, and the FW 200 Condors that were increasingly dominating the skies overhead. Both were handily based on the Biscay coast of France. It was clearly obvious to the Admiralty that if this north-south convoy route was to be kept open, a change of tactics was needed.

Surprisingly, the outward bound OG 75, sailing from the Mersey in early October, managed to win through relatively unscathed, losing only one ship; in this case the corvette HMS *Fleur de Lys*, sunk as the convoy approached Gibraltar. However, OG 75's northbound counterpart, HG 75, was in for a severe drubbing at the hands of the enemy.

HG 75 was scheduled to sail from Gibraltar on the 17 October, but had been held back. Thanks to the breaking of the German Enigma Code in May, Bletchley Park was reading Dönitz's wireless traffic on an hourly basis, and the message coming through loud and clear was that the BdU was preparing a hot reception for the next northbound convoy. Donitz's plan was to strike quickly and strike hard, using a pack of six boats to fall on HG 75 as soon as it passed Tarifa westbound.

As early as the 15th of the month, a patrol line had been set up covering the 23-mile stretch of water between Cape Trafalgar and Cape Espartel. The boats involved, reading from north to south, were U-206 (Herbert Optiz), U-563 (Klaus Bargsten), U-564 (Reinhard Suhren), U-204 (Walter Kell), U-71 (Walter Flachsenberg) and U-83 (Hans-Werner Kraus). Lying submerged at periscope depth during the day, and surfaced at night, no more than 5 miles apart, the boats formed a barrier, through which not even a local fishing boat would pass unnoticed.

Accompanied by ten escorts, including three destroyers and a fighter catapult ship, HG 75 eventually left Gibraltar on the afternoon of 22 October. Walter Flachsenberg in U-71 was first to make contact, sighting the British ships when they were abeam of Espartel late that night. Flachsenberg alerted the other boats, and the group attack began. On the 29th, Dönitz wrote in his War Diary:

> *The boats shadowed the convoy tenaciously in dogged pursuit, and this, together with the air reconnaissance which always managed to pick up the convoy again, has meant that all the boats which were at my disposal came to the attack.*

The reports of the boats on this convoy comprised:

> *U-564 – 6 hits on 6 steamers.*
> *U-563 – 1 steamer and 1 destroyer sunk*
> *3 hits on 2 steamers.*
> *U-83 – 1 passenger steamer and 2 freighters sunk.*
> *U-432 – 2 steamers sunk.*
> *U-206 and U-7 had to break off early in the operation on account of lack of fuel.*
> *U-204 is missing.*

The final reckoning for HG 75 was four merchantmen totalling 8772 tons sunk, and the eventual loss of the destroyer *Cossack*. She was torpedoed by Klaus Bargsten's U-563 on the night of the 23rd, and sank four days later. The fighter catapult ship *Ariguani* was also hit, but remained afloat and was towed back to Gibraltar.

The short career of Walter Kell's U-204 came to an untimely end off Tangiers on 19 October, when she was sunk by the depth charges of the sloop *Rochester* and the corvette *Mallow*. Kell and his crew of forty-five perished with their boat. *Good.*

The next northbound convoy HG 76 sailed from Gibraltar on 14 December 1941, a week after the Japanese had set the Far East aflame, thus bringing America into the war. In the light of such momentous events, the convoy's departure from The Rock went unnoticed, except by German agents on the shores of Algeciras. As the thirty-two loaded merchantmen brought their anchors home and moved out to sea, the telephone lines between Algeciras and Madrid, and then onward to Berlin, ran hot.

HG 76 was a mixed bunch, twenty-five small to medium-sized British steamers, five Norwegians, and two ships flying the blue and yellow flag of neutral Sweden. Their cargoes varied from cork granules to bagged onions, with iron ore in bulk, one of the staples of war, predominating. The British contingent included two ships that had sailed in and survived both OG 71 and HG 73 – Currie Line's *Switzerland* and Ellerman Wilson's *Spero*. The latter vessel carried HG 76's convoy commodore, Vice Admiral Sir R. Fitzmaurice.

It was dark when the last ship cleared Tarifa Point. With the clear water of the open Atlantic lying ahead, the convoy then opened up to form nine columns abreast. As a result of the increasing enemy attacks on the Gibraltar convoys, HG 76 had been marking time in Gibraltar for three weeks while a strong escort force was gathered together for the passage north. This eventually transpired to be Commander F.J. Walker's 36th Escort Group, consisting of the two sloops *Deptford* and *Stork*, and the seven Flower-class corvettes *Convolvulus*, *Gardenia*, *Marigold*, *Pentstemen*, *Samphire*, *Rhododendron* and *Vetch*. In support, but under Walker's command, were the escort destroyers *Blankney*, *Exmoor* and *Stanley*, and the aircraft carrier *Audacity*. By any standards, this was a formidable force.

HMS *Audacity* was a new inovation, the first of the 'Woolworth' carriers specifically designed for convoy escort duty. She had started life as Hamburg-Amerika Line's 5537-ton passenger/cargo ship *Hannover*, but had the misfortune to meet up with the armed merchant cruiser HMS *Dunedin* shortly after the outbreak of war. *Audacity's* conversion to an aircraft carrier had been hurried and basic, involving her superstructure being stripped, and a flight deck laid over her holds. She had no tall bridge island like her big sisters, just a modest steel box offset on the starboard side of the deck. She carried six Martlet fighters of 802 Squadron Fleet Air Arm, which when not in the air were parked on her flight deck. There was no hangar.

Since coming into service on 30 July 1941, *Audacity*, under the command of Commander Donald McKendrick, had escorted three convoys to and from Gibraltar, her aircraft shooting down one FW 200 and creating considerable havoc amongst shadowing U-boats. When her third convoy, OG 76, reached Gibraltar intact, Admiral Dönitz commented: 'The worst feature was the presence of the aircraft carrier. Small, fast manoeuvrable aircraft circled the convoy continuously, so that when it was sighted the boats were repeatedly forced to submerge or withdraw. The presence of the enemy aircraft also prevented any protracted shadowing or homing procedure by German aircraft. The sinking of the aircraft carrier is therefore of particular importance not only in this case but also in every future convoy action.'

However, three convoys in quick succession had imposed a considerable strain on *Audacity* and her aircraft, and when OG 76 arrived in Gibraltar on 11 November, only one of her Martlets was still serviceable. She spent the following month tied up in harbour while her aircraft were ashore for repair and overhaul. When she sailed with HG 76, she still had only four Martlets on her flight deck.

Two hours after HG 76 sailed from Gibraltar, a small group of four merchantmen, a general cargo ship and three tankers, followed in the convoy's wake. The 4972-ton *Empire Barracuda was* loaded with 5,800 tons of ammunition and military stores, while the tankers were sailing in ballast, and all were bound for Suez, via the Cape of Good Hope. Until clear of the western approaches to the Straits of Gibraltar, the southbound ships were to be considered part of HG 76, and under the protection of Commander Walker's escort group.

While Convoy HG 76 was assembling at Gibraltar its progress was closely monitored by Admiral Dönitz's spies. As early as 4 December it was noted in BdU's war diary that: 'In the harbour of Gibraltar there are at present about 55 ships. It is expected, therefore, that the HG convoy, which has been due since the 1st December, will put out very shortly. Particularly strong air cover at present seems to confirm this.'

With the inevitability of the sailing of a large north-bound convoy, Dönitz set about gathering his forces to provide a hot reception for the British ships when they did finally put to sea. Drawing on the U-boats in the area, he formed the wolf pack *Seeräuber* (Pirate) consisting of five boats, Günther Müller-Stockheim's U-67, Günter Hessler's U-107, Klaus Scholtz's U-108, Bruno Hansmann's U-127 and Dietrich Gergelbach's U-574. These boats were ordered to set up a patrol line from 10 miles south of Cape St. Vincent, stretching due south for 95 miles, a long net into which HG 76 must sail. In support of *Seeräuber,* Dönitz called in Arend Baumann in U-131, Wolfgang Heyda in U-434, Engelbert Endrass in U-567 and Gerhard Bigalk in U-751. At the same time, the Condors of KG 40 at Bordeaux-Merignac were moved to a state of readiness to join in the attack. Everything possible was being done to prevent HG 76 reaching its destination.

Admiral Dönitz would have been less confident of success had he known that the thirteen-strong escort group accompanying HG 76 was under the command of an acknowledged anti-submarine expert. Commander Frederick John Walker RN – known those who served with him as 'Johnny'

Walker – who sailed in the sloop HMS *Stork,* was as unconventional as he was ruthless, killing U-boats being his main aim in life. Whereas the accepted means of convoy defence practised by most Escort Commanders of the day was to form a screen around the merchant ships and wait for the U-boats to come to them, Walker believed in actively seeking out the enemy. His policy was to use his fast destroyers and sloops to go after the U-boats, hitting them hard before they came within torpedo shot of the merchantmen. This often meant leaving the convoy defended only by a handful of corvettes, a policy fraught with many frightening risks, but Johnny Walker was to prove that the results obtained far outweighed the risks involved.

For the first forty-eight hours of the passage home HG 76 had air cover provided by Sunderlands of Coastal Command based on Gibraltar. It was one of these aircraft, scouting ahead on the evening of the 14th, that sighted a U-boat some 50 miles south of Cape St. Vincent.

U-127, under the command of Korvettenkapitän Bruno Hansmann, had been the first of the *Seerauber* group to take up position. On the night of the 14th, U-127, a Type IXC on her first war patrol, was idling on the surface 180 miles to the west of Gibraltar, and directly in the projected path of Convoy HG 76. It was a dark night with no moon, and Hansmann was taken completely unawares when the big four-engined flying boat roared overhead. Fortunately for Hansmann and his men, the Sunderland either had no bombs on board, or its pilot was so surprised at sighting the surfaced submarine that he failed to act. Hansmann slammed his hatches shut and took U-127 down at a run. She escaped without damage.

When the Sunderland pilot radioed in his sighting, the Admiralty passed a warning to HG 76, and then called in more reinforcements, consisting of the 36-knot destroyers *Croome, Foxhound, Gurkha* and *Nestor,* which had just left the south bound troop convoy WS 14, and were on passage to Gibraltar. Led by HMAS *Nestor,* the four powerful warships converged on the last reported position of U-127.

Just before midnight, as HG 76 drew abeam of Cape Espartel, the north-western extremity of Africa, the subsidiary convoy of four ships, designated a 'Special Group', broke away from the main body of the convoy and headed south for the Cape. The ships were sailing in two columns of two, the *Empire Barracuda* at the head of the starboard column, a destroyer leading, a corvette on each beam, and a third corvette bringing up the rear. The escorts would accompany the merchantmen only until they were in safe waters a few hours south of Cape Espartel, then they would be on their own.

It was a fine, warm night, dark and moonless, the sky a black velvet canvas splashed with a myriad twinkling stars. Gazing up at this spectacular display from the Empire Barracuda's bridge, Captain Ridley's thoughts inevitably turned to home, soon to be deep in the magic of Christmas. But for him this was the unobtainable. For the next six weeks he would be fully occupied in taking his ship and her cargo of arms and ammunition 10,000 miles, around the Cape and north again to Suez. It was a long haul, made all the more dangerous now that the Japanese had entered the war. The *Empire Barracuda*, formerly the Norwegian-flag *Black Heron*, although twenty-two years old, was powered by a 660 nominal horse power turbine, which gave her a good turn of speed. Given the choice, Ridley would have been tempted to make a dash through the Mediterranean, a mere 2000 miles and seven days steaming, but the Admiralty would have none of it. Overnight, the Mediterranean had become off limits for Allied merchant ships, except in very special circumstances and under heavy escort.

Since its conclusive defeat at the Battle of Cape Matapan, in March 1941, the Italian Fleet had ceased to be a credible force in the Mediterranean, making way for the Royal Navy and RAF to play havoc with Rommel's supply convoys. This was a severe blow to Hitler's vanity, and at the end of August 1941 he ordered all operational U-boats to be sent to the Mediterranean sphere. It was the policy of a madman; it being plainly obvious that, as always, the main threat to the German war effort lay in the Allied convoys bringing supplies and weapons across the North Atlantic from America. Both Dönitz and his immediate superior, Admiral Raeder, protested in the strongest terms against the change of priorities, but their protests were ignored. The transfer went ahead, six boats entering the Mediterranean in September, followed by four more in November. As the end of 1941 drew near, Dönitz was ordered to allocate fifteen boats to set up a patrol line across the Straits of Gibraltar, and a further ten boats to be sent to the eastern Mediterranean – this in spite of the fact that three boats had already been lost in attempting to force a passage of the Straits. Among those now under orders to take the war into the Mediterranean were the 7th Flotilla boats U-74 and U-77.

U-74, a Type VII B out of Bremer-Vulkan's Vegesack yard, sailed from St. Nazaire on 9 December. She was under the command of 35-year-old Kapitänleutnant Eitel-Friedrich Kentrat. Twenty-four hours later, U-74 was followed out by U-77, a Type VII C commanded by Kapitänleutnant Heinrich Schonder. Both boats had orders to break through into the Mediterranean, Kentrat to be based at La Spezia in the north of Italy, and Schonder at Salamis in southern Greece.

On the night of 14/15 December, U-74 and U-77 were to the south-west of Cape Espartel, and making their approach to the Straits of Gibraltar, keeping as close to the African shore as possible. Unknown to Kentrat and Schonder, they were on converging courses with the south bound Special Group led by the *Empire Barracuda*.

Kentrat was first to make contact with the Special Group, reporting to BdU at 2305 on the 14th that he had sighted a convoy of four ships steaming at slow speed on a westerly course. In the early hours of the 15th, Schonder reported sighting four tankers, escorted by two destroyers, on a south-westerly course at 10 knots. BdU ordered both boats to 'utilize the slightest chances of attack, to withdraw at latest before dawn and to proceed further to CH [Mediterranean area]'.

At midnight, with the loom of the powerful light on Cape Espartel sweeping the horizon to port, Captain Ridley, who had been on the bridge of the *Empire Barracuda* since sailing from Gibraltar, decided that the worst of the danger was past, and it was safe to go below. Had he been able to penetrate the darkness astern, he would have thought otherwise. U-74, her low silhouette only a dark shadow on the water, was patiently shadowing the convoy, waiting for U-77 to make contact and join in the attack.

Oblivious to the danger closing in on his ship, Ridley checked the *Empire Barracuda's* position on the chart, wrote up his Night Orders, took one last look around the horizon, and left the bridge, leaving the Second Officer in charge.

During the hours that followed, with the convoy steering an erratic zig-zag course, Kentrat's U-74 lost contact with the ships. However, U-77 was near by, and at 0155 on the 15th, Schonder sighted the convoy. It was then 20 miles south of Cape Espartel. At 0200, he was close to starboard of the *Empire Barracuda*, and was waiting for her to settle down on the next leg of her zig-zag.

At 0205, Schonder fired a spread of two torpedoes from his forward tubes, bracketing the British ship. The first torpedo exploded in the *Empire Barracuda's* after hold, which luckily contained no explosives, the second striking home on her starboard bow, again clear of her lethal cargo. Schonder also claimed to have hit one of the tankers with a third torpedo, but there is no evidence of even a near-miss on any of the other ships in the convoy.

Captain Ridley was sleeping soundly when the torpedoes struck, but his subconcious was so attuned to every movement of his ship, that he was awake and on his feet within seconds. The *Empire Barracuda* was vibrating madly, and despite his dazed state Ridley realised that her propeller shaft, which ran through the after hold, was broken. He ran for the bridge.

By the time Ridley reached the wheelhouse, the *Empire Barracuda* was already going down by the stern. Mercifully, she had not taken a noticeable list either way, but she was still making considerable way through the water. Ridley ordered his crew to their boat stations, but until the ship came to a halt lowering the boats would be courting disaster. However, five minutes later, Ridley was forced to attempt the impossible when the *Empire Barracuda's* bow began to rear out of the water. She was entering her death throes.

The *Empire Barracuda* carried three lifeboats, two large pulling boats on the starboard side, and a motor boat on the port side. Ridley gave the order to lower all three. What followed he described in an interview with the Admiralty in January 1942:

> *Unfortunately, No.3 starboard boat up-ended because, in the darkness, someone let go the after fall and left the boat hanging by the forward fall. It was very difficult to work on the boat deck at all as it was so small and crowded with gear. The forward starboard lifeboat was in the water by this time, having been lowered successfully, and the Chief Officer cast off. He was about four yards from the ship when the vessel started to lurch from side to side, the bows continued to rise out of the water, and the Chief Officer's boat was drawn back over the submerged stern. Meanwhile, the motor boat had been lowered, the forward fall cast off, and the toggle of the painter let go, but the after fall of this boat was still fast when the vessel rose very quickly and we had to leave the boat as it was and slide down the ship's side into the water. Half a minute later I looked round, the vessel was up-ended at an angle of 80°, then she plunged straight down and sank.*

The *Empire Barracuda* was equipped with four wooden liferafts, three of which had been launched before she sank. These were fitted with self-igniting lights, and proved to be the lifesavers for the men now struggling in the water. The corvette *Coltsfoot* was quickly on the scene, and by 0400 had rescued all the survivors, including Captain Ridley, from their rafts. A headcount taken on board the corvette revealed that of the *Empire Barracuda's* crew of fifty-two, thirteen were missing. Ridley was under the impression that these men had probably lost their lives when they rushed out of their accommodation onto the well deck, and fell into the after hold, the deck plating of which had been blown away by the blast of the torpedo.

It was a heavy enough loss of life, but could have been much worse if one of Schonder's torpedoes had exploded in a hold containing explosives.

Captain Ridley praised the bravery of his crew, that of one man more than others:

> *I should particularly like to mention a lad of 20, by name R. Urquhart, a cadet from the New Zealand Shipping Company. He had not yet completed his apprenticeship but as I had sailed without a 3rd Officer he took this position. This lad got away in the Chief Officer's boat, and before the ship sank he noticed the 2nd Officer in the water without a lifejacket. He held on to the 2nd Mate over the side of the lifeboat, until, as I have already explained, this boat was drawn inboard across the deck by the suction of the ship as she sank. He still continued to hang on until his arm was jammed and badly broken between the boat and the ship's side, so that he was forced to let go the 2nd Officer who, unfortunately, was washed away and drowned. The 3rd Officer had only been with me for about six days, but behaved in a cool and courageous manner throughout. He was later made as comfortable as possible on board the* Coltsfoot *and on arrival at Gibraltar was sent to hospital for medical attention.*

As a sad conclusion to the saga of the *Empire Barracuda*, the treatment accorded Captain Ridley and his men after landing in Gibraltar bears witness to a lack of regard, bordering on contempt, so often shown by the British hierachy of the day towards their distressed merchant seamen. Captain Ridley wrote:

> *After being ashore for three weeks, Gibraltar was being evacuated and we were sent home in a Polish ship, s.s.* Batory *with several hundred refugees. These people commandeered all the decent accommodation, as they were first on board. Then the Army, Navy and Air Force personnel came next, and the Merchant Navy last, about 2 hours later, by which time there was no decent accommodation left for us. No berths were allotted to anyone before joining the ship, and it was a case of first come, first served, as there was no organisation of any kind. I do not know who was responsible for the arrangements, but the whole show was chaotic and ludicrous.*

> *On arrival at the Tail of the Bank, Clyde, the Immigration people and Board of Trade representatives came on board. All the service personnel were taken off, leaving the Merchant Navy personnel last again. We were lined up from*

11 a.m. until 5 p.m. before being allowed to leave in a tender; the Immigration people seemed to treat us as spies. They showed no consideration; when I reached the table these officials decided to go to lunch, leaving everyone still standing in a queue. I eventually got through about 4.30 p.m. along with a bunch of Chinese.

There were about 250 people crowded into the tender, and they took us alongside three other tenders which were moored at the Pier. It was dark and there were no gangways between any of these tenders. It was difficult and dangerous enough for uninjured men, but my 3rd Officer had a broken arm, and the 2nd Officer from the Paracoombe had lost an arm, and these two men were practically helpless. It was with the utmost difficulty that these men were eventually assisted ashore.

There was no one to meet us when we got ashore, although the ship had arrived on the Sunday afternoon and it was now 6 p.m. on Monday evening. In fact, the arrangements for the Merchant Navy personnel, right from Gibraltar, were disgusting and totally inadequate. Eventually, we were met by our Agents who arranged for the men to go to the Sailors' Home if they wished, and travelling vouchers were issued for everyone, so I proceeded at once to my home in Glasgow.

On the morning of 15 December, while the *Empire Barracuda* survivors were being rescued from their rafts by HMS *Coltsfoot*, U-127 was on some 34 miles south of Cape St. Vincent, and heading in for the Straits of Gibraltar on the surface. Bruno Hansmann had apparently learned no lessons from his earlier brush with a Sunderland, for instead of diving at dawn, he remained on the surface long after the sun was up. Unfortunately for Hansmann, his submarine lay in the path of the destroyers *Croome*, *Foxhound*, *Gurkha* and *Nestor*, who were steaming in line abreast. Their radars and Asdics were probing above and below the sea, but in the end it was down to the Navy's tried and tested 'Mark 1 Eyeball' to find the enemy.

At 1042, one of *Nestor's* lookouts reporting an object on the surface right ahead at approximately 7 miles. *Nestor* increased speed to 22 knots, and when 6¼ miles off, with the target identified as submarine, she opened fire with her forward 4.7s. The Australian destroyer fired eight salvoes, and with the shot falling too close for comfort, Hansmann took U-127 down at a rush.

Hansmann might have got clean away, but the other three destroyers had joined *Nestor*, and the Asdic beams of all four were locking onto the disappearing boat. At 1114, *Nestor* had a firm echo at 1600 yards, and she went in to attack, dropping pattern after pattern of depth charges turning the sea around the fleeing U-boat into a boiling maelstrom. The other destroyers joined in, and at 1122, hammered by the combined blast of dozens of 300lb Torpex-filled cannisters, U-127's pressure hull finally burst, spewing forth a great gush of oil that welled to the surface, bringing with it a pathetic mixture of charred wreckage, scraps of clothing and human remains. *Korvettenkapitän* Bruno Hansmann and his crew of fifty died with U-127, leaving behind them not one single enemy ship sunk or damaged to justify their deaths.

Chapter Twelve

Retaliation

With the help of air reconnaissance and watchers ashore, Lorient had been carefully watching the progress of HG 76 since sailing from Gibraltar. Then, on the night of 14/15th, all contact was lost. In the early hours of the 15th, an Italian agent in Tangiers reported that the ships had reversed course, and were retracing their steps towards Gibraltar. Confusion reigned in Lorient, but not for long. The Italian report was quickly discredited by agents in Gibraltar, who reported the harbour and its approaches empty, except for small craft and the occasional ship calling for bunkers. Incredibly, in spite of all the watching eyes at Lorient's disposal, it seemed that HG 76, a huge fleet of thirty-two merchantmen, escorted by thirteen naval vessels, had disappeared from sight on entering the broad Atlantic. An entry in BdU's War Diary on 15 December read:

> *Convoy: No reports of sightings were received from the boats. The air reconnaissance sent out has achieved nothing. Control considers the reconnaissance line report (from the Italian agent in Tangiers) as very unlikely. The operation against the convoy is being continued. U-434 will join Group Seeräuber. In order to have boats in the area of air reconnaissance planned for the 16th December, and in order to prevent them falling behind the convoy, a patrol line has been ordered for 0900 on the 16th December from CG 8171 to 8744 (36° 51′ N 11° 26′ W to 35° 15′ N 11° 26′ W). Sequence: U-434 – 107 – 127 – 574 – 131 – 67 – 108. 7.5 knots has been laid down as the maximum possible speed of advance.*

U-131 was stationed the middle of the long line of U-boats which, on the morning of 16 December, lay submerged across the predicted course of Convoy HG 76. Commanded by 38-year-old *Korvettenkapitän* Arend Baumann, U-131 was a Type IX C, built on the Weser, and commissioned only five months earlier. Her career to date had been a disappointment, to say the least. Whilst working up in the Baltic she had narrowly missed being torpedoed by a Russian submarine, had similarly escaped an attack by a fellow U-boat, and had rounded off her training by ramming a set of anti-torpedo nets. As a result of the last incident, U-131's hydrophones were severely damaged, and although repaired, were still not operating at full capacity when she sailed from Kiel on her first war patrol on 1 November.

U-131's fortunes took a turn for the better when she was on station some 400 miles south of Iceland, patrolling the North Atlantic convoy route. On 6 December, she sighted and sank the 4016-ton British steamer *Scottish Trader*, bound from the US to Liverpool with a full cargo of steel and foodstuffs. This was a very promising start to a first war patrol, but it proved to be a false dawn. A few days later, Baumann was in pursuit of a 12,000-ton Allied ship sailing alone, when U-131's port diesel failed. Before repairs could be effected, the target ship was out of sight over the horizon.

As December moved on, and the constant search for enemy ships proved fruitless, Baumann and his men anxiously awaited the expected order to join the 2nd Flotilla in Lorient, with the almost certain prospect of spending Christmas in port. This was not to be. On 12 December, Baumann received instruction from BdU to proceed south to the Gibraltar area, and there wait for further orders. The disappointment at missing Christmas was exacerbated by the suspicion that they would soon be called upon to run the gauntlet of the Royal Navy in the Straits of Gibraltar and attempt to break through into the Mediterranean. A cloud of depression descended on the boat.

When U-131 joined the other *Seeräuber* boats on the 16th, word had been received from Lorient that the British convoy had left Gibraltar two days earlier, and was sailing westwards at approximately 7 knots. The boats were ordered to move slowly eastwards to meet the convoy.

Submerged below periscope depth, and moving slowly towards the rendezvous with HG 76, Arend Baumann was completely unaware that the repairs made to his hydrophones following the collision with the anti-torpedo nets in the Baltic were makeshift, to say the least. That night, with U-131's hydrophone operator reporting no ships within range, Baumann decided to surface. Luckily, before surfacing, he raised the main periscope and took a quick look around. To his horror, and consternation, Baumann found that he was about to surface in the middle of an armada of slow-moving ships. Recovering from the shock Baumann was tempted to try a quick shot at one of the merchantmen, but then he saw the sinister silhouettes of a number of escort vessels hovering on the outskirts of the convoy, and decided to return to the depths before the Asdic beams came reaching out for him.

Baumann remained submerged and on strict silent routine until he was satisfied that the enemy ships had passed overhead. Returning to periscope depth, he slowly and deliberately scanned around the horizon, assuring himself that U-131 was alone. Only then, with the approaching dawn chasing away the shadows of the night, did he set off in pursuit of the convoy. An hour running on full speed was sufficient to bring the rearmost ships of HG 76 within sight. Reducing speed to avoid overtaking the convoy, Baumann sent out a brief signal, reporting, 'Contact established'. U-434 and U-574 were within listening range, and acknowledged. BdU's powerful station at Lorient also picked up Baumann's signal, and relayed it to all *Seeräuber* boats.

Günther Müller-Stöckheim in U-67 was first to join up with Baumann, sighting U-131 at 0605. However, at 0745 Baumann reported to Lorient, 'Contact lost'. Lorient then alerted Air Reconnaissance at Bordeaux, and a long-range Condor was despatched with orders to find the convoy and stay with it. Reports from the aircraft throughout the day enabled Lorient to keep track of HG 76.

The sight of the *Focke-Wulf* circling low on the horizon alerted Commander Walker to the probability that U-boats were being homed in on the convoy. Darkness was already setting in, and he resisted the temptation to detach escorts from the screen to search for an enemy who might, or might not be there. He did, however, radio Commander MacKendrick in the carrier *Audacity*, requesting that he launch an aircraft next morning at first light.

At daybreak on the 17th, HG 76 was 400 miles out into the Atlantic, and still making a westerly course. As soon as there was light enough, *Audacity* headed up into the wind, and the first Martlet of the day trundled down her short flight deck, and roared into the air.

The Grumman Martlet, a single engined, single-seat fighter – known to the Americans as the 'Wildcat', was a sturdy, reliable and highly manoevrable aircraft having a maximum speed of 315 mph, and armed with four .50 calibre machine-guns. The primary task of the Martlets of 802 Squadron Fleet Air Arm carried by the *Audacity* was to keep the *Focke-Wulf*s at bay, but on this occasion Walker was after U-boats. The lone Martlet was not long in delivering.

U-131 had regained contact with the convoy during the night, and continued to shadow on the surface until first light. She then dived to avoid detection. At about 0930, Baumann brought his boat back to the surface to take a quick look around. Although U-131 was then 22 miles to port of the convoy, it so happened that as she came to the surface *Audacity's* Martlet was within visual range. Arend Baumann was quick to recover from he shock of seeing the British plane suddenly drop out of the sky, her guns blazing. He immediately dived, and took U-131 down to 250 feet.

Left with only a patch of disturbed water to mark the escape of the U-boat, the Martlet's pilot radioed back to *Audacity* reporting his sighting, and then began to circle the spot, acting as a beacon for the carrier's radar to lock on to. Alerted in turn by *Audacity*, HMS *Stork* raced westwards at maximum speed. On her open bridge, Commander Walker crouched over the bearing compass, conning the sloop towards the circling Martlet. At the same time, he gave orders for the nearest escorts, the destroyers *Blankney*, *Exmoor* and *Stanley*, and the corvette *Pentstemon* to join him.

The 27-knot Hunt-class destroyer *Blankney*, commanded by Lieutenant Commander P.F. Powlett, quickly overhauled Walker's sloop, and went in to drop a single depth charge on a patch of oil indicated by the Martlett. No Asdic contact was obtained, but Powlett found other oil patches leading in a west-south-westerly direction. Following this trail, he dropped a pattern of charges, but again with no result.

Walker now ordered *Blankney* and *Exmoor* to form up in line abreast with *Stork*, and then began a sweep on a course of 270°. His assessment of the situation was that the U-boat had been shadowing the convoy on a westerly course, and would most probably have continued on that same course after being forced to dive. This assessment proved correct when, at 1053, more than four hours after the sighting by the Martlet, a firm underwater contact was obtained at a range of 1,600 yards.

Blankney went in first, dropping a pattern of six depth charges set to medium depth as she went through a widening patch of oil. *Pentstemon* followed at 1106 with a pattern of ten charges, six of which were set to explode at 150 feet, and four at 385 feet. Contact was not regained after the attack, but a later interrogation of survivors from U-131 revealed the devastating effect of the charges:

At 1108, as one prisoner stated, a number of depth charges exploded around the U-boat. Three were particularly close and the damage within the U-boat was severe. A considerable quantity of water entered aft and, according to one prisoner the U-boat lay at an angle of nearly 40 degrees and began to sink. A number of gauges in the control room were smashed and the electric motors damaged, although they did not become entirely useless. Oil from a leaking tank began to pour into the diesel room. The hydrophones, which had been working at irregular intervals only, now went completely dead. The lights were not extinguished.

Prisoners alleged that U-131 had sunk to a depth of over 600 feet before she could be got under control. This statement must be taken with reserve; survivors are always inclined to exaggerate the depth to which they sink during attack. Steel plates were cracking, as if they would give way at any moment. Paint was peeling in blisters from the inside of the hull; locker doors were warped and jammed shut by the tremendous pressure...

While Baumann was fighting to save his command, Walker, unaware of the drama being enacted in the depths, had taken his ships further to the westward. He then altered course 90 degrees to port and steamed south for several miles, before coming round onto an easterly course to cover new ground. *Stanley* had now joined the search, and the five ships formed up in line abreast 1 to 2 miles apart on a course of 090°. The order of steaming, from north to south, was *Penstemon, Stanley, Blankney, Stork,* and *Exmoor.*

Beneath the waves, U-131 had lost the battle to stay submerged. Baumann had managed to regain the trim, but the damage to his boat was so severe, that he had no other option left but to try to reach the surface. The supply of compressed air was all but exhausted, but there was just sufficient to blow all tanks in a last desperate attempt to escape a lingering death in the cold depths of the Atlantic. The tanks were blown, and for what seemed like hours to the forty-seven men trapped in her sweating hull U-131 hung motionless, then with a groan that sounded almost human, began to rise. When the U-boat reached the surface, she had just 8 kilograms of compressed air left in her bottles.

The ex-US Navy destroyer *Stanley,* commanded by Lieutenant Commander David Shaw, had a lookout at the masthead, and was first to sight U-131. Shaw immediately reported to Walker, 'Submarine on surface bearing 060°'. Walker signalled the chase, and the five escorts altered onto the bearing, and increased to maximum speed.

As might be expected, the two Hunt-class destroyers, *Blankney* and *Exmoor,* surged ahead, closely followed by *Stanley,* which although of 1918 vintage, was still capable of a good turn of speed. The corvette *Pentstemon,* anxious not to be left out at the kill, was making black smoke and straining every rivet to keep up with the others. Likewise, *Stork,* top speed 18¾ knots, was breaking all previous records. On her bridge, bareheaded and fuming with impatience, Johnny Walker was directing operations.

Arend Baumann watched in horror as the enemy warships thundered down on him like a pack of avenging hounds. He could not take the risk of submerging again, for without compressed air U-131 would never rise again.

He must either surrender, or make a run for it. Baumann decided on the latter course. Sending his guns' crews to their stations, he put U-131 stern on to his pursuers, and ordered his engineer to go to maximum emergency speed.

U-131 was equipped with two 1800 horse power, 9-cylinder, four-cycle M.A.N. diesels, which gave her a cruising speed of 18 knots on the surface. In an absolute emergency – and this was certainly that – with the speed governors removed, her diesels were said to be able to produce 22 knots, perhaps more.

While U-131 had been submerged, the Martlet that first spotted her had been forced to return to the carrier for lack of fuel. Unfortunately for Baumann, just as he began his desperate flight, the relief Martlet from HMS *Audacity* arrived overhead. The pilot, Sub-Lieutenant George Fletcher, had orders to delay the U-boat until Walker's ships caught up with her. Without hesitation, Fletcher dived to the attack, his four .50 calibre guns spraying the apparently helpless U-boat.

In his eagerness to cripple U-131, Fletcher had ignored the U-boat's ability to hit back, and as he dived Baumann's two anti-aircraft guns mounted abaft the conning tower opened up. The Martlet ran straight into a lethal curtain of 37mm and 20mm shells. A 20mm shell hit the cockpit, probably killing the pilot outright, while a 37mm shell scored a direct hit on one of the fighter's wings, tearing it off. The Martlet failed to pull out of its dive, crashing into the sea close alongside U-131. Sub-Lieutenant George Fletcher thus earned the posthumous distinction of piloting the first aircraft to be shot down by a U-boat in the war. His death also left HMS *Audacity* with just three aircraft operational.

Unfortunately for Baumann and his men, any advantage they gained by shooting down the Martlet was short-lived. The destroyers *Blankney* and *Exmoor* were by then within gun range, and their 4-inch shells began to straddle the fleeing U-boat. *Stork, Stanley* and *Pentstemon* joined in as they closed the range.

With the British shells falling all around him, and unable to answer their fire with his 105mm without bringing U-131 broadside on, Baumann had to accept that he was in a hopeless situation. Although U-131 had not yet been hit, it could only be a matter of time before the enemy shells found her and blasted her out of the water. Baumann decided, albeit reluctantly, to scuttle the boat and rely on the enemy to show mercy to his men. As U-131, her vents and hatches open to the sea, began to settle, her crew abandoned her, and were picked up by the destroyers *Exmoor* and *Stanley*, while *Blankney* stood guard. It then fell to *Stork* to retrieve the body of Sub-Lieutenant George Fletcher. The pilot was buried at sea early next morning under a leaden December sky with the sloop, her ensign at half-mast, rolling gently in the Atlantic swell. There was great sadness in Commander Walker's voice as he committed the body of the young pilot to the lonely deeps of the Atlantic.

Although visibly moved by the loss of Sub Lieutenant Fletcher, Walker was well satisfied that his action in taking the destroyers away from the main body of the convoy had been vindicated by the sinking of U-131. However, a preliminary interrogation of the prisoners had confirmed Walker's suspicions. Other U-boats were somewhere in the vicinity – perhaps as many as six.

The rest of the *Seeräuber* pack was closer at hand than Walker feared. In fact, while the destroyers were pounding U-131, just 10 miles away U-434 was on the surface, a witness to the destruction of her fellow U-boat.

U-434, a Type VII C commanded by 28-year-old Wolfgang Heyda, was another boat with a disgruntled crew. She had sailed from St. Nazaire on 1 November, and for more than a month Heyda had haunted the convoy lanes without finding a single target for his torpedoes. On 9 December, he had sighted the southbound convoy OG 77, but was unable to mount an attack. By this time, U-434 was running short of fuel and, more importantly in the eyes of her crew, she had been without bread and potatoes for five days. To forestall any unrest, Heyda decided to put into Vigo where, despite Spain's declared neutrality, he was able to take on fresh stores.

U-434 entered Vigo Bay under the cover of darkness on the 14th December, and made fast on the seaward side of a merchant ship which was moored parallel to the shore. She was the 1878-ton *Bessel* of the Neptune Line, registered in Bremen. Heyda learned that the *Bessel* had been at Vigo since the outbreak of war, acting as a supply ship for U-boats. Her captain, Heyda was told, obtained a regular supply of provisions from various Spanish sources by posing as a ship's chandler. On average, a U-boat was being supplied by the *Bessel* every night. It is inconceivable that an operation of this scale could be hidden from the Spaniards for long, and it surely must have had their blessing.

U-434 sailed from Vigo early on the 15th, having taken on board a good stock of fresh meat, vegetables and fruit. She was also able to top up her fuel tanks from the *Bessel*. Heyda had by then received orders from Lorient to proceed south and join *Seeräuber*.

Soon after sailing from Vigo, U-434 received signals from a Condor of Air Reconnaisance reporting that HG 76 had left Gibraltar and was heading west. Later, Heyda began receiving regular position reports from U-131, which was then shadowing the convoy. Homing in on U-131's signals, U-434 sighted HG 76 on the morning of the 17th some 150 miles north-east of Madeira. For the time being,Heyda kept his distance from the convoy, intending to move in after dark. That afternoon he had a grandstand view of Walker's attack on U-131.

Following the sinking of U-131, Heyda submerged to periscope depth, and keeping a wary eye on Walker's destroyers, tagged on behind the convoy. He surfaced again after dark, but lost contact with the convoy altogether at 0400 on the 18th. He left the conning tower in disgust, and went below to rest.

Oberleutnant Frank, U-434's First Watch Officer, took over the watch at 0800, and shortly afterwards sighted four destroyers dead ahead. U-434 was still on the surface, but Frank did not submerge, neither, for some unexplainable reason, did he call Heyda to the conning tower. It is reported that the officer ordered full ahead on both engines and steered for the destroyers, an action he and all his comrades were to bitterly regret.

HMS *Stanley*, with her lookout at the masthead, was again first to see the enemy, breaking R/T silence at 0906 to report to *Stork* that she had sighted a surfaced U-boat on her port quarter at 6 miles.

Commander Walker used his already proven method of attack, ordering the destroyers *Blankney* and *Exmoor,* and the sloop *Deptford* to form up in line abreast on *Stanley* and move in at full speed, while he directed operations from *Stork.*

Wolfgang Heyda arrived breathless in the conning tower of U-434 to be greeted by the fearsome sight of a pack of warships bearing down on him at 24 knots, their forward guns already spitting fire. Without hesitation, he cleared the conning tower and crash-dived. As U-434 submerged in a flurry of white water, more in defiance than in hope of finding a target, Heyda fired a single torpedo at the enemy ships. Not surprisingly, the torpedo missed.

Once under water, Heyda intended to go deep and creep away, but as the U-boat slid down into the depths the probing fingers of several Asdic beams could be heard pinging towards them. The depth charges followed soon afterwards.

Overhead, *Stanley* was first to reach the patch of oil and disturbed water marking the spot where U-434 had gone down. *Stanley's* Asdic was out of action, so Lieutenant Commander Shaw reduced speed to 12 knots and began to mark out the area for the others by dropping single depth charges in a square around the position. He had completed three sides of the square, dropping nineteen charges in all, when *Blankney* arrived on the scene. *Blankney* dropped a five-charge pattern set to 150 and 250 feet, then stood off, passing her Asdic bearings and ranges to *Stanley,* allowing the four-stacker to move in with a fourteen-charge pattern set to explode deep. Determined to give the U-boat no time to recover, Walker then ordered *Blankney* to attack again, which she did, dropping a pattern of six charges set, as before, to 150 and 250 feet.

Below the surface, U-434 was in serious trouble. The first depth charges dropped by *Stanley* had damaged her conning tower hatch, which was leaking badly, the water streaming down into the control room. Then, as *Blankney* joined in the attack, and depth charge after depth charge came spiralling down to explode alongside the U-boat, she was thrown from side to side, her hull resonating to the powerful blasts. The lights went out, the steering gear jammed, the hydrophones failed, and the bow started to drop as the water poured in through the broken hatch. All the gauges were shattered, with the exception of one depth gauge in the motor room, and this showed that the boat was sinking rapidly.

As their boat bucked and heaved under the onslaught of the British charges, in the dim glow of the emergency lighting the crew of U-434 looked to their commander to save them. The only functioning depth gauge now showed 300 feet, and the needle was still climbing.

Wolfgang Heyda knew he had only seconds to chose the fate of himself and his crew – surface and perhaps live, or stay down and almost surely die. He hesitated only briefly, then ordered all main ballast to be blown.

U-434 shot to the surface with her motors still running. As she appeared, Walker's ships closed in to 500 yards, firing with all guns that could be brought to bear. Unable to steer, and bow-heavy, Heyda accepted that he could not run. Having seen that the time fuses of the scuttling charges were set, he ordered his men over the side.

Seeing the U-boat break surface, *Blankney* opened fire, and increased speed to ram, but at the last moment Lieutenant Powlett saw that the enemy boat was being abandoned. He tried to sheer away, but *Blankney* was committed, and she struck U-434 a glancing blow, the destroyer receiving minor damage.

As he ran clear, Powlett realised that there might be a possibility of boarding, and perhaps saving this U-boat. He ordered the whaler to be sent away with an armed party. Unfortunately, U-434 had not been entirely deserted. Even though all the others were in the water, including her commander, Wolfgang Heyda, his Number One, *Oberleutnant* Frank – either very brave, or very foolish – had stayed with his boat. As *Blankney's* whaler hit the water, Frank opened fire with the 20mm gun, sending tracers arcing across the intervening stretch of water at the broadside-on destroyer. Luckily for *Blankney*, at that precise moment, the scuttling charges set in U-434's hull when Heyda abandoned her, choose to explode. The submarine, with her bottom blasted open, sank like a stone, taking *Oberleutnant* Frank with her.

Blankney picked up forty-two survivors, only two men, Frank and Maschinengefreiter (Stoker 2nd Class) Brandes, being lost. It is believed that Brandes was killed by *Blankney's* propellors as she moved in to rescue the swimmers. *< Hof- CHoP!*

With the sinking of U-434 Commander Walker had good cause for satisfaction. His unorthodox tactics, untried before HG 76, had been thoroughly vindicated. Every U-boat sent to the bottom meant a dozen Allied ships remaining afloat, and the count, only four days into the voyage, was in his favour. But Walker was aware – as was every man sailing in HG 76 – that the battle was far from over. Between them and the safety of British waters lay nearly a thousand miles of hostile ocean. Furthermore, the odds against the convoy reaching its destination without further loss were lengthening. That afternoon, the destroyers *Blankney* and *Exmoor*, the cutting edge of Walker's attack group, were recalled to Gibraltar. He was left with the sloops *Stork* and *Deptford*, seven corvettes, the escort carrier *Audacity* – in herself something of a liability – and just one destroyer, *Stanley*.

In the hands of 35-year-old Lieutenant Commander David Shaw, who had retired from the Royal Navy in 1937, returning to the service when war broke out, *Stanley* had proved herself to be a formidable U-boat hunter. However, she was a visibly ageing ship. Built for the US Navy as USS *McCalla* in 1918, and laid up between the wars, *Stanley* was one of the fifty destroyers handed over to the Royal Navy in September 1940 in exchange for bases in the West Indies. Known in the Navy as 'four-stackers' for their distinctive four funnels, they were not liked by their new owners. Narrow in the beam, and therefore totally unsuited for the North Atlantic weather, in which they rolled hideously, they also had an excessively large turning circle, a distinct disadvantage when tackling a U-boat. But for all their faults, the 'four-stackers' were a godsend to the Royal Navy, filling the gap left by the destroyers lost at Dunkirk and Norway.

Stanley was responding to the challenge of HG 76 magnificently, but she was, in the words of Lieutenant Commander Shaw, suffering from 'various defects and difficulties'. Having escorted a troop convoy out to Freetown in November, she had spent some time in that port while essential repairs were carried out to her dynamos and boilers. Leaving Freetown, bound for Gibraltar, boiler leaks had forced her to put into Bathurst to take on water, and later to top up from a merchant ship she was escorting. She had been experiencing trouble with her Asdics since leaving Londonderry, and on the way north these failed altogether. Then, to exacerbate an already bad situation, her radar also failed. There were neither the spares nor the expertise on board to repair either set, so *Stanley* had no means of detecting a submarine underwater, and her surface visibility depended on the eyesight of her lookouts. When *Blankney* and *Exmoor* left, *Stanley* was ordered to cover the rear of the convoy, which, given her deficiencies, was probably the best place for her.

CHAPTER THIRTEEN

An Eye for an Eye

As the shadows lengthened and the day drew to a close, HMS *Stanley* was standing guard astern of the convoy, zig-zagging in broad sweeps in the wake of the ships. She was without functioning radar and Asdic, her own safety dependent entirely on the vigilance of her lookouts. And this was the danger hour when the U-boats began to stalk the unwary in earnest.

At 1830, a strange four-masted steamer was seen to be overtaking HG 76 on the quarter. Lieutenant Commander Shaw altered to investigate, challenging the ship by lamp. After some hesitation – there was obviously a language difficulty – the four-master identified herself as the 4372-ton, Portuguese-flag, *Mello*, bound for Lisbon. While *Stanley* was thus engaged, *Pentstemon* reported sighting a U-boat 8 to 10 miles on the port beam of the convoy. *Pentstemon* was joined by *Convolvulus*, and the two corvettes were ordered to attack. *Stanley*, being close by, dismissed the Portuguese ship and joined in the chase.

The three ships swept the area of the sighting thoroughly, but no contacts were made. During the search, *Convolvulus* reported that torpedoes were fired at her, but this was not confirmed. At 2136, *Stork* ordered the corvettes to rejoin the convoy, while *Stanley* resumed her position astern. The attack had been inconclusive, but Walker assumed that at least one U-boat must be in the vicinity of HG 76. His assumption was correct.

Later events showed that the furore had been caused by U-574. A Type VII C commanded by 27-year-old *Oberleutnant* Dietrich Gengelbach, U-574 was another boat on her first war cruise, having left Kiel on 13 November. Gengelbach had sailed with orders to break out into the Atlantic, and then, in company with several other boats, mount an attack on an important British convoy which was then assembling off Halifax, Nova Scotia.

Winter North Atlantic being what it is, Gengelbach had a very rough crossing, battling westerly gales all the way. When he was approaching Newfoundland weather conditions had become so bad that the proposed attack on the convoy was abandoned. This was hardly a good start to a maiden voyage – and there was worse to come. Lorient ordered all boats involved in this operation to return to French bases, with the exception of U-574. As he had not yet fired any of his torpedoes, Gengelbach was instructed to make for an area off the Azores, where a Freetown bound convoy was expected to pass. Having done as much damage as possible to this convoy, he was to take U-574 to Brest. Christmas in port once more became a distinct possibility.

U-574 arrived in the designated position 120 miles north-east of the Azores on 28 November, and lay in wait for Convoy OS 12, which Lorient reported would be passing on the 29th. Other U-boats were in the vicinity, but Gengelbach had no contact with them.

OS 12 duly hove in sight next day, but turned out to be under unusually heavy escort. For two days Gengelbach tried to approach the convoy, but was driven off by the escorts, as were the other U-boats. Only one boat was successful, Wolfgang Lüth's U-43, which sank the 5569-ton steamer *Thornliebank* early on the 29th.

When OS 12 had gone on its way, U-574 made a rendezvous with U-434, at which Wolfgang Heyda had passed a secret dispatch from BdU to Gengelbach. The gist of this dispatch was that U-574 was to proceed to Vigo, where she would receive fuel and stores from the *Bessel*. She was then to return to the Azores and remain in the area for another six weeks, or until she had used up all her torpedoes, whichever came first.

Having already spent two weeks in the North Atlantic subjected to the most atrocious weather, the very thought of enduring another six weeks of this purgatory did not appeal to the crew of U-574. There were murmurs of discontent, but these were quickly silenced by Gengelbach, who had other more serious worries to contend with, paramount among them a serious shortage of fuel. In fact, U-574's bunker tanks were so low that he was forced to make the passage to Vigo on one engine at 5 knots.

U-574 entered Vigo Bay under the cover of darkness on 13 December, leaving at 0330 on the 14th, having received 90 tons of diesel oil and fresh provisions from the *Bessel*. Acting on orders from Lorient, Gengelbach, went south after sailing from Vigo, and took up a position in the western approaches to the Straits of Gibraltar. On the 15th, he received a signal from a Condor of Air Reconnaissance reporting that a British convoy was northbound from the Straits. He was also contacted by U-131, which was then shadowing HG 76. With no orders to the contrary from BdU, Dietrich Gengelbach decided to join in the attack on the convoy.

Just before dark on the 18th, U-574 sighted a large freighter, apparently sailing unescorted, and Gengelbach gave chase on the surface. Another U-boat – unidentified, but probably Klaus Scholtz's U-108 – joined in the pursuit. Their quarry was undoubtedly the Portuguese ship *Mello*, which unfortunately for the U-boats, was then about to be investigated by HMS *Stanley*, with the corvettes *Convolvulus* and *Pentstemon* in support. Both U-boats suddenly found themselves under attack, and were lucky to escape.

Dietrich Gengelbach brought U-574 back to the surface an hour later, under the cover of full darkness. It was a fine night, the sky partly overcast, with a pale moon occasionally breaking through gaps in the cloud. The wind was still fresh from the north-east, the sea slight to moderate, while the unrelenting westerly swell gave the surfaced boat an uncomfortable roll.

Gengelbach set off after the convoy at full speed, coming in sight of the rear ships at 0200 on the 19th. He narrowed the gap as much as safety would allow, and then submerged, maintaining contact by listening to the beat of the ships' propellers. U-574, with an underwater speed of 7½ knots, had no difficulty in keeping up with the slow moving merchantmen.

At around 0400, Gengelbach rose to periscope depth to take a look at the convoy. He found that the visibility had deteriorated, and he could see nothing through the periscope but the nearest wave-tops. He surfaced, but when he threw the conning tower hatch back and clambered out into the fresh air, he was astonished to see a column of ships passing close to starboard. Two smaller ships at the rear of the column were quite obviously escorts.

In his eagerness to catch up with HG 76 Dietrich Gengelbach had walked into a trap. If he stayed on the surface, the escorts would pick him up on their radars, and if he dived, their Asdics would instantly search him out. He followed the only course of action left open to him and took the fight to the enemy.

The two escorts seen by Gengelbach were the destroyer *Stanley*, which was zig-zagging astern of the convoy, and Walker's flagship *Stork*, then making a high-speed inspection of the defence screen. Ironically, *Stanley*, with no radar and no Asdic, was first to sight U-574. Lieutenant Commander Shaw used his R/T to warn *Stork*, reporting 'Submarine in sight'. A few minutes later, one of *Stanley's* bridge lookouts saw torpedo tracks approaching from the port quarter, and shouted a warning. Shaw immediately altered to starboard to comb the tracks, and increased to full speed. The destroyer responded promptly to helm and engines, and the torpedoes passed harmlessly astern of her. Shaw used the R/T again to warn Walker that he was under attack.

Stork was with the main body of the convoy, about 6 miles ahead of *Stanley*, and Walker immediately reversed course to go to the destroyer's aid. However, in the excitement Lieutenant Commander Shaw had omitted to give his exact position, and as *Stork* raced back there was a near-collision between the two escorts. This led to a flurry of lamp signalling as both demanded identification of the other. The beams of the flashing signal lamps, although shaded, were visible to Gengelbach.

Hidden in the darkness – the moon was only a dim glow behind the clouds – U-574 was still on the surface, and only 1200 yards off on *Stanley's* port quarter. Taking careful aim, Gengelbach fired a spread of three torpedoes from his first, third and fourth bow tubes.

Two of Gengelbach's torpedoes missed *Stanley*, but the third struck her just abaft her bridge, probably her most vulnerable spot. The torpedo exploded in one of her after fuel tanks, breaking the veteran destroyer's back and turning her into a blazing inferno from which very few would escape alive.

Yeoman of Signals Alexander McEwen, who was on *Stanley's* bridge, later reported:

We came in sight of the convoy and the Stork, *and the* Stork *challenged us and I made our pennants and* Stork *made hers. She was on our starboard bow about 20 degrees.*

Just after that there came a warning "torpedo port". Just prior to that the Captain tried to make certain whether it was a submarine or not and we made a signal "submarine not sighted". That was the last R/T we made. I was on the bridge watching the Stork *when the torpedo hit us and the bridge collapsed and I went in the water. The bridge seemed to break to pieces and I went through and finished up in the water. When I looked up the bows of the ship were almost above me and I swam away...*

HMS *Stanley* was torpedoed at 0409 in full sight of Commander Walker, who witnessed the drama from the *Stork's* bridge. He had been watching the destroyer through his binoculars when she erupted in a sheet of flame. His reaction was characteristic; he immediately ordered all escorts to fire starshell and charge headlong at the enemy.

Stork was in the van, her Asdics indicating a firm contact on the port bow, in the vicinity of *Stanley*. Taking care not to approach within half a mile of the burning wreck, to avoid injuring any men in the water, Walker led off with a pattern of five depth charges set to 50 feet. He then continued past the wreck for 1000 yards, reversed course, and ran in again dropping a ten-charge pattern set to 50 and 150 feet.

Following the spectacular demise of HMS *Stanley*, U-574 ran away from the scene of her victory at full speed for about five minutes before Gengelbach took her down. She was creeping away underwater when Walker's second pattern of ten charges came spiralling down, exploding immediately above the U-boat.

Walker's judgement was unerring, and the effect of the powerful charges exploding close to the U-boat was catastrophic. The shock blew the main fuses on the switchboard, started a fire in the control room, and put both electric motors out of action. Gauge glasses were shattered, all lights went out, and a bank of compressed air bottles burst, adding to the confusion reigning. When one of the frames of the pressure hull fractured, and water spurted in, shock gave way to panic. U-574's engineer officer, Leutnant (Ing) Lorenz was of the firm opinion that the boat was doomed, and demanded that Gengelbach surface before they were all condemned to death on the bottom. Gengelbach thought otherwise, and a fierce row ensued between the two officers.

Eventually, Lorenz won the argument, and Gengelbach ordered his crew to don lifejackets and blow tanks. Slowly, for there was little compressed air left, U-574 began to rise. She reached the surface only to be bathed in the light of spectacular display of starshell and snowflake fired by HG 76's escorts. As soon as the conning tower was clear of the water, Gengelbach called for full ahead on the diesels, his intention being to escape on the surface. Unfortunately for him, *Stork* was only 200 yards away, and bent on revenge. Commander Walker's log reads:

As I went in to ram he ran away from me and turned to port. I followed and I was surprised to find later that I had turned three complete circles, the U-boat turning continuously to port just inside Stork's turning circle at only two or three knots slower than me. I kept her illuminated with snowflakes and fired at her with the four-inch guns until they could not be sufficiently depressed.

161

After this the guns' crews were reduced to fist shaking and roaring curses at an enemy who several times seemed to be a matter of feet away rather than yards.

A burst of 0.5 machine-gun fire was let off when these could bear, but the prettiest shooting was made by my First Lieutenant, Lieut. G.T.S. Gray, DSC, RN, with a stripped Lewis gun from over the top of the bridge screen. He quickly reduced the conning tower to a mortuary. No men were seen to leave the U-boat although they must have jumped some time judging from the position in which we found the survivors later.

Contrary to the latter entry in Walker's log, one of U-574's petty officers taken prisoner stated that although the conning tower was raked by machine-gun fire, no one was hit as they jumped overboard. This prisoner also said – and his statement was backed by others – that Dietrich Gengelbach made no attempt to save himself. While his crew were abandoning ship, he disappeared down the conning tower hatch, and perished with U-574. It was also stated that Lieutnant (Ing) Lorenz shot himself after carrying out Gengelbach's orders to open the valves to scuttle the boat.

Before she sank, U-574 suffered the indignity of being rammed by *Stork*. The sloop hit the U-boat a glancing blow forward of the conning tower, rolling her over. As *Stork* pulled clear, Walker dropped a pattern of depth charges set to the shallowest setting blowing the U-boat apart. It was a brilliant and successful spur-of-the-moment attack, but it cost *Stork* dear. The collision with the U-boat caused serious damage to the sloop's bows, bending them sideways, and put her Asdic dome out of action. For the remainder of the voyage *Stork* would do no more U-boat chasing.

Having disposed of the U-574, Walker's next thought was to search for survivors from *Stanley*, if any existed. But as *Stork* began to move away from the area, voices were heard calling in English. Walker being of the opinion that no one could have survived the sinking of the U-boat, assumed that it must be *Stanley's* men in the water. He hove to and dropped his boats. Five men were pulled from the water, while the corvette *Samphire* picked up another thirteen, but all eighteen men proved to be survivors from U-574. Those who were saved later said that twenty-six men had drowned, some being so panic stricken that they forgot to inflate their lifejackets, while others were blown to pieces by *Stork's* depth charges.

As soon as the German survivors were aboard, Walker took *Stork* at full speed to the estimated position of *Stanley's* wreck. Given the intensity of the explosion and subsequent fire on board, there seemed little hope that anyone could have survived, but as *Stork* approached the area cries for help were heard. Walker's boats found twenty-five men in the water, all that remained of HMS *Stanley's* crew of 145, which included twenty-six survivors from the aircraft carrier *Ark Royal*, sunk in the Mediterranean in early November. One of *Stanley's* survivors died later on board *Stork.*

The Board of Inquiry into the loss of HMS *Stanley*, held at Devonport in January 1942, concluded that it was highly likely that many of the survivors in the water were killed when *Stork* dropped her first pattern of depth charges close to them. Their deaths were unintentional and regrettable, but served to illustrate Walker's determination to kill U-boats, even when there was a possibility that some of his own men might also lose their lives.

The story of U-574 did not end there. Just before dawn on 22 December, *Deptford* and *Stork* were in collision, *Deptford* striking Walker's ship on the port side of her quarter deck. The damage to either ship was not great, but *Deptford's* stem sliced into a cabin containing the five German prisoners from U-574. Two of them were crushed to death. Only sixteen men of the boat's crew of forty-four survived to see the war out in a British prisoner of war camp.

While Stork and a substantial part of HG 76's escort force were preoccupied with the sinking of U-574 and the rescue of the *Stanley* survivors, another member of the *Seeräuber* group, U-108, had penetrated the weakened screen around the convoy.

U-108, a Type IX B under the command of *Korvettenkapitän* Klaus Scholtz, sailed from Lorient on 9 December, and had made contact with HG 76 late in the afternoon of 16 December. Unlike the unfortunate U-574, she was a war-seasoned boat, on her fifth patrol, with a well experienced captain and crew. Commissioned by Klaus Scholtz in October 1940, she had already sunk eleven Allied ships totalling over 56,000 tons, her most recent victim being the 4751-ton Portuguese steamer *Cassequel*, sent to the bottom only five days earlier. That Scholtz had deliberately sunk a neutral ship sailing with all her lights on was indicative of the ruthlessness with which Dönitz's U-boats were now prosecuting the war at sea.

Scholtz approached HG 76 from the east at about 0400 on the 19th, and quickly sighted the escort carrier *Audacity*, which was outside the convoy on her night station, and zig-zagging at 14 knots. The high-sided flattop was clearly visible in the glare of the starshell and snowflake being fired in the hunt for U-574, as were the merchantmen beyond. Scholtz, who had only two torpedoes left on board, had intended to use them sparingly, sinking two merchant ships, if possible. An aircraft carrier, however, was a prime target that warranted a full salvo.

Trimmed well down, and keeping a weather eye on what appeared to be a corvette hovering between the carrier and the convoy, Scholtz came up on *Audacity* on her starboard quarter. This was the dark hour before the dawn, with no moon, and an overcast sky. The carrier, not being equipped with radar, was completely unaware of the approach of her attacker.

At 2000 yards, Scholtz lined up his sights on *Audacity*'s engine room, allowed the necessary deflection, and fired both remaining torpedoes. The stopwatch clicked, the count began. But when the estimated running time for the torpedoes had elapsed, and the British carrier was still afloat and continuing with her lazy zig-zag pattern, Scholtz reluctantly conceded that he had missed. Contrary to his assumption, however, his torpedoes were not entirely wasted.

When, at the Commodore's Conference prior to sailing from Gibraltar, his ship had been allocated No.11 in the convoy, Captain Walter Ross was far from pleased. At No.11, leading ship of the port outside column, the 2869-ton *Ruckinge* would be first in line for the torpedoes of the U-boats as they came in from seaward. She was well armed – exceptionally so for a non-descript Cardiff tramp – mounting a 4-inch gun aft, a 12-pounder HA/LA on the poop, two Hotchkiss machine-guns amidships, and no less than four Lewis guns on the bridge. She also carried three depth charges aft, although at her top speed of 10 knots she would be in danger of blowing her own stern off should she ever dare to drop them. But for all this formidable array of armament, and the six DEMS gunners carried to maintain and man the guns, the *Ruckinge* remained a slow-moving, slow to manoeuvre, merchant ship. She was a target not to be missed.

The *Ruckinge*, owned by Constants (South Wales) Ltd., had loaded at various Biscay ports, arriving at Gibraltar with 820 tons of chemicals, 620 tons of timber, 638 tons of foodstuffs and 51 tons of base metal on board. Her initial destination was Oban, where she expected to pick up a convoy bound for East Coast ports. In addition to her crew of thirty-eight, which included the six DEMS gunners, the *Ruckinge* also had three passengers on board – two survivors landed in Gibraltar from another ship, and one stowaway.

Captain Ross was on the bridge of the *Ruckinge* as the dawn approached. His attention was focused on events happening astern, where the sky was lit up by the starshell and snowflake fired by Walker's ships as, having depth charged U-574 to the surface, they went in for the kill. The weather was improving, with the promise of a fine day, and Ross was not alone in speculating that perhaps the worst was over for HG 76; Lisbon was abeam, with only 800 miles to go to the Western Approaches. But Ross was also aware that in a little over forty-eight hours they would be crossing the mouth of the Bay of Biscay. There they would be within easy reach of the U-boats bases on the Atlantic coast of France, and less than a couple of hours flying time for the *Focke-Wulf Condors*.

Ross was still surveying the situation astern when one of Klaus Scholtz's errant torpedoes found a target in the rust-streaked hull of the *Ruckinge*, penetrating her thin plating and exploding in her boiler room with a muffled boom like the sound of distant thunder. Captain Ross later recorded:

After the torpedo had struck the ship I do not remember anything until I found myself on my back on the bridge. A lot of water was thrown on to the bridge, but I do not know if there was a flame. All the watertight doors were closed at the time...Everything on the bridge was shattered and the concrete protection (around the wheelhouse) collapsed. I scrambled into the wheelhouse but could not switch on the electric lights, and even the oil lamp had been smashed by the explosion.

Immediately the ship listed to port and began to settle slowly. The bunker hatches were blown off, the doors of the accommodation were smashed off their hinges and the furniture in the saloon wrecked...

The devastation in the *Ruckinge*'s engine room was even greater. The blast from the explosion cracked the boilers, filling the space with scalding steam, while the sea poured in through the jagged hole in the ship's side. The three stokers on watch were forty-three-year-old David Norwood, veteran of the trenches in the First World War, a 16-year-old trainee named Townsley, both from the Scottish port of Ardrossan, and an unnamed Welshman. They all died in the devastating explosion that suddenly ripped apart their warm enclosed world in the quiet hours of that morning. It later transpired that the three men would not normally have been on watch below at the time. They were standing in for three others, who had ended their night ashore in Gibraltar hopelessly drunk, and were still languishing in jail on the Rock.

Captain Ross, having recovered from the trauma of the attack, made a quick assessment of the situation, and came to the conclusion that his ship was severely damaged, and probably sinking. She was stopped and listing heavily, slowly falling astern of the other ships. With the escorts busy elsewhere, there seemed to Ross to be a high probability that the *Ruckinge* would be given the coup de grâce by the enemy before the day was much older. He ordered the boats to be lowered, abandoned the ship, and pulled clear, intending to reboard when daylight came. Two hours later, Ross and the thirteen men in his boat were picked up by HMS *Stork*, while General Steam's *Finland* rescued the remaining twenty-five in the other lifeboat.

The *Ruckinge* was still afloat when Ross reached the deck of the *Stork*, which prompted Commander Walker to raise the question of reboarding the steamer. When Ross explained that his ship's boilers were wrecked and her engine room flooded, Walker realised the futility of going back, and ordered the corvette *Samphire* to sink the *Ruckinge* by gunfire.

Discounting the *Empire Barracuda*, the *Ruckinge* had been the first merchantman to be sunk in the *Seeräuber* pack's attack on HG 76; one too many, of course, in Johnny Walker's book. But, on the other hand, Dönitz had sacrificed three of his U-boats in the process of ending the voyaging of one Bristol Channel tramp. At a time when the U-boats were sinking thirty Allied ships a month in the Atlantic, this was a major victory, and a vindication of Walker's unorthodox methods.

Perhaps fortuitously for HG 76, the *Seeräuber* boats lost contact following the sinking of the *Ruckinge*, and the convoy enjoyed a few hours of blessed peace in which to recover from the mayhem of the night. But at first light on the 20th Dönitz's Condors were back in the air and searching. They found the convoy without much difficulty, two of these great four-engined predators appearing on the northern horizon while a quick breakfast was being prepared in ships' galleys throughout the convoy.

As soon as the Condors were sighted, *Audacity* launched two Martlets, piloted by Sub. Lieutenants Brown and Lamb. Brown took one of the FWs unawares, meeting it head-on with his guns blazing. Caught like a rabbit in the headlights of an approaching car, the German pilot desperately tried to avoid the hail of bullets from Brown's four .50 calibre guns. It seemed that he might succeed, but then the Condor staggered, banked sharply, and with black smoke pouring from her fuselage, dived into the sea.

Sub. Lieutenant Lamb took on the other Condor, but its pilot had no stomach for the fight. Before the Martlet was within range, he turned tail and escaped in the clouds. The damage was done, however. As the German plane fled northwards, its wireless operator was heard tapping out the convoy's position to Lorient.

During the afternoon, another Condor appeared, and began to shadow the convoy. *Audacity* once again sent up the Martlets, one of which, piloted by Sub. Lieutenant Sleigh, attacked the *Focke-Wulf* from astern, but failed to shoot it down. Taking a leaf out of Brown's book, Sleigh tried the head-on approach, which again was successful. The Condor went down, but as it went it came near to taking the Martlet with it. Sleigh had been so close to the bomber when he pulled up that his tail wheel that he scraped the enemy plane, carrying away its wireless aerial.

Audacity's Martlets were in the air again at dusk, and one reported seeing a U-boat on the surface 15 miles to the west. Walker sent *Deptford*, *Marigold* and *Convolvulus* to intercept, but by the time they reached the area of the sighting, the U-boat had disappeared.

The U-boat in question was Harald Gelhaus' U-107, guided onto HG 76 by the Condors. Before he was forced to dive, Gelhaus had reported the convoy to be in a position 435 miles due west of Cape Roca, and steaming north at 8 knots. Lorient contacted U-71, U-108, U-567 and U-751, and ordered them to home in on U-107.

An entry for the day in Admiral Dönitz's War Diary reads:

At 2000 U-107 made contact in 9225. The boats of Group Seeräuber *were ordered to operate on the basis of this report, mean course then being 330°, enemy speed approx 6–8 knots. According to a report at 2111 U-107 was driven off again immediately after sighting the convoy. At 0315 on the 19th U-574 made contact. T 0455 U-108 came up with the convoy in square CF 6815. At 0759 U-108 reported last convoy position in 6815 at 0620 course 340°, speed 7 knots and a further ship sunk, a third probably sunk (U-108 observed a flash on one ship after a two torpedo salvo and a large black smoke column, and heard two detonations). Since then there has been no contact. Although all her torpedoes were expended U-108 was ordered to maintain contact. At 1526 U-127 and U-434 were asked for their position. No report up to now.*

CHAPTER FOURTEEN

The Final Act

A t daybreak on 20 December, HG 76 was 400 miles west of Oporto, and on a north-easterly course for the Western Approaches. After the excitement of the previous night, the convoy had tightened its ranks in anticipation of more attacks as it drew nearer to Biscay. Commander Walker, pacing the bridge of the *Stork* restlessly, realised that now, more than ever, the odds were weighted in the enemy's favour. His two best destroyers, *Blankney* and *Exmoor* were on their way back to Gibraltar to refuel, *Stanley* had gone, left lying on the bottom nearly 200 miles astern, and his own ship *Stork was* damaged and severely restricted in her ability to fight. Walker feared for his convoy, and his fears were well grounded. Had he been able to read the entry in Admiral Donitz's War Diary for the day concerning HG 76, he would have been even more worried.

Donitz wrote:

Müller (U67) reported at 1120 a convoy in square 2965. At the same time Scholtz (U108) and Gelhaus (U107) also reported the convoy in sight. Last report of contact from U108 was at 2029, convoy being in square 2832, course NE. At 2230 U107 reported contact lost, she suspected northerly course of the convoy since she passed 2 escorts at 2118, course North, in square 2576. No further contact up to the morning.

Three U-boats were on the fringes of HG 76, and to replace those sunk by Walker's ships, Dönitz had now called in three more. U-71, U-567 and U-751, all commanded by experienced men, would soon be in position to join in the attack.

The Condors, the eyes of the U-boats, were never far away, hovering out of gun range, their coded Morse signals crowding the ether. *Audacity's* three Martlets did their best, one of chasing a Condor for nearly 60 miles, before being forced to turn back for fear of running out of fuel. During the afternoon, another Martlet sighted two U-boats on the surface right ahead of the convoy and, forewarned, the ships were able to make a radical alteration of course to avoid the danger.

Thanks largely to the vigilance and aggressive patrolling of *Audacity's* aircraft, at least one of which was in the air throughout the daylight hours, the U-boats lost all contact with the convoy, and so lost the advantage. The night then passed without incident, allowing a few hours refreshing sleep for men whose endurance had been sorely tested over the preceding days and nights.

Sunday 21 December opened fine and clear, with a fresh north-easterly breeze ruffling the tops of the waves. The weather was marred only by a rising swell, indicating a blow far out in the Atlantic. This was not good news for *Audacity*. Obliged to head into the wind for her Martlets to take off and land, she would be beam-on to the swell, and rolling heavily much of the time. It was not a good day for flying.

The first patrol took off as soon as it was light enough, and began to search around the fringes of the convoy. Within minutes, Sub.Lieutenant Brown, was reporting back that he had sighted two U-boats were on the surface at 25 miles. The boats were alongside one another, and appeared to be transferring stores or spares. Walker dispatched *Deptford* and three corvettes to investigate, but by the time they reached the spot, the U-boats had dived out of sight. No Asdic contacts were obtained.

At 1130, a patrolling Martlet spotted two more U-boats skulking to the west, and the corvettes *Convolvulus* and *Marigold* were ordered to take care of them. Once again the U-boats evaded their pursuers. Shortly afterwards, a Martlet sighted another U-boat 10 miles off on the port bow which appeared to be keeping pace with the convoy. At 1500, yet another was discovered astern, discreetly shadowing the ships. Walker was not surprised when he received a signal from the Admiralty warning of at least six U-boats believed to be concentrated around the convoy. Dönitz's War Diary confirmed much of this:

Contact was again made by U-108 at 1254 on 21st. At 1352 U-67 also reported convoy in BE 8788…Requests for position check showed that U-108 confirmed the position and suspected possibility of a part-convoy. At 1740 U-567 sighted the convoy in 8755, last report was at 1908, square 8728, course 020°. At 1600 U-67 was forced by an aircraft to submerge, subsequently depth charge pursuit by destroyer, type 'Eskimo'.

HG 76 was now steering directly for the North Channel, Walker having decided that as the enemy had the convoy well targeted there was little point in attempting to fool him. He did, however, consider it worth while confusing the U-boats by staging a mock battle. As soon as darkness fell, the convoy made a bold alteration of course to starboard, while *Stork* and two corvettes carried on to the north-east. When the main body of the convoy was well clear, the three escorts created a diversion on the horizon by firing snowflakes and starshell and engaging in a great deal of excited R/T chatter. The whole effect of the diversion was spoiled by an unidentified merchantman, believing she was under attack, firing snowflake and bathing the escaping convoy in light.

One of the U-boats searching for HG 76 was U-567. A Type VII C, commissioned in April 1941, U-567 was on her second war patrol, with nothing to show for her efforts but one merchantman of 3485 tons sunk. She was, however, now sailing under a new and highly successful commander. Engelbert Endrass, an ex-merchant service officer, had been First Lieutenant to the legendary Günther Prien when, shortly after the outbreak of war, he took U-47 into Scapa Flow and sank the battleship *Royal Oak*. Promoted to command in U-46, Endrass sank 137,000 tons of shipping in eighteen months, thus earning himself the coveted Knights Cross with Oak Leaves, before taking over U-567. Now that Prien, Schepke and Kretschmer were gone, *Kapitänleutnant* Endrass had become one of Admiral Dönitz's top aces. *THEY MET A DEPTH CHG. WITH THEIR NAME ON IT!*

Seeräuber having suffered the unprecedented loss of three boats in six days, Dönitz was looking to Endrass to restore the fortunes of the group. As a newcomer to the operation, Endrass had only a vague idea of the position and movements of HG 76, but the luck that seemed to follow the commander throughout his career was with him again that night. While Walker was away staging his mock battle, U-567 had been unwittingly overtaking the convoy, which was then invisible in the darkness. When the nervous merchantman fired his snowflake rockets and turned night into day, Engelbert Endrass was presented with a whole convoy of prospective targets.

The rear ship of the centre column of HG 76 was the 3324-ton steamer *Annavore*, one of the five Norwegian-flag ships in the convoy. The *Annavore*, commanded by Captain Gerhart Reichelt, was owned by Gunnstein Stray & Son of Farsund, but had been under British control since the fall of Norway in June 1940. She carried a total complement of thirty-eight, which included four British DEMS gunners, and two passengers. Her cargo consisted of 4,800 tons of iron ore, loaded in Huelva for Aberdeen.

No one aboard the *Annavore* saw U-567 creeping up on her from astern, neither were the tracks of Endrass's torpedoes spotted as they sped towards the ship. The first, and only, warning of danger came when the ship heeled over under the force of an explosion as a torpedo slammed into her side. The sea rushed into her half-empty holds, she lost her reserve buoyancy, and dragged down by weight of her ore cargo, she sank within minutes. Only four men, Able Seamen Leonard Karlsen and Knut O. Johannessen, Stoker Johan Malmin, and Trimmer Torleif Værøy, survived. All were found drifting half-conscious in the sea of oil and debris left by the sinking ship and picked up by one of the escorting corvette.

Walker's instinctive reaction to the torpedoing of the *Annavore* was to order his escorts to fire starshell and snowflake, which in turn prompted the merchant ships to join in the firework display. As a result, HG 76 and the sea around it was again bathed in brilliant light, offering an open invitation to any shadowing U-boat to pick a target.

It is estimated that as many as eight U-boats were now assembled around HG 76, one of which was the newly arrived U-751, under the command of Gerhard Bigalk. U-751 was approaching on the convoy's starboard quarter when the lights went on.

Thirty-three-year-old *Kapitänleutnant* Bigalk's career to date had been far from conventional. After a number of years as an officer in merchant ships, he joined the Naval Air Service as a midshipman in 1934, subsequently flying twenty-one combat missions in the Spanish Civil War. In November 1939 he transferred to the U-boat-arm, reaching command in January 1941, when he took the newly commissioned U-751 out of Wihelmshaven. Thereafter he had not enjoyed much success, his only notable triumph being the sinking of the British steamer *Saint Lindsay* in June. Now, presented with such an array of easy targets, Bigalk was spoilt for choice. Then something special caught his eye.

Since sailing from Gibraltar, a nightly routine had been agreed by Commander Walker and Commander MacKendrick for the protection of the vulnerable escort carrier *Audacity* during the hours of darkness. At dusk, she would either move inside the convoy, or take up a position close on its port side, where she was protected by one of the corvettes. As soon as it was light enough, she would then steam clear of the ships and head up into the wind to fly off her dawn patrol.

Before dark on the 21st MacKendrick decided he would take station on the starboard side of the convoy. Walker's Battle Report stated:

For the last three nights, Audacity with one corvette had zig-zagged independently well clear of the convoy. Before dark tonight she had asked for a corvette and proposed to operate on the starboard side of the convoy. I regretfully refused the corvette since I had only four escorts immediately around the convoy. I also suggested that she should take station to port of the convoy since I anticipated any attack from the starboard side. Audacity replied that the convoy's alterations of course to port would inconvenience her and eventually she went off to starboard alone.

There seems to have been some friction between Walker and MacKendrick on this occasion. The two men were equal in rank, but Mackendrick's appointment as commander predated that of Walker, which theoretically made MacKendrick the senior man. In which case, Walker was unable to overrule him, and at dusk *Audacity* took up a position 8–10 miles off the starboard beam of HG 76, zig-zagging and alone.

It may be that being so far removed from the convoy, *Audacity's* presence was not revealed by the display of fireworks prompted by the sinking of the *Annavore*. However, it just so happened that at the time only one of the carrier's aircraft was serviceable, and that needed a new starter motor before it would be ready to fly the dawn patrol. Being a 'Woolworth' carrier, *Audacity* had no hangar deck, and any repairs to aircraft had to be carried out on the open flight deck. This was being done by mechanics using shaded blue torches.

Perhaps it was one of the flickering blue lights that caught Gerhard Bigalk's eye, or being an ex-Air Force man, it may have been the distinctive shape of the carrier seen in the glow of the starshell that attracted his attention. Whatever the reason, Bigalk had found a target worthy of his torpedoes. He broke away from the convoy and sheered off to starboard. *Audacity,* not being equipped with radar, had no warning of the U-boat's approach.

The carrier was steaming at 14 knots, and executing a wide zig-zag pattern, making a 60-degree alteration, first to port and then to starboard, and maintaining a steady course for eight minutes between each alteration. Lieutenant David Price had the watch on the bridge. Like Gerhard Bigalk, he was an ex-merchant seaman, well experienced in the ways of ships and the sea. As U-751 moved in for the kill, Price was in the port wing of *Audacity's* bridge, his attention largely focused on mayhem taking place in the rear of the convoy, and not a little concerned that his ship might be silhouetted against the night sky by the pyrotechnics. Also on the bridge were the midshipman of the watch, the helmsman, Chief Yeoman of Signals T. Pearson, and two signalmen.

No one on *Audacity's* bridge saw Bigalk's torpedo approaching. The alarm was given by Able Seaman Bailey, on lookout in the port after Oerlikon platform, which projected out over the ship's side. Bailey saw the feathered track streaking in from the port quarter and lunged for the bridge telephone. His warning came too late.

Leading Air Mechanic Bruce Burgess, supervising repairs on the flight deck, also saw the torpedo:

Some time after 2100 hours I stopped for a breather and lent on the port side windshields amidships. I looked down at the sea and saw the trail of a torpedo heading straight towards me. I shouted "Torpedo, portside amidships!", and then ran to the Martlet that I had been working on and clasped the starboard wheel but was overtaken by a rush of water from the initial strike. Something, flying past, hit me on the head.

The torpedo struck *Audacity* on her port side aft of the engine room, in what had been her No.4 cargo hold in her days of commercial trading. The explosion was barely audible on the bridge, but the damage done was catastrophic. Lieutenant Commander (E) S.L. Parker, *Audacity's* chief engineer, was in the engine room at the time:

The generator room was flooded. I went down to the lower platform. There was about 2 ft of water and I could see the water rushing from the tunnel entrance. There had been a watertight door in the bulkhead of the tunnel, but they had taken the door out at Blyth and put a new bulkhead in further aft, because we had a pump inside the door. The watertight bulkhead had carried away. The ship's side connections had been put into cemented boxes and I looked round to see if there was any water coming in through the boxes. There was no water coming in from there.

By the way the water was rushing in it looked to me as if it was the tunnel bulkhead that had gone. One other thing it might have been – No.7 tank may have been holed. The ship kept perfectly upright except that she started to go down by the stern right away, which would have been improbable if she had been hit in the bomb room. The Second Engineer told me that he had instructions to flood the bomb room, but he could not operate the valves. All the gear had been bent.

174

Audacity was crippled, her engine room flooded, her steering gear smashed, but she was still afloat, and on an even keel. There was no panic; men stood to their posts, damage parties were already at work. Within minutes they were reporting to Commander MacKendrick that although the ship was badly hit, she was in no immediate danger of sinking. However, after reporting his predicament to *Stork*, MacKendrick ordered his Number One, Lieutenant Commander Walter Higham, to lower the boats to the water and launch the Carley floats. In the event of having to abandon ship, MacKendrick wanted to give his men a fair chance of survival. When *Stork* signalled that the corvettes *Convolvulus*, *Marigold* and *Samphire* were coming to his aid, the Commander decided to await their arrival before abandoning ship.

And that might have been that. But, at 2110, *Marigold*, leading the rescue ships, was unable to see *Audacity* in the darkness, and requested that the carrier fire a rocket to indicate her position. Unfortunately, while the rocket might guide in the corvettes, it must undoubtedly have been seen by other eyes, namely those of Gerhard Bigalk, who was awaiting the opportunity to deliver the coup de grâce.

Chief Yeoman of Signals Pearson stated:

The Captain told me to send a signal saying: 'I will fire a rocket at 2145. That signal was made just after 2130 and the Navigating Officer gave me the ship's chronometer to check the time with, and I fired the rocket. After I had fired the rocket I looked out on the starboard quarter and I saw a little blue light calling us up, so I gave one of the signalmen a pair of glasses and the other a lamp to answer the corvettes. As they were answering I heard 'two torpedoes approaching' from the flight deck. I saw the submarine almost on the beam about 3½ to 4 cables. I could see two torpedo tracks coming towards the ship, so I jumped down into the starboard bridge because I thought the flight deck would crumble, which it did.

Audacity, dead in the water and unable to manoeuvre, clearly visible in the light of her own rocket, was an unmissable target, but Bigalk was leaving nothing to chance. He brought U-751 in so close to the carrier that she came under fire from *Audacity*'s Oerlikons, which were still manned. This was a futile gesture, for the two torpedoes seen by Yeoman Pearson were racing in. One struck the *Audacity* beneath the bridge house, and the other went home abaft the bridge. The combined effect of the double explosion broke her in two.

HMS *Audacity's* remaining time was now numbered in minutes, and Commander MacKendrick was forced to give the order to abandon ship. Chief Yeoman of Signals Pearson again:

I remained on the bridge with the Captain. He sent everybody away. The Captain had a rubber dinghy. He told me to throw it into the water, and the Captain and Mr Strickland (Gunnery Officer) joined me. We got off away from the ship and we did not see anybody else. It was a quarter of an hour after everybody had gone before we left the ship. She broke in two and each piece came out and then sank and broke away. The stern portion seemed to stand on its fore end for a moment before it sank. Just as she was going I noticed a blue flash in the after part and felt a small explosion, as if something had blown up inside the ship.

There was one corvette coming in our direction. This was only six yards away, and I tried to call her, but there were so many people shouting that she passed us twice and we were in the water for nearly 1¾ hours when we saw one corvette, which happened to be Pentstemon, *and as we drifted along I got hold of a line and passed it to the Captain and I caught the next line. I was still holding on to the dinghy with one arm and could only hold the rope with the other. I was hauled up by one arm and as soon as I left the water I remember nothing more.*

Using his own initiative, Lieutenant Commander J. Byron, RNR brought *Pentstemon* into the rescue operation. The cutter was dropped and sent away to look for survivors, while Byron manoeuvred to present a lee for the boat. It was then that Commander MacKendrick was seen in the water, struggling to stay afloat. MacKendrick was quite obviously exhausted, and nearing the end of his tether. To make matters worse, he was on the weather side of the corvette, which was rolling her gunwales under in the heavy swell. *Pentstemon's* First Lieutenant, Lieutenant Williams, who was supervising operations on deck, realised that MacKendrick was in danger of being sucked in under the keel of the corvette, and jumped into the water to help him. Williams managed to get a rope around the Commander, who was now unconscious, and signalled the deck to haul on the rope. *Pentstemon* chose that moment to give a particularly heavy roll, and the rope was snatched out of the hands of the men on deck. Williams was pulled from the water, but Commander MacKendrick drifted away. He was never seen again.

HMS *Audacity*'s brief career with the Royal Navy came to an end at 2210 convoy time on 21 December 1941, when, broken and waterlogged, she sank into a watery grave 420 miles north-east of the Azores. After she went down, the search for survivors continued, but hampered by the darkness and the fact that *Audacity*'s crew had not been issued with lifejacket lights, none were found. Out of aircraft carrier's total complement of 400, Commander Douglas MacKendrick, eight of his officers, and sixty-three men were lost.

There was a payment to be made for *Audacity*. At 0040 on the 22nd, as she was carefully combing the area for survivors, the sloop *Deptford* surprised a U-boat on the surface. *Deptford* fired starshell, which brought *Stork* racing to the spot, but the U-boat – which was later identified as Engelbert Endrass' U-567 – had by then dived. Walker then began a painstaking Asdic search, which went on for more than two hours without success. Eventually, when even Walker himself must have been on the point of giving up, *Deptford* had a firm contact, and moved in to drop pattern of depth charges. The charges must have exploded right on top of U-567. Only a patch of oil spreading on the water remained to mark the graves of Engelbert Endrass and his crew of forty-six.

The night was not yet over. U-67 had penetrated the screen, and Günther Müller-Stöckheim had his sights on the CAM ship *Darwin*, whose catapult launched fighter aircraft could yet play a vital part in the defence of HG 76. Walker's escorts were everywhere, dashing to and fro, and Müller-Stöckheim was nervous. He fired too soon, and his fan of torpedoes went wide of the *Darwin*. Misfortune followed on misfortune as the starshell went up again, and U-67 found herself suddenly bathed in light. Müller-Stöckheim dived at once, but the U-boat had been seen by the corvette *Rhododendron*, which immediately attacked. *Deptford* joined in, and over the next two hours forty-one depth charges were dropped, some of them very close to U-67. She escaped, but not without suffering serious damage. At 0430, Müller-Stöckheim brought his boat to the surface again, well astern of the convoy. Most of his instruments had been smashed, and the boat was leaving a wide oil slick in her wake. It was time for U-67 to go home.

At sunrise on the 22nd, HG 76 was less than 500 miles from British waters, but the eight days spent at sea constantly under attack by U-boats and *Focke Wulf*s were beginning to take their toll on the ships. The convoy had lost two merchant ships and their precious cargoes, a destroyer and an aircraft carrier, and in return had sunk four U-boats. The two sloops,

Deptford and *Stork,* had suffered considerable, though not serious, damage, and all escorts were low on depth charges. Moreover, there was an air of total exhaustion hanging over all ships, naval and merchant, whose crews had been without proper rest since leaving Gibraltar. But perhaps the greatest weakness suffered by HG 76 was the loss of HMS *Audacity* and her gallant covey of Martlets, which had provided such valuable early warning of the approach of U-boats.

And still the enemy kept coming. During that day, two more boats made contact; Walter Flachsenberg's U-71 and Ulrich Folker's U-125. Both these boats, U-71 on her fifth war patrol, and U-125 on her third, were yet to sink their first enemy ship. They had been on their way across the Atlantic to American waters when they were diverted to HG 76, and were anxious to join in the chase. Unfortunately for them, their approach to the convoy coincided with the arrival of the destroyers *Vanquisher* and *Witch*, sent out to reinforce Commander Walker's escort force. When Flachsenberg and Folker sighted the convoy, it was surrounded by a screen of escorts they could not hope to penetrate.

On the morning of the 23rd, HG 76 came within range of Liberators of Coastal Command based in southern England, which then maintained patrols over the convoy throughout the daylight hours. For the U-boats their foray against Convoy HG 76 was over. The damaged U-67 was ordered to return to Lorient for repairs, while the remaining boats of *Seeräuber* were sent to other hunting grounds. Admiral Dönitz noted in his War Diary:

The success achieved from the convoy up to now is slight. One aircraft carrier, 3 ships, also 2 tankers, which, however, were shot up in the first night from a group separated from the convoy. As against this, the loss of 4, possibly 5 boats. The weather conditions were also very unfavorable; very little wind no seaway therefore favorable conditions for location. The chances of losses are greater than the prospects of success. No contact with the convoy. Therefore the decision has been made to break off operations.

The men of HG 76 missed their Christmas at home, but when the 25 December dawned they were safe in British waters, with the west coast of Ireland in sight to starboard and friendly aircraft overhead. They had won and the U-boats had lost, the victory due, in the main, to Commander Johnny Walker's aggressive defence of the convoy. The instructions he had issued to his ships read: 'Our object is to kill, and all officers must fully develop the spirit of vicious offensive. No matter how many convoys we may shepherd through in safety, we shall have failed unless we slaughter U-boats. All energies must be bent to this end.' Walker's methods were unorthodox, completely uncompromising, even bordering on brutal, but they were to change the face of war in the North Atlantic for ever.

The efforts of those who had brought Convoy HG 76 home were not appreciated by everyone. Leading Air Mechanic Bruce Burgess, who survived the loss of the carrier *Audacity,* had a bitter tale to tell:

...Eventually reaching Lee-on-Solent we reported to the OOD who promptly told us that the galley was closed but that we were being put on a charge for being out of the rig of the day! He was some snotty-nosed subbie with some obscure degree in (say) Egyptology. There are many RNVR officers with a lot of enemy action experience behind them but there were also a lot of useless idiots who had only obtained their commission by patronage.

Petty Officer Dick Turner of HMS *Vetch* summed up the stress suffered by men sailing in a convoy:

The uncertainty of convoy work was extremely wearing on the nerves. During the passage it was impossible to grab more than a couple of hour's doze. There was no opportunity for any restful sleep – the bell that announced 'Action Stations' could, and would, ring at any time of the day and night.

This was brought home to me when we were in Liverpool following a convoy passage. For the first time in some weeks I thought that I could get a decent night's sleep. However, in the morning when the alarm bell went off I leapt out of bed, grabbed my clothes, dressed and headed for the door when I was interrupted by my wife saying, 'What on earth are you doing, Dick?' In my mind I was still on the ship and the Action Stations alarm had just sounded. It had become a completely automatic reaction and was a sign of the high state of nervous tension in which we all lived our lives in those days.

CHAPTER FIFTEEN

Epilogue

Harassed by U-boats and *Focke-Wulf* Condors throughout the passage, both north and south, the Gibraltar convoys also had to contend with undeclared, though no less dangerous, enemies. Ostensibly neutral, Spain was undeniably hostile to Britain, while her neighbour Portugal choose to straddle the fence throughout the war. Gibraltar Bay was under constant surveillance by agents of the *Abwehr*, Germany's intelligence service, based in nearby Algeciras. They kept watch on the movements of all Allied shipping in and out of Gibraltar, reporting to the German Ambassador in Madrid, who in turn passed their observations on to Berlin. There were other *Abwehr* agents in Spanish Morocco, who regularly reported the progress of the convoys through the Straits.

That the U-boats were receiving stores and fuel in Vigo Bay from the supply ship *Bessel* has already been mentioned. The *Bessel*, owned by the Neptune Steamship Company of Bremen, was said to have a crew of eighteen German naval personnel who wore civilian clothes, she did not fly a national flag, and had not moved from her anchorage since arriving soon after the commencement of hostilities in 1939. In her forward holds she carried provisions, and a large tank built into one of her after holds held diesel oil. A U-boat requiring stores or fuel would arrive off Vigo on a prearranged date, enter the bay at night, and heave-to 500 metres off the *Bessel* to await one of her boats coming alongside with instructions. She was then allowed to tie up alongside the supply ship. The transfer of stores and fuel usually took between five and six hours, during which time the U-boat's crew boarded the *Bessel* for a much-needed bath and a meal. The U-boat was required to sail again before daylight.

The Vigo operation was highly organised, carried out under the eyes of, and presumably with the blessing of, the Spanish authorities. A crew member from

U-574, who stated under interrogation that he had visited the *Bessel* at Vigo whilst serving in another boat, alleged the Master of the *Bessel* periodically scoured Spain for provisions, adopting the guise of a civilian corn chandler for such excursions. The Master was reputed to be in close contact with the Gestapo. Another prisoner declared that the German Ambassador to Spain was on board the *Bessel* when U-574 arrived for supplies. The main items transferred were fresh meat, vegetables and fruit. In addition, the prisoner stated that U-574 took on 100 cubic metres of fuel oil.

Portugal was Britain's oldest ally, the association between the two countries dating back to the Anglo-Portuguese Alliance of 1373. From the outbreak of war in 1939, although sympathetic to Britain's cause, the Portuguese Government maintained a policy of strict neutrality. When France fell in June 1940, and Britain faced the might of Germany alone, many hitherto friendly countries, Portugal amongst them, began to reconsider their options.

With the capture of the German Enigma machines from the weather ships *Munchen* and *Lauenberg* and U-110 in May and June 1941, for the first time Britain's codebreakers were able to accurately track the movements of U-boats. As the summer wore on, German radio traffic intercepted indicated that Dönitz was using the Portuguese administered Cape Verde Islands to supply his U-boats.

The Cape Verde Islands consist of an archipelago of ten islands and five islets lying 400 miles off the African mainland, and close to the main trade routes between Europe and the Cape of Good Hope. The islands were discovered in 1450 by Antonio Noli, a Genoese in the service of Portugal, and colonised by Portugal in 1462. For many years they were a major provisioning station for the sailing ships, but with the coming of steam they faded into insignificance again.

Tarafal Bay, lies on the southern side of San Antão, the westernmost of the Cape Verde Islands. An entry in the North Atlantic Memoir of 1879 reads:

This watering place of Terrafal Bay is one of the most convenient for the purpose amongst the Cape Verde Islands. The bay is spacious, and had a black sandy bottom. Vessels anchor in 20 fathoms, at three-quarters of a cable's length from the shore, sheltered from the N.E., and South winds and sea; and when the wind comes to the westward of South or North there is always, from the extreme high land, a calm in the bay, the wind never blowing home, but only occasioning a swell to set in.

From the high mountains over the bay a small stream descends, which is never dry; on the first level spot a large pond has been formed as a reservoir to receive the stream, with a sluice to conduct it to the sands between the flat and the beach, which is a gradual descent...

Tarafal Bay had changed little over the years, and in 1941 afforded an ideal rendezvous for U-boats operating against the Freetown and Gibraltar convoys,

In September 1941, U-111, a Type IX B commanded by *Kapitänleutnant* Wilhelm Kleinschmidt, was patrolling off the lonely St. Paul's Rocks, just north of the Equator. On the 20th, she sighted the 8474-ton British motor vessel *Cingalese Prince*, sailing unescorted from Bombay to Trinidad. The unsuspecting merchantman was despatched with a single torpedo.

While Kleinschmidt was stalking his prey, further north, off the Canary Islands, U-67 and U-68 were shadowing the northbound Freetown convoy SL 87. Karl-Freidrich Merten, in U-68, struck first, on the 22nd using his last remaining torpedo to sink the 5302-ton motor vessel *Silverbelle*. Günther Müller-Stöckheim, commanding U-67, followed up two days later by sending the 3753-ton steamer *St. Clair II* to the bottom.

Both Merten and Müller-Stöckheim then contacted Lorient requesting permission to return to Biscay. Although neither boat had been at sea for more than ten days, both commanders considered a return to base warranted, U-68 having used up all his torpedoes, while U-67 had a sick man on board.

Soon after U-67 sailed from Lorient, Müller-Stöckheim discovered that one of his radiomen had contracted VD while on a run ashore in France. Medically, this was not serious, but having a contagious disease at large in the cramped confines of a submarine was extremely bad for morale. Müller-Stöckheim wanted rid of the man as soon as possible.

Admiral Dönitz had no intention of allowing the boats to return to port after such short voyages, and he arranged for them to make a rendezvous in Tarafal Bay with U-111. Kleinschmidt had spare torpedoes and provisions on board, and having been at sea for six weeks, was due to return to Lorient within days. Before he set out for Biscay, he was ordered to meet U-68 in Tarafal Bay on the night of 27/28 September for the transfer of torpedoes. U-67 was instructed to enter the bay on the following night to hand over the sick man into Kleinschmidt's care.

Lorient's coded messages were intercepted and deciphered by Bletchley Park, and the British submarine HMS *Clyde*, which had recently left Gibraltar to patrol off the Canary Islands, was ordered to investigate.

HMS *Clyde,* commanded by 38-year-old Commander David Ingram, DSC, RN, was a large River-class submarine displacing 2,206 tons. She was armed with six 21-inch torpedo tubes and a 4-inch deck gun, and had a surface speed of 22 knots. Under Ingram's command, *Clyde* had distinguished herself in the Norwegian campaign by torpedoing the 26,000-ton German battleship *Gneisenau,* putting her out of action for six months.

Ingram arrived off Tarafal Bay just before midnight on 27 September, and not knowing what he might find inside, submerged before entering. Once inside the bay, he took a look around through his periscope, and was not surprised to see two submarines silhouetted against the shoreline. They were tied up alongside one another, and using shaded lights. U-111 and U-68 were engaged in the delicate task of manhandling torpedoes from one to the other.

Ingram decided to attack at once. He surfaced, and approached the enemy boats stealthily, his bow tubes ready to fire a full salvo. Unfortunately for Ingram, the Germans had lookouts posted, and they were alert. There was a commotion aboard the U-boats, the lights were extinguished, and they separated quickly, the outside boat turning to meet *Clyde* head-on.

The challenger was Wilhelm Kleinschmidt's U-111, and she seemed to be intent on ramming the British boat. Ingram took violent evasive action, and brought his deck gun to bear. Seeing this, Kleinschmidt crash-dived, and U-111 passed under *Clyde's* keel with only inches to spare as she fled out to sea.

Recovering from the shock of the near-collision, Ingram swung *Clyde* back on course, and fired his bow torpedoes at U-68. He was again frustrated, for Merten was already under way and diving. Ingram's torpedoes exploded harmlessly on shore, disturbing no one, except, perhaps, a group of Portuguese soldiers, who were said to be watching the proceedings from a safe distance.

Fearing an underwater attack, Ingram now submerged to listen with his hydrophones. He was unaware that the situation had been further complicated by the arrival of U-67. Müller-Stöckheim was twelve hours early for his appointment with U-111, but he decided to enter the bay. There were now four submarines in the vicinity of Tarafal Bay, and the resulting hydrophone effects must have been enough to make Müller-Stöckheim's hair stand on end. He surfaced to investigate.

Ingram brought *Clyde* to the surface at the same time, and there followed a deadly game of cat-and-mouse as the two submarines tried to ram each other. They were well-matched, circling each other like a pair of seasoned prize-fighters. Müller-Stöckheim had the advantage; U-67 being the smaller boat by 100 feet, and with a tighter turning circle than *Clyde*.

This bizarre contest, enacted in this remote island bay far out in the Atlantic was short-lived. Ingram saw an opportunity to ram, rang for emergency full speed, and charged at his German opponent. Müller-Stöckheim had anticipated this. He slipped inside *Clyde's* turning circle, and attempted to return the compliment. But as U-67 bore down on him, Ingram threw the helm hard over to starboard. As a result, U-67 struck *Clyde* only a glancing blow. The British submarine suffered superficial damage, whereas U-67's bow was badly buckled, three of her four bow tubes being unusable. Günther Müller-Stöckheim now had no other choice but to return to Lorient, where U-67 remained under repair for six weeks.

Lieutenant Commander Ingram reported the Tarafal Bay incident to the Admiralty, and the anti-submarine trawler HMS *Lady Shirley* was despatched from Gibraltar to search for the U-boats involved. The 472-ton *Lady Shirley*, commanded by Lieutenant Commander Arthur Callaway, RANVR, was an ex-Hull trawler with a top speed of 10 knots. She was armed with a 4-inch gun, two 0.5 calibre Vickers and two .303 Hotchkiss machine guns. She was equipped with Asdic, and carried a limited number of depth charges.

On 4 October, a week after Tarafal, the *Lady Shirley* was patrolling 300 miles west-south-west of Tenerife, when she surprised U-111 on the surface. Callaway opened fire on the U-boat with his 4-inch, but Kleinschmidt was already diving when the first shell landed.

Callaway was an anti-submarine specialist, and he soon had U-111 in his Asdic beam. He pounced, dropping a pattern of five depth charges directly over the U-boat. Several minutes later, much to Callaway's surprise, Kleinschmidt surfaced. It is not clear whether U-111 was damaged, or Kleinschmidt had decided he could outgun his insignificant looking opponent; U-111 was more than twice the size of the *Lady Shirley*, she had a surface speed of 18½ knots, and she mounted a 105mm deck gun, one 37mm and four 20mm canons.

U-111's superior armament came to nought when she fired her 105mm. In the rush to man the gun, the crew had forgotten to remove the watertight tampion from the barrel. The gun blew up, killing or wounding all those around it. This terrible accident took a lot of the fight out of the U-boat's crew, but they manned the 20mm guns, raking the *Lady Shirley's* bridge, killing one man and wounding three others.

Eventually, the trawler's heavy gun began to exact a grim toll, Wilhelm Kleinschmidt was killed, and those of his crew left uninjured decided that this was a fight they could not hope to win. They abandoned their guns, opened the vents, jumped over the side. Seeing that the U-boat was clearly finished, Callaway gave the order to cease fire. The battle had lasted just twenty-three minutes, ending in the destruction of another of Dönitz's grey wolves.

As 1941 drew to a close, records showed that in the first two years of the war Britain and her allies had lost nearly 9 million tons of merchant shipping. Most of this had gone to the U-boats, who were riding on the crest of a wave, virtually sinking at will. But the day of retribution had dawned with HG 76, sailing under the protection of Commander 'Johnny' Walker and his brave little band of sloops and corvettes. Walker's aggressive and unorthodox tactics had taken the U-boats by surprise, and they had suffered accordingly. The Battle of the Atlantic was by no means won, but the tide was on the turn.

The Last Voyage of the *Auditor*

An Extract from the Diary of Second Radio Officer George V. Monk

Captain E. Bennett in command

Officers:

Chief Officer H.T. Wells

2nd Officer D.O. Percy

Senior 3rd Officer J.F. Tooth

3rd Officer H. Proctor

Chief Radio Officer H. Walker

2nd Radio Officer G.V. Monk

3rd Radio Officer A. Graham

Chief Steward R. Doyle

Chief Engineer D.C. Smith

2nd Engineer J. McAuley

3rd Engineer R.A. Catterall

4th Engineer P.J. Murphy

On 14th June 1941 I joined the s.s. *Auditor* (T & J Harrison), 5444 grt. We sailed from the Royal Albert Docks, London on 15th June for Cape Town, Durban and Beira fully loaded with export cargo, Army stores and aircraft.

At Southend on Sea we joined a northbound convoy, first calling at Methil before passing round the North of Scotland to Oban. When the convoy had just passed Flamborough Head, the ship ahead – a motor ship of Ellermans – set off an acoustic mine which exploded just under our bows. Fortunately, the mine had been laid in deep water and although it gave us a severe hammering, it did not damage the hull or the engines. At that time, the merchant ships in East Coast convoys were provided with an anti-aircraft balloon. One was delivered to us at Southend which we would keep until Methil. It was flown just above the top of the foremast and let out several hundred feet when an aircraft attack was imminent. The balloon wire was wound on to a large drum attached to a cargo winch, but when the mine exploded the shaking was so severe it loosened the controls and allowed the balloon to rise. It was some time before we realised what had occurred, and that our balloon was at the end of its tether. The Commodore made some comments about playing with our balloon, not realising what had caused the problem.

The coastal convoy arrived at Oban on 20th June and the ocean convoy of some 45 ships – OB 337 – sailed the next day. A week later it dispersed and the merchantmen then sailed independently, bound for their first ports.

Naval Control at Oban had given our Master a route which was to take the *Auditor* due south to the Brazilian coast and then across the South Atlantic to Capetown. This route was planned to take us away from the area of U-boat activity, but it was never completed.

On 4th July 1941, just as the moon was setting about 2 am, the Auditor was torpedoed by U-boat 123 (Lt. Hardegen). A violent explosion took place in way of No.4 hold port side, and it destroyed No.4 lifeboat. I was asleep at the time the torpedo hit but quickly put on some clothes and grabbed my 'hammer bag' and lifejacket. Making my way to the radio office, which was on the boat deck aft of the funnel, I found that my Chief was already there and had started transmitting our distress message:-

SSSS SSSS SSSS AUDITOR 25.47N 28.23W TORPEDOED

The emergency spark transmitter was being used as the ship's power supply and had failed. He knew the ship's position at the time because at the start of each watch the radio office was given a half-hourly position report, which ensured no delay in getting the position.

The radio office had emergency lighting and I could see that it was in a shambles. Fortunately, the emergency transmitter was in working order and the aerial was intact. My Chief called out to me, 'Get the lifeboat transmitter into No.1 boat and I'll carry on here'. I left and made my way to No.1 boat station under the bridge.

Whilst at sea, lifeboats were always kept swung out and lowered to deck level so that, if required, they could be lowered without delay. However, just as I had lifted the portable transmitter into the lifeboat, the crew at the falls lowered away. When it was launched the boat's rope ladder came down. As my station was in the Chief Officer's boat – No.2 port side – I was now in the wrong boat, so I had to climb up the rope ladder to get back to the boat deck. Whilst I was doing this I passed the 3rd Officer who was descending. When I got back to the boat deck I saw Captain Bennett dressed in his shore clothes (he was concerned about being taken prisoner by the U-boat), and he called out, 'Go and get your Chief – she's going fast'.

By this time, about 7 minutes after the explosion, my eyes had become accustomed to the darkness and, as it was a clear night with stars shining brightly, I was able to move around the ship easily. When I got back to the radio office I found that my Chief was still transmitting our distress message. He asked me to get his coat from his room which was on the lower deck.

This I did and, when I got there I could hear the sea pouring into the engine room below, just like the sound of a large waterfall. On returning to the radio office we checked that the code books had been thrown overboard, and my Chief then screwed down the Morse key (so that any ship could get a bearing on us). We then quickly made our way back to the bridge deck.

The only lifeboat alongside was No.1 – the Captain's boat. I went down the rope ladder (the one I had recently climbed) followed by my Chief and the Captain. The boat rope was cut and we pulled away. When about 80 yards off and about 15 minutes after the torpedo hit, the *Auditor's* bow slowly rose up until vertical, then she sank gracefully into the Cape Verde Basin, some 3000 fathoms below. What was so ghastly to us was the noise of the ship breaking up. The engines, boilers and cargo breaking loose, and the flashes as wire ropes supporting the masts and deck cargo snapped and whipped around hitting other objects, also the anchor chains coming adrift. Besides wreckage floating around, all that was left of a fine ship were a number of large crates (deck cargo), and three boats.

A little later the sound of diesels could be heard; it was U-123 cruising around. Obviously Lt. Hardegen wanted to make sure that the *Auditor* had sunk, but he did not contact us.

There were 23 survivors in the Captain's boat, which included the Chief Engineer, Chief Steward, Third Officer, Chief Radio Officer (my Chief), myself, one AB, one Gunner and 15 Lascars. Nothing could be done until daylight, except to keep in touch with the other two boats. As our boat was leaking it was necessary to bail continuously.

At sunrise on Friday stocks were taken of our provisions and these were found to be one and a half kegs of water (about 9 gallons), one case of small tins of condensed milk and a large quantity of hard ship's biscuits. The daily ration was:-

Half dipper of water (3 fluid ounces).

One spoonful of condensed milk (spoon made from the wood of the case).

One biscuit (biscuits were so hard that they could not be eaten).

Later the three boats closed and the Captain had a conference with the Chief Officer and Second Officer who were in charge of boats No.2 and No.3 respectively. My Chief told them that our distress messages had been acknowledged. Subsequently, it transpired that several ships had received it and one with HF transmission had passed it direct to London. The Naval authorities knew that we had been in action and the ship had sunk. The question was – 'Would we be rescued or would we have to sail to the nearest land?'

The conference was held while the boats were riding to sea anchors, which had been put out at daybreak. As we were in the zone of the NE trade winds there was a stiff breeze blowing with a choppy sea, and it was difficult for the boats to keep together. So we secured a rope to each boat to avoid drifting apart.

Whilst the position given in our distress message was accurate, a decision had now to be taken as to the islands or lands we should make for if we were not rescued. It was necessary to bear in mind the prevailing winds and ocean currents, and that we would be sailing a lifeboat – without a keel and liable to drifting. Unfortunately, there were no Atlantic charts available, and the only navigational aid in each boat was a compass.

For many years prior to the war I used to buy a pocket Shipping Diary, and when in London in December 1940 I purchased one for 1941. Little did I know then how useful it was going to be, because when the officers were conversing I suddenly realised that I had my diary in my coat. Many times in the past I had seen a couple of pages giving latitude and longitude of bunkering ports, and when I looked at this page it gave the co-ordinates for St. Vincent – the port of the Cape Verde Islands. As I also had my pay book in my 'hammer bag', I was able to draw a chart and lay off a course to St. Vincent which was some 600 miles S.S.E. of our present position. With this information it was decided that should we not be rescued, these islands were the obvious choice for a landfall. And so, the officers worked out a course for each to steer which would allow for the effects of the N.E. trade winds, ocean current and drift. The estimated time for the voyage was 11 to 12 days. However, a factor which greatly influenced this decision was that the islands were mountainous. In fact, Captain Bennett had visited St. Vincent many years ago and remembered that these mountains were very high, around 6000ft to 9000ft, and therefore could be seen from a great distance, perhaps 40 miles or more. If they had been low lying the decision would have been, no doubt, to set course for the N.E. coast of South America – some 1,700 miles distant and a voyage of around 21 days or more.

At the Ocean Convoy Conference in Oban, the Naval Control Officer had advised all Masters that should you be attacked and sunk and your distress message and position had been sent and acknowledged, then do not attempt any long distance lifeboat voyage. He said there was always a naval vessel within 2 days-sailing distance from your position, so just wait for rescue. My Chief, who was with Captain Bennett at the Conference, confirmed that this was the instruction given.

So we waited all through Friday and Saturday, the three boats riding to sea anchors and drifting westwards. Captain Bennett was adamant that we must wait as it was a Naval Control instruction; but by Saturday evening the officers 'rebelled' and said that our provisions were limited, so 'let's get sailing!' So it was agreed that if no rescue had taken place by Sunday morning the boats would set sail independently for St. Vincent, C.V.I.

During these two days the lifeboat transmitter sent distress messages at regular times, and in particular at the 'silent period' time.

Early on Sunday morning the sea anchors were hauled in and each boat set sail on the pre-arranged course. By sunset, the Chief Officer's boat was well ahead, and the Second Officer's boat was hull down astern of us. The N.E. trade winds were blowing steadily, and our speed was estimated at 2.5 to 3 knots. The boat was sailing well, but a good lookout could only be maintained when we rode the crest of the swells.

By Monday morning both of the other boats were out of sight. At the outset it was agreed that each boat would sail independently; this would ensure that if one was found by a rescue ship a search could be organised for the other two. It was fine weather and during the day it became very warm; some of the crew were already suffering from sunburn. At night it was very cold. As the boat was still leaking it was necessary to bail frequently, but during the day we would sit with our feet in the water in the hope that our bodies might absorb some moisture this way. Steering the boat was the main task of Captain Bennett and the Third Officer, although occasionally the other officers would relieve them. Steering at night was difficult as there was no light in the compass. Lifejacket lights were used to check the course, but mainly we steered by the stars and moon.

During the next three days the weather was fine with fleecy clouds and a strong wind. At times the sea became choppy which reduced our speed. When in the valley of a swell one could look up at the side of it and see many varieties of fish swimming above the level of the boat. In this area the sea was a marvellous colour and so clear but, of course, undrinkable.

On Friday – the 8th day – the Master estimated that at dawn we had made some 300 miles since setting sail. It was cloudy and during the morning there was a light rain shower. The inside cover of the transmitter was used to collect some of the drops of rain, after which it was licked dry. As thirst was our main problem, Captain Bennett increased our water ration to two and a half dippers a day. On this basis our stocks should last for another seven days. If our present speed could be maintained then one of the islands should be sighted before the water ration was exhausted. Ship's biscuits provided for lifeboat use were a disaster, being so dry and hard that no one could eat them. The only food that could be eaten was condensed milk, and the ration of this was increased to two spoonfuls a day. Unfortunately, the Third Officer, who was unwell when we took to the boats, became delirious. In fact, he tried to go overboard but we caught him in time and laid him under the thwarts. He recovered a day or so later.

Monday – 11th day. During the previous three days the weather has been good and, fortunately, we had remained in the zone of the N.E. trades, which enabled us to maintain a steady speed in spite of a heavy swell. Captain Bennett estimated that by dawn we had sailed about 550 miles, an average speed of 2.5 knots. As we were obviously getting near to the islands we transmitted distress signals at regular times, but as we had not been supplied with a radio receiver we did not know if any station was trying to contact us. In the late afternoon a bird was sighted which meant that land must be near.

Tuesday – 12th day. It was cloudy and the crew, who were on lookout at dawn, thought that there was a grey smudge on the horizon on our port beam. Could this be an island? If so, then we were some 40 miles off course. The effects of wind and current must have been greater than estimated.

This smudge on the horizon was watched by all of us for at least an hour to see if there was any movement – like a dark cloud. It did not move, so it must be one of the islands. The lifeboat's course was now altered to East-North-East, and now we met a head wind which meant frequent tacking. This gave us severe problems straight away for the sea was rough with quite a swell running. Shortly after the course had been altered the heel of the mast broke. It was fixed but we had no tools to carry out a proper repair. It broke again in the forenoon and afternoon, and again was fixed as best as was possible. The boat was being put under severe strain due to constant tacking and received a great pounding but, fortunately the mast stays held. Whilst tacking the boat shipped a lot of water so it was all hands to bailing. Headway was slowly made, and as the day wore on, the island became larger, but by sunset we were still some 20 miles away.

Wednesday – 13th day. I was at the tiller for the night watch; the light of a lighthouse at one end of the island was seen and this helped us to maintain a course. The wind dropped and the sea became calmer as we sailed nearer to the island. Later, when some 8 miles from the shore, the Master said to me to 'Hold her there'.

It was not wise to approach too close to the shore until we could see what it was like. When dawn broke we could make out the layout of the island, and it looked very menacing; the steep rocky cliffs came down to the sea with no place to land. We sailed in a little closer, and as the sun rose behind the mountains it began to get very warm. We were now in the lee of the island and the wind dropped completely. For the first time since the *Auditor* sank our lifeboat was steady and on an even keel. It was now time to ship the oars and row, and as the cliffs looked less steep to the south, that was the way we headed.

Every man took turns at the oars but it was hot and very tiring, particularly as we had not eaten anything substantial for 13 days. After rowing for 3 hours some colours appeared on the mountainside, and these turned out to be the roofs of some small houses. At last there appeared to be some habitation. Later we saw two boats making for us; they had brought out two carafes of fresh water. How good it tasted. The boats, manned by local Portuguese fishermen, took our rope and towed us for the last mile or so to the village of Tarrafal on the island of Sao Antao.

Around noon our boat was brought alongside a stone jetty and we disembarked. How wonderful to walk on the land again. Most of the villagers were there to meet us. The Third Officer was carried ashore, as were most of the Lascars. The remaining survivors walked ashore (although a little unsteady) and climbed the hillside track to the Manager's house where a room had been made available for us. It was sheer luxury to be able to lay on the floor and relax with gallons of fresh water available. Captain Bennett warned us not to eat any solid food for several days as our stomachs would not be able to accept it – and so, the good villagers made us soups. Strange to say, we had arrived at a water loading terminal. High in the mountains above Tarrafal is a fresh water lake. The Portuguese had piped a supply down to the jetty. Every alternate day a small tanker arrived and loaded water to take to St. Vincent – the capital of the Cape Verde Islands. The next day we would board the tanker to take us to the capital.

On arrival at Tarrafal the Manager of the settlement told us that the Second Officer's boat had arrived on Monday – two days ahead of us. All of us were delighted to hear that his boat had made it but were intrigued to know how they had beaten us. Apparently, the Second Officer, who had a steel lifeboat, was very disappointed when, at dusk on the first day's sailing, he was well astern of the other two boats. The next day he found a length of canvas (possibly a boat cover), and from this he made a jib and hoisted it. Fortunately, as he had a steel boat it did not leak and so, with less weight and an extra sail he made a faster passage.

The next day, just before noon, the water tanker arrived and loaded its cargo of fresh water. We went aboard and sailed at 2.30 pm, arriving at St. Vincent at about 6 pm. Our lifeboat, which had served us so well during the last two weeks, and which had brought us safely to the island, was left at Tarrafal. News had gone ahead that we were arriving on the water boat. When it docked at the main quay there were not only our Chief and Second Officers with their crews to greet us, but many survivors from the *Clan Macdougall*, the *Silveryew* and a Dutch motor ship.

The Chief Officer's boat, which had raced ahead of us had made a good passage. By Tuesday (12th day) the islands had not been sighted and so he assumed that they had passed them. He then altered course for the South American coast. This proved to be a good decision, because next day they were sighted by a Portuguese ship which brought them and their boat to St. Vincent. After he initial wait of two days, all three lifeboats had finally made their objective, the Cape Verde Islands.

When discussing our voyages with the other officers they all said that they were very impressed with the performance and seaworthiness of their boats. In hindsight, they should have been better equipped and provisioned, with a larger supply of water. With just the basic equipment of a compass, set of oars, tiller, mast and sail they had taken severe punishment from heavy swells and choppy seas, but they had completed the voyage. As the name implies, they were indeed life boats.

The day after our arrival, Captain Bennett reported to the British Consul and met his staff – all of whom were R.N or R.N.R officers who formed the Naval Control Service for this port. They said that our distress – SSSS – message was received, and after checking their charts, estimated that our boats would arrive in about 11 days time. When Captain Bennett told them that we had waited for 2 days for rescue (as instructed by Naval Control at Oban), they all burst out laughing, and said, 'You can't be serious; we've never heard of that joke before'. Captain Bennett was so incensed with the Oban Naval Control for issuing such a misguided instruction to shipping that he promptly cabled Harrisons at Liverpool and asked them to lodge a complaint with the Admiralty. Captain Crocker, RN, the senior Naval Control Officer at St. Vincent, to*ld Captain Bennett that there were no British naval vessels in the area of the *Auditor*'s sinking, and so there was no hope of any rescue being carried out. It was fortunate that we did not wait any longer and set sail for the islands.

With some 240 merchant seamen survivors at St. Vincent accommodation was at a premium. My Chief and I were placed with a local family for a week and then moved to Wilsons, who were T & J Harrison's agents. Their premises had offices on the ground floor and living accommodation on the floor above.

The day after our arrival we received an advance of pay. This was essential as we had to visit some shops to buy suitable clothes. Jackets were not available 'off the peg', but had to be made to measure, taking about 10 days; shoes were also made to measure and the local cobblers turned out a good pair in a few days.

All the *Auditor*'s survivors made the most of the next few weeks to relax and recover from the ordeal they had been through, the effects of exposure and lack of food and water. The weather was ideal with blue skies and temperatures in the 70s.

The Cable and Wireless Company had a large station at S. Vincent, and their staff and families were exceptionally good to survivors. We were invited to their social events, parties, and on occasions entertained at private dinner parties in their homes. I am certain that their kind hospitality helped us considerably in making a quick and good recovery.

A week after our arrival we said goodbye to the survivors of the *Clan Macdougall*, *Silveryew* and the Dutch ship, who were being repatriated to the UK via Freetown. About that time we learnt that more survivors had arrived in the port, so we went down to the main quay to greet them. These survivors were from the motor tanker *Hornshell,* which was torpedoed around the end of July when bound from Gibraltar to Trinidad. In charge of lifeboat No.3 was the Second Officer, who had a crew of 15, which included 11 Chinese. He told us that they had been in the boat for about two weeks when a ship was sighted. It came very near to them, and although they shouted and burnt flares, it did not stop. Fortunately, the ship's cook came out of the galley to empty a bucket over the side when, on looking aft, he saw their boat. He alerted the Mate (who had been asleep on the bridge), and the ship turned back to pick them up. It was a Spanish vessel on passage to the Cape Verde Islands.

There was little to do in St. Vincent, and to occupy our time we used to go for walks each morning, either around the port, or to the bays and beaches on the other side of the island. The afternoons were spent resting and in the early evening most of us went to the Plaza to walk around this large square. It appeared that half the town's population carried out this ritual each evening, using the occasion to chat with friends and relatives before going home to an evening meal.

During the morning walks I found it was difficult for me to face the bright sunlight. Even using a pair of dark glasses did not improve my sight. Captain Bennett thought I should see a specialist (there were no special facilities in St. Vincent), and so the Agents arranged for me to be sent to Lisbon to go into the British Hospital and possibly see an Ophthalmic Surgeon.

It was Friday the 19th August that we had another unusual event. I was awakened about 4.00 am by rumbling noises, only to find my wash basin dancing around the marble-topped table. I suddenly realised that St. Vincent was being hit by an earthquake. I quickly got out of bed, and ran down the outside stairs to the quadrangle below. All the other people in the building did the same thing, and we waited there until the earthquake had subsided. Apparently, it was not too severe, and there was only superficial damage. However, I well remember seeing the street lights swinging to and fro, and wondering if Wilson's building might collapse.

A few days later I was told that a passage had been booked for me and the Chief Steward of the *Auditor* in the Portuguese liner *Serpa Pinto,* 8489 tons, which was calling at St. Vincent next weekend en-route to Lisbon (incidentally, the *Serpa Pinto* was built for Royal Mail Lines in 1915 as the *Ebro.* The Portuguese shipping company Cia. Colonial of Lisbon purchased her in 1940 for their New York and Central American Service. As Portugal was neutral, it was essential to have her name and country written in very large letters on each side of the ship).

On Saturday 23 August, 5 weeks after arriving in the islands, I said farewell to the *Auditor's* crew, and with the Chief Steward embarked in the *Serpa Pinto*. The Second Officer and the Third Engineer of the *Hornshell* also joined us –as their company – Anglo Saxon Petroleum – were repatriating them to the UK via Lisbon. We sailed early next morning, calling at Madeira on Wednesday, and arrived at Lisbon late on Friday evening.

At night the *Serpa Pinto* was floodlit so that any U-boat sighting her knew it was a neutral ship. There had been one or two occasions previously when she had been stopped and searched. In fact, in early 1941 she had been stopped by the British and ordered into Bermuda, where a 3-day search was carried out for Germans believed to have been aboard. Fortunately for us, she was not stopped this voyage.

Although the *Serpa Pinto* had accommodation for some 500 1st and 2nd Class passengers, she was not fully booked for her return voyage to Lisbon. One of her passengers was a British Consulate Inspector who was returning from a South American tour of duty. The four of us got to know him quite well, and it transpired that his relations lived very near to my home in Essex. On arrival at Lisbon the four of us were met by a Consulate official, who cleared us through the Immigration and Customs in record time, and took us to the Braganca Hotel in the centre of the city.

The next day the same official called early and took me to the English Hospital, where I was examined and arrangements were made for me to see an eye specialist later that day. The same official came with me and stayed for a long time to interpret as I could not speak Portuguese. He left me with the specialist who worked on my eye during the next eight days. I stayed at his surgery during the day and he would call me in several times to give me treatment. I found out later that I had corneal ulcers which the specialist had been able to disperse, and so saved my sight.

With my sight greatly improved, the Chief Steward and I reported daily to the British Consulate to check if they could arrange repatriation for us to the UK. There was a possibility that we could be flown back, but at the last minute it was cancelled due to other people having greater priority. On Monday 15th September I was asked to call at the Consulate and was told that a Danish ship, the s.s. *Ebro*, required a radio officer for a voyage to the UK. As I wanted to return home as soon as possible, either working or as a D.B.S., I accepted and signed on. The Consulate also arranged for the Chief Steward to return to Liverpool as a passenger in the s.s. *Cortes*.

The *Ebro* (1600 tons) had just completed loading a cargo of cork when I joined her. Shortly after my arrival a lady and her two children came aboard; they were the only passengers, as this ship had very limited accommodation. A Scottish engineer, whose ship had been torpedoed, had reached Lisbon by a roundabout route also joined as Third Engineer. Prior to the war, the *Ebro* had been sailing on short-sea voyages mainly from the Baltic to the Mediterranean.

Leaving Lisbon at dusk, we hugged the Portuguese coast that night and all next day, arriving at Gibraltar at 3.00 pm. As we were entering port a convoy of 24 ships was leaving. Hardly had we anchored in the bay when a launch came alongside and a Naval Control Officer came aboard. He instructed us to join Convoy HG 73, which had just sailed, and briefed us on the operational procedures and gave us a convoy plan. As the *Ebro* had a good turn of speed we had no trouble in catching up with this convoy. We were allotted position No.54, the third ship astern of the Commodore. I was instructed to discontinue normal radio watches and to assist the Master (Danish) and the two deck officers (one Danish, the other Norwegian) with convoy instructions and signalling with the Aldis lamp and flags.

Letter from John P. Cox to Geoffrey Drummond dated 5 June 1990

Randburg
Transvaal
June 5th 1990

At that time I was serving on board the Liverpool based Flower-class corvette HMS Campanula, and our station was out on the port stern wing of OG 71.

We had gathered at Rothsay and were going as far as Gibraltar. The Aguila was carrying the Commodore of Convoy and we heard there was a party of Wrens and VADs on board for Singapore as well as other passengers.

The Aguila was a distinguished vessel to look at because she wore three masts and a tall funnel. She was owned by the Yeoward Brothers of Liverpool, her peacetime run had been to and from the Atlantic Isles, Liverpool and Belfast.

Our course on this occasion took us uncomfortably close to the French Biscay coast, and the attacks when they came were reputedly carried out by submarine training crews out of Brest. It has also been said that we were so close in because of a very large convoy far to the west of us containing many troopships and other vessels carrying materials for General Montgomery's Middle East build up, which ended up for the Battle of El Alamein. Therefore OG 71 was a decoy and as such was expendable

For several days and nights after we sailed, the convoy had a quiet time. But as we moved down towards the Portuguese coast, things began to change. There were two heavy attacks on the convoy, a Tuesday and Thursday, so the 19th must have been a Tuesday, and this began soon after sunrise with the spotting of a large Focke-Wulf Condor *which remained with us during daylight, no doubt radioing the number of ships and escorts and their positions to the advancing U-boats and directing them into the most favourable situation for a night attack.*

I think the Aguila *was hit about 2200 followed by other vessels all through the night. One vessel near our position was hit and as we closed in to search for survivors there was a strong smell of beer everywhere. This probably was the Irish ship* Clonlara *and she was supposed to be carrying Guiness destined for the NAAFI of Gibraltar. We recovered several badly injured seamen from this and other casualties. Meanwhile we had been approaching the position where the* Aguila *had occupied and there were many lights in the sea and the cries of people dying coming from amongst them. Just then the* Alvar *was hit and we dropped back to assist. We picked up some of her crew several of whom were horribly scalded, then by the time we had got back into position, all those lights on the water had gone.*

So far as our injured survivors were concerned, we carried no Surgeon, not even a Sick Berth Attendant, so it had to be rough and ready medical aid and we did the best we could for them.

That night ended and daylight came, but the attacking force must have become scattered because it was quiet all that day and all that night. But by daylight on Thursday 21st the Condor was back and stayed with us all day and doubtlessly directing the U-boats into position for another attack Then soon after dark the slaughter began all over again. On two occasions during the night we had to lower our boat to pick up survivors most of whom were seriously injured.

Sometime during that terrible night, we picked up the Mate and an Engineer from the tug Empire Oak *which had been bound for Singapore, and some time later the Mate told us they had rescued one Wren from the* Aguila, *but sadly she did not survive this time.*

Just about now there was a massive explosion and a horrible spread of fire across the sea where the Stork *had been, and as we circled the blazing area we must have presented a marvellous target by being silhouetted against the fire, but nothing happened, there was no sign of life – and the convoy moved on. The* Stork *had* been carrying aviation spirit for the carrier HMS Ark Royal, then in Gibraltar. The Stork had been owned by the General Steam Navigation Co. of London. For what remained of that night, sometimes counter-attacking with depth charges, sometimes picking up survivors, amongst which was one man who had both his eyelids split from side to side, yet assured us that he could see well enough, but both his legs were mangled too, but he was manfully fighting his pain.

At daylight on the 22nd while investigating gunfire we came upon the Norwegian steamer Spind and she was being attacked by gunfire, obviously the U-boat had no torpedoes left, and just before day broke had surfaced and fired on the vessel. She was going down by the head, her stern high in the air. There were no boats near her so we assumed that if there were survivors they must have been picked up by someone else. As the sun came up, but for the convoy far ahead, the ruffled surface where the Spind had gone down, and ourselves, the sea seemed empty.

Eventually we regained our position in the convoy but we were so full of survivors, most of them needing urgent medical and surgical attention, that later that day we were ordered to detach from the convoy and make for Gibraltar with all haste. Berthing there on Sunday 24th where doctors and ambulances met us.

Nicholas Monsarrat was the 2nd Lieutenant of the Campanula at that time. These incidents of OG 71 are mentioned in his book 'The Cruel Sea'. If you have read it you may recall the incident of the horribly scalded fireman from one of the sunken ships who would not die. He lay inside the break of the fo 'castle for days suffering God knows what.

Some weeks later we were dry docked up in the Dingle area of Liverpool, my mate and I were having a drink in the local Social Club there, we were the only sailors present. At a table across from us sat a pale and shabbily dressed woman perhaps in her late 30s who bought us a drink each. We thanked her for her gesture but said she need not have spent her money on us, however she would have none of it and told us she was only carrying out the wishes of her husband who some weeks previous had been reported as 'Missing at sea'. Apparently he had already lost two ships and on each occasion had been picked up by a Royal Navy vessel upon which he had been kindly and carefully treated. So he had told his wife that whenever she was at the Club and there were Royal Navy men present to buy them a drink by way of his thanks.

We sympathised with her about her husband and asked from what ship he was reported missing. She said he was on the Stork.

We did not say anything about what we knew, deeming it better that she learn of the circumstances of his loss from official sources.

Long, long ago, deep within myself I dedicated my Atlantic Star medal to the victims of OG 71 as their headstone – it was the only one they had then. When I have occasion to look back at it, I see again those many lights on the sea where the Aguila had been and hear the despairing cries from people who knew they were about to die – think of the unfortunate Wren who survived one nightmare only to perish in another just over twenty-four hours later – or of that hideous, burning patch of sea – and of the lady who bought us a pint just because the sailors had been kind to her husband.

We endured many similar experiences afterwards and had our share of losing – we went to Russia and back – all the way across the Atlantic and back time after time, the alarm bells sounding day and night – do you wonder then that when the time came to hit back, we were equally as merciless? <u>We must never forget.</u>

I was spared to become a parent, grandparent and great grandparent. So many others were not.

My thoughts will be with you all on Sunday August 19th in your place of memorial, we cannot bring them back – they may not have wanted to if they could – because after their initial terror was over in the cold water of an Atlantic night and their realisation that death was all that was left – they went quietly and with dignity to lie in peace and tranquillity on the deep oceanfloor. No one could hurt them any more.

I am

Yours faithfully,

John P. Cox ex-Royal Navy 1937–52

Bibliography

Admiralty, **Bay of Biscay Pilot**, Hydrographic Department, 1956

Blanford, Edmund, **Target England,** Airlife, 1997

Churchill, Winston, **The Second World War,** Cassell, 1950

Collier, Richard, **1941: Armageddon,** Hamish Hamilton, 1981

Forde, Captain Frank, **The Long Watch,** Gill & Macmillan, 1981

Findlay, A.G., **North Atlantic Memoir,** Richard Holmes Laurie, 1879

Hague, Arnold, **The Allied Convoy System 1939–1945**, Vanwell Publishing, 2000

Hancock, H.E., **Semper Fidelis,** General Steam Navigation Company, 1949

Haldane, R.A., **The Hidden War**, Robert Hale, 1978

Holm, John, **No Place to Linger,** Holmwork Publishers, 1985

Jones, Geoffrey, **Defeat of the Wolf Packs,** William Kimber, 1986

Ludlam, Harry & Lund, Paul, **Nightmare Convoy,** W. Foulsham, 1987

Mallman-Showell, J.P., **U-Boats Under the Swastika**, Ian Allan, 1973

Monsarrat, Nicholas, **The Cruel Sea,** Cassell, 1953

Padfield, Peter, **Dönitz – The Last Führer,** Cassell, 2001

Paterson, Lawrence, **First U-boat Flotilla**, Leo Cooper, 2002

Robertson-Evans, Terence, **Walker R.N.,** Evans Bros. Ltd., 1956

Tennant, Alan J., **British & Commonwealth Merchant Ship Losses to Axis Submarines 1939–1945,** Sutton Publishing, 2001

Thomas, David A., **The Atlantic Star,** W.H. Allen, 1990

Slader, John, **The Fourth Service**, Robert Hale, 1994

Terraine, John, **Business in Great Waters,** Leo Cooper, 1989

United States Navy, **Sailing Directions for the West Coasts of Spain, Portugal, and Northwest Africa,** Hydrographic Office U.S. Navy, 1942

Williamson, Gordon, **Wolf Pack,** Osprey Publishing, 2005

Woodman, Richard, **The Real Cruel Sea,** John Murray, 2004

Other Sources

Company of Master Mariners of Canada, Daily Mail, Daily Telegraph, Flower Class Corvette Association, Journal of Commerce, Journal of Strategic Studies, National Archives, Kew, National Archives, Washington.

The Author also wishes to acknowledge the help of:

Geoffrey Drummond, George Monk, Grahame Morris and Captain T.C. Rooney

Index